# Enhancing Primary Care
# of Elderly People

Garland Reference Library of Social Science
Volume 1142

# Enhancing Primary Care of Elderly People

Edited by
F. Ellen Netting
Frank G. Williams

Garland Publishing, Inc.
A member of the Taylor & Francis Group
New York & London
1999

**Library of Congress Cataloging-in-Publication Data**

Enhancing primary care of elderly persons / edited by F. Ellen Netting
and Frank G. Williams
    p.  cm. — (Garland reference library of social
science ; v. 1142)
   Includes bibliographical references and index.
   ISBN 0-8153-2532-0 (paperback : alk. paper). —
ISBN 0-8153-2531-2 (case)
   1. Aged—medical care. 2. Primary care (Medicine)
I. Netting, F. Ellen. II. Williams, Frank G.  III. Series
RA564.8.E54  1999
362.1'9897—dc21          98-21725
                   CIP

Paperback cover: Bill Brown Design

Printed on acid-free, 250-year-life paper
Manufactured in the United States of America

*Dedicated*
*To the enhanced primary care of elders*

# CONTENTS

# FOREWORD

The John A. Hartford Foundation, headquartered in New York City, is a nationally oriented health foundation with assets in excess of $450 million. Since 1995, an increasing share of the foundation's grant payments has been devoted to projects related to aging and health. For 1997, these payments exceeded $17 million.

For over two decades, the foundation's trustees have sought to improve the nation's capacity to provide effective and affordable health care to its citizens. In particular, the foundation has recognized that our health system—from academic training and research to service delivery—is not prepared to deal with the needs of a rapidly expanding elderly population. While we have devoted substantial resources to all of these areas, service delivery is the focus of this book.

Part of our current health care crisis relates to a variety of insurance and financing problems that work against comprehensive services. Equally important, in the foundation's view, has been the lack of conceptual models for provision of individualized, yet comprehensive, services. Practical ways for health professionals to develop the capacity to provide such services economically and effectively have been in short supply.

The foundation's Generalist Physician Initiative, featured in this book, grew out of these concerns, along with the recognition that our health care "system" in 1990 was no sane person's answer to the question, "How might we as a nation provide better care for an aging population?" In May 1992, we committed to a new service-oriented initiative to develop and assess innovative models to improve primary physician's care for their older patients. We felt a sense of urgency in this task as we watched physicians' time for direct patient care, contact, and planning diminish just as older patients' needs for such care expanded. Thus, we sought to develop models that addressed these practical difficulties for doctors facing patients with complex and intertwined biopsychosocial issues. While the project was directed at improving the care of elders, the resulting models should be relevant to the care of any patient with complex needs.

Central to the initiative was an assumption that the consumer movement in health care had focused primarily on younger generations of patients. Older patient cohorts seem more likely to turn to their physicians than to computers or consumer activists, for expert advice, information, and guidance. For them, we believe that generalist physicians, that is, primary care internists and family physicians, are not only the first line of defense when illness strikes, but a continuing source of reassurance. Since physicians routinely see elderly patients in their office practices long before serious decline occurs, they are in the best position to initiate preventive as well as therapeutic steps. Yet the relatively low payment from Medicare for patients with both subtle and overtly complex conditions, combined with the slowly changing traditional biomedical model of training, neither encourages nor prepares physicians to think holistically.

Given these constraining forces, the foundation believed that introducing other health professionals—most typically nurses and social workers—into primary-care office practices offered our best hope for more effective care. Therefore, we sought models to enhance the range of health-care response capacity offered in primary-care office practice. Further, we felt that such models could be affordable and perhaps even cost-saving, particularly if all relevant health care settings, such as inpatient, emergency, and home, were considered.

In evaluating these models, we recognized that a strict randomized trial approach to outcome evaluation was not feasible. Too many variables, including physician/hospital relationships and loyalties, physician participation in health maintenance organizations (HMOs) and preferred provider organizations (PPOs), patient relationships, and stability of physician practice size and structure, could not reasonably be controlled. Further, the many variations across the country in such factors as patient preferences and expectations and supply of physicians and other personnel mitigated against any single answer for all settings and circumstances. Thus, project diversity was sought to bring about models to address a broad range of problems as well as variations in geography (both population density and region), health financing, population diversity, practice size and structure, and the nature and targets of the interventions.

Projects totaling in excess of $9.5 million in foundation commitments were implemented during the following 6-year period. The foundation balanced concern about investing in projects that might not show the desired results, due to forces beyond their control, with the commitment to demonstrate needed change. We chose to believe that traditionally trained physicians could and would alter their accustomed practice styles in order to yield better patient care. Less certain was whether new care models could be fully implemented and remain stable over the time period needed to demonstrate positive clinical and/or financial results.

When the initiative began, relatively few elders were enrolled in Medicare HMOs. Although this participation has more than quadrupled in the past decade, the logic of the interventions developed by the projects remains compelling. Particularly for those managed care systems in which relatively decentralized primary care is the norm, the new efforts represent sharp but feasible advances.

The individual and collective project efforts are described and analyzed in this book. The foundation has learned that components of several projects might be combined to address particular local situations. Out of this project have emerged other initiatives that focus on the importance of interdisciplinary, collaborative teams. In addition, a foundation-supported national dissemination partnership, under the leadership of Frank G. Williams, is ongoing as this book goes to press.

There are many people to thank for the incredible efforts that have made this initiative a reality. While the individual project leaders and participating primary care physicians come immediately to mind, of equal importance are the many nursing and social work professionals and paraprofessionals who willingly entered into new "careers" to make these projects a reality. Most important, however, are the thousands of older patients and their families who willingly gave their time to help us learn.

At a June 1997 conference in Denver, where the personnel from the project sites described on the following pages gathered to discuss final results, I stated that what we have learned from the Generalist Physician Initiative is that it has enhanced not just physician practice, but our whole notion of what excellent primary care might be and how it might be provided. It is our hope that the nation's elders will be the immediate beneficiaries of the rapid and widespread adoption of these and many other patient care enhancements.

*Donna Regenstreif, Ph.D.*
Senior Program Officer
The John A. Hartford Foundation, Inc.

# ABBREVIATIONS AND ACRONYMS

ADLs  activities of daily living
ARNP  advanced registered nurse practitioner
CCEAs  Centers of Excellence for the Aging
CDSM  chronic disease self-management
CGA  comprehensive geriatric assessment
DCCT  Diabetes Control and Clinical Trials
FASE  Functional Abilities Screening Evaluation
FFS  Fee for Service
GEM  geriatric evaluation and management
GITT  Geriatric Interdisciplinary Team Training
HAP  Health Alliance Plan (of HFHS)
HDFP  Hypertension Detection and Follow-Up Program
HFHS  Henry Ford Health System
HMO  health maintenance organization
IADLs  instrumental activities of daily living
IPA  Independent Practice Association
IPIC  Intervention Pathways to Integrated Care
NEON  Northeast Ohio Neighborhood Health Services, Inc.
PA  physician assistant
PACE  Program of All-Inclusive Care for the Elderly
PCC  patient care coordinator
PCP  primary care physician
PPO  preferred provider organization
RN  registered nurse
SC GRIP; *also* GRIP  South Carolina Geriatric Rural Initiative Project
SCC  Senior Care Connection
SCM  System Case Management

**SCN**  Senior Care Network
**SJH**  St. Joseph Healthcare
**SW**  social worker
**UHS**  United Health Services
**UMA**  United Medical Associates (of UHS)

# ACKNOWLEDGEMENTS

Our first acknowledgement is to The John A. Hartford Foundation's trustees, program officers, and staff who supported this endeavor. Special appreciation is due to Donna Regenstreif, senior program officer, from whose vision this initiative developed. Dr. Regenstreif's foreword provides a perspective that sets the stage for this book.

The 32 contributors to this volume are extremely busy leaders and practitioners in health care. We want to acknowledge their creativity and the special efforts that went into each chapter. Biographical sketches of contributors contained at the end of this volume attest to the experience, expertise, and competency represented here. On behalf of the contributors, we extend our thanks to the professionals at each site who worked with them to realize their improved models of care for elderly persons.

There are two persons who have worked hard behind the scenes to make this publication a reality. We are especially grateful to Tracy Kirkman-Liff, who worked with us to provide comprehensive feedback when first drafts were received. Her patience and ability to focus on detail assisted us in strengthening each manuscript and in reconciling stylistic and structural differences. The second person who has worked behind the scenes is Dr. Anne Kisor, who has attended to assorted essential formatting details. Tracy Kirkman-Liff and Anne Kisor have not only provided technical assistance, but offered helpful suggestions on content that have contributed to the quality of the final product.

We want to thank David Estrin, senior editor at Garland Publishing, for his faith in this project and for his sense of humor that spurred us along the way. His unfailing commitment to publishing this book was obvious from the very beginning, and we are grateful for his support and assistance throughout the process.

Special appreciation goes to our colleagues, Dr. Brad Kirkman-Liff and Dr. Mark Sager, who joined us in the dissemination and analysis phase of this initiative. They read the first draft of every chapter and provided excellent feedback for contributors, and then they joined us in the actual writing process.

And last, we thank those who made this book possible, the older persons who participated in intervention and comparison groups. Their names are kept in strictest confidence but their stories are interwoven into each chapter. Elderly persons are the unsung heroes and heroines in the daily interactions that are recounted in the following pages, and to them we are most grateful.

# Enhancing Primary Care
# of Elderly People

# Medicare Managed Care and Primary Care for Frail Elders

*Bradford L. Kirkman-Liff*

The provision of primary care for an increasing elderly population has assumed increased importance in the last decade with the rapid expansion of contracting by health maintenance organizations (HMOs) and other forms of managed care with the Health Care Financing Administration (HCFA). In 1985 HMOs covered 1,025,000 Medicare recipients, and by October 1997 this number had grown more than fivefold to 5,731,527 (Health Care Financing Administration, 1986, 1997). Fiscal year payments to HMOs under contracting rose from $556,000,000 in 1985 to $25,608,000,000 in 1996. The number of plans contracting has grown from 205 in 1985 to 415 in 1997, with 57 plans awaiting approval. The Congressional Budget Office (1997) projects Medicare enrollment in managed care to reach over seven million recipients in 1999 and over fifteen million recipients in 2007. As a percentage of total Medicare beneficiaries residing in each state, the highest Medicare managed care penetration is found in California and Arizona, where 38 percent of beneficiaries are in risk contract plans. In 7 states over 20 percent of all Medicare beneficiaries are in HMOs and there are no recipients enrolled in managed care plans in 11 states (Health Care Financing Administration, 1996).

The voluntary enrollment of Medicare recipients in managed care has been and remains encouraged by the more generous benefit packages available through such enrollment. Traditional Medicare provides no coverage for outpatient prescriptions, and coverage for such drugs under HMOs has become a major attraction for elders. Other benefits include lower physician and hospital co-payments. The cost for elderly persons to purchase an indemnity supplemental policy (so-called "Medi-gap" coverage) has always been far more than the nominal premium required for selection of a Medicare risk contractor. In recent years in most markets, Medicare contractors have offered basic coverage at no additional premium for expanded benefits. By the end of 1996, only 37 percent of Medicare managed care enrollees are paying any premium, and the average premium for those who are paying is $13.52 (Lamphere, Neuman, Langwell & Sherman, 1997, p. 129).

## The Promises of Medicare Managed Care

Although greater coverage at no or lower cost is important, the promise of managed care for Medicare recipients goes further. It was hoped that most Medicare contractors would be organized systems of care with a strong emphasis on primary care, disease prevention, and health promotion. Traditional Medicare coverage, as in traditional indemnity insurance, pays on a fee-for-service basis with no mechanism to assure the appropriateness or quality of patient referrals or the necessity of treatment. The enrollment of elderly persons in such plans would hopefully improve the quality of their care and their outcomes. In such structured, integrated systems, each elderly person would have a central primary care provider responsible for all aspects of their health, since managed care has the potential to add aspects of nutrition, exercise, and psychosocial counseling to the medical model of acute illness treatment. It was hoped that managed care could move the model of health services for elders from an episodic treatment orientation to a continuous health maintenance and improvement strategy. It was also hoped that voluntary enrollment of Medicare recipients in HMOs would lower the costs for the federal government.

Indeed, over the last two decades large public and private sector employers have seen a stabilization (and in some areas a decline) in their employee health care benefits costs due to the switch from indemnity insurance to managed care. The funding formula for HMOs under the Tax Equity and Fiscal Responsibility Act of 1982 (TEFRA) set HMO premiums as 95 percent of the average adjusted per capita cost (AAPCC) for traditional Medicare in each county served by the HMO (Gabel, 1997). It was hoped that this 5 percent savings would provide some reduction in total Medicare expenditures.

# The Reality of Medicare Managed Care

Unfortunately, the benefits of the rapid growth of managed care for older persons have only partially appeared. Medicare recipients in HMOs are continuing to receive substantially improved benefits, and the marketing efforts of risk contracts continue to emphasize the lower out-of-pocket costs, especially for prescription drugs. Medicare recipients enrolled in HMOs have very high levels of satisfaction. However, these findings must be tempered by the fact that Medicare recipients are not "locked" into their HMO for one year as are participants in commercial HMOs. Medicare recipients can switch out of an HMO and back to traditional fee-for-service Medicare with only one month's notice (Langwell & Hadley, 1990). Also, there is little evidence of improved quality and outcomes from enrollment in Medicare managed care plans (Wagner, 1996). For example, one study found indications of poorer health outcomes for elders in HMOs than in traditional Medicare (Ware, Bayliss, Rogers, Kosinski, & Tarlov, 1996), while another found no differences between Medicare HMO and fee-for-service (FFS) patients in quality and outcomes (Retchin et al., 1992).

A second area where the promise of Medicare recipient enrollment in HMOs has not been fulfilled is in the costs of the program. As documented by the General Accounting Office (1994), the current payment methodology for risk-bearing HMOs substantially overpays HMOs for the services that they provide to members. This is due to the favorable risk selection that HMOs achieve and the reliance on a noncompetitive rate setting formula that is tied to the traditional Medicare fee-for-service costs. A number of proposals have been developed for improved risk-adjustment payments and the use of competitive contracting. However, it is likely to be several years before current demonstration projects result in policy implementation that will result in programmatic savings.

A third area in which the promise of managed care for the Medicare population has not been achieved is tied to the restructuring of the field of managed care itself. The original hopes of Medicare managed care were based on the HMO models that existed in the 1960s and 1970s. These models were not-for-profit, locally controlled organizations, structured around multispecialty group practices with salaried physicians, and had a strong integration among their hospital, physician, and insurer components. In the last decade, particularly since 1992, the nature of HMOs and managed care has changed. Most managed care organizations offer HMO coverage and various forms of point-of-service plans, preferred provider organizations, and indemnity coverage. HMOs are just one form of managed care—a product, not *the* product—and the HMO product itself has changed. Most plans are now organized along the lines of a loose network, with little strong integration among the physicians, hospitals, and insurer. There has been rapid consolidation within the managed care field. Community rating for the employer-sponsored coverage has generally disappeared. Patient cost sharing has increased, as has the use of capitation to pay physicians (Gabel, 1997). Most managed care plans continue to use the traditional utilization management techniques of prior authorization, concurrent review, and discharge planning. While case management is increasingly used, it generally takes the form of case management intervention after the occurrence of a catastrophic acute episode. Together, the reliance on micro management techniques and the many changes in the field of managed care have produced an increasingly strong backlash against managed care. While this backlash is not entirely warranted, and has not yet had the effect of reducing the growth of Medicare enrollment in HMOs, the movement from fee-for-service to HMO coverage is now a more controversial issue.

Primary care physicians are increasingly expected to serve as "gatekeepers" by managed care organizations. Patient problems are diagnosed and treated and referrals are made to specialists and other sources of care as necessary. Using this approach, patients are not typically allowed to visit other providers without a referral from their primary care physicians. While this process may work well for episodic illnesses, the Generalist Physician Initiative described in this book raised questions about this approach for chronically ill patients.

A gatekeeper model also does not lend itself to a team approach because everything still has to go through one person. Direct access to other providers can be overly constrained when it may be quite appropriate. Chronic care patients develop relationships with a variety of providers who come to understand their complex problems. As a gatekeeper, the primary care physician can become an unnecessary barrier to social workers, counselors, and other providers of psychosocial services, as well as to specialist physicians seen on an ongoing basis. For elderly patients with chronic problems the primary care physician can efficiently manage and oversee care without being consulted for every referral. Cost control can be maintained by having all professionals participate in the appropriate incentive systems.

# Moving Managed Care Forward

Managed care must continue to evolve if the promises for improved care and lower costs are to be achieved. The easy cost savings from improved primary care gatekeeping, discharge planning, and aggressive selective contracting by managed care plans have been achieved. Now the more difficult work remains—examining the production process of health services and finding innovative approaches to provide improved care for frail elderly persons. As presented in this book, the Generalist Physician Initiative sponsored by The John A. Hartford Foundation supported the development of ten innovative approaches that should serve as examples for further developments in managed care.

## References

Congressional Budget Office (January, 1997). Appendix G: Medicare managed care projections. In *The economic and budget outlook, fiscal years 1998–2007* (pp. 358–381). Washington, DC: Author.

Gabel, J. (1997). Ten ways HMOs have changed during the 1990s. *Health Affairs, 16*(1), 134–145.

General Accounting Office (September, 1994). *Medicare managed care: Growing enrollment adds urgency to fixing HMO payment problem* (GAO/HEHS-96–21). Washington, DC: Author.

Health Care Financing Administration (April, 1996). *Medicare managed care* (Publication No. HCFA 02195). Washington, DC: Author.

Health Care Financing Administration, Office of Managed Care (December, 1986). *Medicare managed care contract report.* Washington, DC: Author.

Health Care Financing Administration, Office of Managed Care (October, 1997). *Medicare managed care contract report.* Washington, DC: Author.

Lamphere, J., Neuman, P., Langwell, K., & Sherman, D. (1997). The surge in Medicare managed care: An update. *Health Affairs, 16*(1), 127–133.

Langwell, K.M. & Hadley, J.P. (1990). Insights for the Medicare HMO demonstrations. *Health Affairs, 9*, 74–84.

Retchin, S.M., Gurnick-Clement, D., Rossiter, L.F., Brown, B., Brown, R. & Nelson, L. (1992). How the elderly fare in HMOs: Outcomes from the Medicare competition demonstration. *Health Services Research, 27*(5), 651–669.

Wagner, E.H. (1996). The promise and performance of HMOs in improving outcomes in older adults. *Journal of the American Geriatric Society, 44*, 1251–1257.

Ware, J.E. Jr., Bayliss, M.S., Rogers, W.H., Kosinski, M. & Tarlov, Alvin R. (1996). Differences in 14-year health outcomes for elderly and poor chronically ill patients treated in HMO and fee-for-service systems. *Journal of the American Medical Association, 276*(13), 1039–1047.

# CHAPTER 1

# An Overview of Primary Care and the Generalist Physician Initiative

*Mark A. Sager, Frank G. Williams, and F. Ellen Netting*

Primary care is the provision of integrated, accessible health care services by clinicians who are accountable for addressing a large majority of personal health care needs, developing a sustained partnership with patients and practicing in the context of family and community.

—Institute of Medicine, 1996

The growth and expense of the United States health care system have renewed interest in the potential of primary care practice to improve patient outcomes and control health care costs. This renewed interest in primary care represents a historic shift in emphasis away from sub-specialty–dominated high-level technical care toward a more integrated system of care capable of addressing a wide spectrum of personal health care needs. This reorientation toward primary care is supported by federal efforts to encourage the training of more generalist physicians and by the growth of health maintenance organizations, which rely on generalist physicians to provide first-contact care.

The re-emergence of primary care has also highlighted the limitations of our current primary care system. The structure and function of primary care reflect fiscal incentives which have rewarded episodic, urgent care and discouraged more broadly based efforts to maintain health. As a result, current primary care practice tends to be disease-oriented, office-based, and restricted to reimbursable services. This narrow scope of primary care has unfortunate consequences for an elderly population, which requires a more comprehensive system of care in which prevention and health promotion are integral components. These limitations threaten to exacerbate the economic and social consequences of an aging society in which the most rapidly growing segment is age 85 and over. Without improvement in the health of older persons, health care costs for this segment of the population alone are projected to increase sixfold in constant 1987 dollars by the year 2040 (Schneider & Guralnik, 1990, p. 2335). Cost-containment strategies alone will be insufficient to contain the health care costs of an aging population. The implication is that unless our society is willing to devote additional resources to health care in the future, medical care—especially primary care—must shift toward a proactive system of care in which the maintenance of health and function are primary goals.

The potential economic burden of an aging society and the urgent need to reform current medical practice are reflected in statistics from the Medicare program, which now accounts for 20% of all personal health care expenditures. Davis and O'Brien (1996) report that 29% of Medicare enrollees now have at least one disability in activities of daily living (p. 184), 26% rate their health as fair or poor (p. 185), and 44% are age 75 and older (p. 187). The poorer health status of the elderly is associated with a hospitalization rate four times that of the rest of the population (Levit et al., 1996). In 1994, 37% of all admissions to non-federal short-stay community hospitals were for care of elderly persons, and Medicare now accounts for 30% of this country's spending for hospital services (Heffler, Donham, Won & Sensenig, 1996, p. 223). In constant 1987 dollars, Medicare costs are expected to double by 2020 (Schneider & Guralnik, 1990, p. 2337).

Physicians, like the hospital industry, have become progressively more dependent on Medicare funding. In 1994, 37% of the Medicare budget or $39 billion was paid to physicians (Health Care Financing Administration [HCFA], 1996, p.66). Medicare now pays for 19% of all personal health care expenditures to physicians, one-third of which are for office visits (HCFA, 1996, p.97). In 1994, Medicare enrollees made 537 million office visits, accounting for 48% of the 1.1 billion physician and supplier services provided in the program. Twenty-seven percent of these physician services were provided by general practice, family practice, and internal medicine physicians who received $6.5 billion or 17% of Medicare payments (HCFA, 1996, p.190). Physicians listing geriatrics as a specialty received the lowest total Medicare reimbursement of any specialty, exceeding only the payments received by the specialties of pediatrics, nuclear medicine, oral surgery provided by dentists, and manipulative osteopathy (HCFA, 1996, pp. 324–325).

The low proportion of Medicare payments to physicians listing geriatrics as a specialty reflects the small number of physicians with formal training in geriatric medicine. A call to the Association of American Medical Colleges revealed that in 1995–1996 only 235 internal medicine and 32 family practice physicians were receiving training in geriatrics. The implications of this are clear. The majority of care for older patients will be provided by generalist physicians, most of whom will become increasingly dependent on Medicare patients to support their practices. In the Medicare program, the number of physician and non-physician services increases dramatically with age. This suggests that in the future, physician practices, and health care in general, will be increasingly dominated by the older patient and the special challenges of geriatric care.

## The Challenges of Geriatric Care

Most elderly persons live healthy and active lives without significant functional disability or health-care resource consumption. However, within the geriatric population is a unique group of frail elders characterized by lowered physiological reserves and an increased risk of functional loss and long-term institutionalization. Age-related changes in physiology, pharmacology, and illness presentation make the health care of frail elders a challenge to the average clinician. The presence of multiple illnesses complicates diagnosis and treatment and significantly increases both the risks associated with having multiple providers and the likelihood of polypharmacological and iatrogenic complications. Frail elders are particularly vulnerable to the adverse effects of medications, not only because of age-related changes in drug pharmacokinetics and pharmacodynamics, but also because of the large number of drugs taken, many prescribed inappropriately. In one study, 24% of people age 65 and over received at least one of 20 drugs contraindicated in older persons (Wilcox, Himmelstein & Woolhandler, 1994, p. 292). The combination of adverse drug events, inappropriate prescribing, and poor compliance with treatment regimens make drug-related complications expensive and a potentially avoidable cause of 10 to 19% of nonsurgical hospitalizations in persons age 65 and older (Chrischilles, Segar & Wallace, 1992, p. 634; Grymonpre, Mitenko, Sitar, Aoki & Montgomery, 1988, p. 1092).

The health care of frail elderly persons is also characterized by many medical conditions not commonly seen in younger populations. These geriatric syndromes—falls and immobility, osteoporosis, dementia, delirium, urinary incontinence, visual and hearing impairments, and polypharmacy—represent a significant challenge to practitioners and a substantial cost to society. Twenty-five million Americans suffer from osteoporosis, of which hip fracture is the most serious consequence. Approximately 90% of hip fractures occur in persons age 70 years and older and 90% of hip fractures occur as the result of a fall (Grisso et al., 1991, p. 1326). The economic costs of falls, hip fractures, and osteoporosis alone are between $10 and $18 billion annually (Schua-Haim & Gross, 1997, p. 54). The personal costs of these geriatric syndromes in impaired quality of life and loss of independence are incalculable.

Previously uncommon conditions are now major public health problems in an aging society. Diseases like dementia that were once considered rare now affect 5% of the population over age 65 and up to 50% of those over age 85 (Evans, et al., 1989, p. 2551). The clinical landscape is therefore changing. Clinicians, many without formal training in geriatric medicine, are now being asked to care for increasing numbers of elders with chronic conditions that have medical as well as psychosocial consequences.

Approximately 13% of elders living in the community (as opposed to institutions) report visual impairment and 30% report hearing impairment. The prevalence of visual and hearing impairments increases to 28 and 48% respectively for those persons age 85 and older (Reuben, 1991, p. 160). Sensory impairments represent barriers to communication that would be expected to increase the length of an office visit by prolonging history taking and increasing the time required for explanations of treatment regimens. Nevertheless, information from the National Ambulatory Medical Care Survey (Sloane, 1991) and other studies (Radecki, Kane, Solomon, Mendenhall & Beck, 1988a, 1988b) consistently show that individual office visits for the elderly are shorter and less comprehensive than for younger patients. For women age 55 to 64, 61% received a breast exam and 56% a pelvic examination during a general medical examination, while the percentages of women age 65 to 74 receiving those same services were only 36% and 34%, respectively (Sloane 1991, p. 42).

Optimal geriatric care is distinguished by the need to identify and skillfully manage psychosocial, economic, and environmental problems that may be difficult to identify during a typical office visit. Social isolation, untreated depression, and inadequate support services are frequent explanations for noncompliance with treatment regimens, potentially avoidable hospitalizations, and premature long-term institutionalization. Comprehensive and potentially time-consuming psychosocial and environmental evaluations are not part of routine primary care practice and usually require a home visit. In one study, the home visit resulted in the identification of an average of four new problems, 23% of which could have resulted in death or significant morbidity. The most common problems identified related to psychobehavioral-, safety-, and caregiver-related difficulties (Ramsdell, Swart, Jackson & Renvall, 1989, p. 17). Importantly, clinical information obtained during an office visit could not predict the kinds of problems identified by the home visit, illustrating the potential benefits of extending primary care beyond the office visit for this population.

The complex and multifaceted psychosocial, as well as the biomedical, aspects of geriatric care require a broader focus by the geriatric practitioner. One way to achieve this broader focus is to employ interdisciplinary teams capable of assessing and managing illness and promoting well-being in older patients. Geriatric teams are most frequently composed of a physician, nurse, and social worker who work with pharmacists, rehabilitation specialists, and other professionals to provide and coordinate geriatric care. Interdisciplinary teams in outpatient geriatric programs have been shown to lower mortality and to improve patient satisfaction and functioning as well as the quality of health and social care (Engelhardt et al., 1996; Hendrickson, Lund & Strømgård, 1984; Melin, Wieland, Harker & Bygren, 1995; Rubenstein, Stuck, Siu & Wieland, 1991; Stuck et al., 1995; Toseland et al., 1996). However, because Medicare does not pay for many non-physician services, interdisciplinary teams in non-academic primary care settings are rare. When non-physician practitioners are employed in primary care practices, they are often limited to providing reimbursable office-based services.

## The Potential of Primary Care

Integrated primary health care services that address a large majority of medical problems would seem to have the potential for providing high quality and efficient geriatric care. Long-term physician-patient relationships should allow for more comprehensive management of multiple problems, the substitution of less expensive outpatient care for hospital care, earlier communication about changes in condition, and more comprehensive health promotion and education. Available data suggest that elderly persons benefit from long-term doctor-patient relationships and are remarkably loyal to their physicians. In a representative sample of enrollees participating in the Medicare Current Beneficiaries Survey, 55% reported a tie to a physician of five or more years and 36% reported a tie to a physician lasting ten or more years. The benefits of these sustained physician-patient relationships were lower inpatient and outpatient Medicare costs (Weiss & Blustein, 1996, p. 1742). Having a usual source of primary care has been shown in other studies to improve patient satisfaction and reduce health care use without compromising quality of care (Institute of Medicine, 1996, pp. 62–63; Mark, Gottlieb, Zellner, Chetty & Midtling, 1996).

In spite of the potential benefits of primary care, the U.S. health care system has no clearly defined method for primary care delivery. In contrast to most industrialized countries, primary care in the United States is provided by diverse practitioners in a variety of settings and has been criticized for its narrow disease orientation. Poorly reimbursed aspects of primary care, such as patient education and health promotion, are often neglected by a system designed to respond to acute needs and characterized by an emphasis on diagnosis and treatment. For patients with chronic diseases, there is no integrated system of care that effectively combines disease management with the ability to provide a full range of coordinated personal health care services, including preventive and rehabilitative care (Franks, Nutting & Clancy, 1993; Wagner, Austin & Von Korff, 1996).

The potential benefits of reorganizing the primary care system and the weaknesses of the current system are illustrated in two randomized controlled trials, the Hypertension Detection and Follow-Up Program (HDFP) and the Diabetes Complications and Control Trial (DCCT). These clinical trials evaluated therapeutic interventions for both diabetes and hypertension and incorporated comprehensive efforts into their design to develop and reorganize the medical care delivery system for patients with these diseases. In both the HDFP and the DCCT trials, models of care were designed to improve follow-up, the frequency and quality of systematic assessments, and patients' involvement in the management of their illnesses. Importantly, each trial delegated major aspects of care to non-physicians to improve the continuity and comprehensiveness of care management. The findings were impressive. The HDFP trial reduced mortality by 17% (Hypertension Detection and Follow-Up Cooperative Group, 1979, p. 2562) and the DCCT Research Group trial significantly reduced the complications of diabetes (Diabetes Complications and Control Trial Research Group, 1993). Although both of these clinical trials were designed to test disease-oriented therapies, their outcomes emphasize the importance of reorganizing primary care into collaborative teams for better chronic care management. Primary care of elderly people should be no less likely to benefit from an organized effort to enhance and broaden primary care services.

The organization and economics of primary care in the United States have worked to restrict non-hospital practice to physicians' offices and to discourage a team approach to patient care. The narrow focus of current primary care, centered around an office visit, limits opportunities for intervention and prevention. In one study, an in-home preventive assessment program conducted by trained volunteers identified an average of four new or sub-optimally treated conditions in a community dwelling population age 70 and over. Home visits at 4-month intervals achieved a 31% reduction in smoking, a 94% compliance rate with recommendations for vaccinations, and improved functioning among participants (Fabacher et al., 1994, p. 630). In another study, the therapeutic benefits of in-home assessment and monitoring were evaluated in a 3-year randomized and controlled trial in which persons age 75 years or older were visited every three months at home by a nurse practitioner working in collaboration with a geriatrician. The nurse practitioner made recommendations for self-care (e.g., exercise, medication management), identified new or suboptimally managed conditions, assisted with community services, and monitored for compliance with recommendations and changes in condition. The intervention significantly reduced disability and long-term nursing home placement in the experimental population. The estimated cost of a disability-free year was only $6,000, significantly less than the annual costs of institutionally based long-term care (Stuck et al., 1995, p. 1184). These two studies illustrate the potential benefits of collaborative, continuous, and preventive primary care that is not restricted to an office visit.

## The Generalist Physician Initiative

Office-based attempts to enhance primary care services are hampered by a busy schedule and the absence of trained personnel specifically assigned to fill the system's gaps in health education, promotion, and prevention. In spite of the potential benefits of reorganized primary care, most primary care practices have little time or financial incentive to develop or even implement new delivery systems. In recognition of the need for improved models of primary care and the very real barriers to change in primary care practice, The John A. Hartford Foundation undertook the Generalist Physician Initiative in 1992. This initiative was based on the premise that the generalist physician, working in tandem with nurses, nurse practitioners, social workers, physician assistants, and others, should play a central role in managing the integration of care for elderly persons. The nine health care organizations selected to participate in the initiative developed alternative models to enhance primary physician care. Project sites varied in setting, organization, allied personnel, method of operation, and other factors. "Enhancing primary care" in this program was defined generally as expanding the scope of the primary physician's practice to identify and be responsive to a broader set of psychosocial, economic, environmental, support, and other factors affecting the health and welfare of frail elderly persons. This initiative was not a standard multi-site demonstration in which a specific model or theoretical approach was implemented and tested in several locations. Instead, each participating site was asked to develop its own model to demonstrate what worked in its particular environment. While this approach made comparative evaluations very difficult, it added much to the richness, scope, and diversity of the results because sites were selected based on their experience and expertise in developing creative and successful programs for health care delivery.

Each model required a means to motivate physicians, staff, and administrators to expand the scope of their primary care practices. Each needed a method to assess patients' needs and their personal environments. Processes for communicating this information and incorporating it into patient care were also critical for each model. Most models utilized collaborative personnel to complete these tasks. As a result, teamwork became an important factor.

These models represented significant changes in the delivery of primary care for their host organizations. Effective, enthusiastic clinical and managerial leadership was important to maintain project viability at every site. Project managers needed to identify and continually focus on costs and organizational benefits, which often changed throughout the demonstration.

In the chapters to follow, each site is described with a particular emphasis on its local environment, practice cultures, project design issues, role and relationship development, and lessons learned. Keeping in mind that each model was developed to enhance the physician's ability to provide primary care to older persons, there are common themes that emerge amid the remarkably creative differences in how sites approached this challenge.

In Chapter 2, Whitelaw, Tupper, Early, and Collier describe how the Henry Ford Health System, based in Detroit, Michigan, tested the Complementary Geriatric Practice model for integrating care for elderly patients. Designed to integrate the geriatric care continuum by restructuring the delivery process in the primary care setting, this model teams geriatric nurse practitioners with generalist physicians to provide more comprehensive and coordinated care to high-risk geriatric patients in the clinic setting. In this model, the role of the generalist physician includes providing medical assessment and diagnosis, working in consultation with the nurse practitioner to develop and revise care plans, and managing complex and unstable patients. In addition, the generalist physician actively monitors sub-specialty care. The nurse practitioner works with the physician to develop the care plan and ensures that the patient and caregiver understand the plan. The nurse practitioner also assesses the functional and psychosocial status of the patient, ensures that these issues are addressed, manages the clinical care of stable patients, and facilitates transitions between care settings.

In Chapter 3, the team of Schraeder, Shelton, Britt, Turngren, and Nagele write about the Carle Clinic Association, located in Urbana, Illinois. The Geriatric Collaborative Care model was built on a team approach in which the physician, nurse, and patient collaborate to develop cost-effective, quality health care services. Primary care physicians identify panels of their patients that would benefit from collaborative care. Nurse partners' and primary care physicians' caseloads are aligned to develop and tap the resource of collaboration when managing individual health care plans. This strategy has also eased the integration of the model into Carle's existing health delivery system. Nurse partners provide comprehensive nursing assessment, monitoring, support, and health education and promotion in the home or clinical setting. They work in collaboration with the patient, physician, and other providers in assessing, planning, care managing, providing care, and arranging, authorizing, and coordinating services. The nurse synthesizes data from a variety of sources including assessments, patient reports, clinical records, research reports, and service utilization histories. The role of the case assistant, who follows through on connections with community agencies and supports the nurse's role, is unique in this project design.

Battaglini and Czerenda's Chapter 4 features System Case Management (SCM), the model developed by United Health Services (UHS) in Broome County, New York. This model is designed to help primary care physicians resolve problems their older patients have in negotiating the health care system, such as coordinating social, medical, and preventive health services and managing costs. Participating physicians are internists providing primary care services through United Medical Associates, a multi-specialty medical practice affiliated with UHS. SCM is designed to demonstrate that the continuum of services available at UHS can be integrated and coordinated for the benefit of the patient through the addition of the patient care coordinator (PCC) in the physician's practice. The PCC is a master's-level prepared nurse with advanced training in a primary care area: family, adult care, or geriatrics. Located within the physician's practice, the PCC closely collaborates with the physician on clinical as well as case management issues.

Weinberg authors Chapter 5, in which the model developed at Mt. Sinai Medical Center in Miami Beach, Florida, is presented. Intervention Pathways to Integrated Care is designed to promote comprehensive geriatric care, improved outcomes for older persons, and increased generalist physician productivity and satisfaction in working with elderly persons. Groups of generalist and sub-specialist physicians participate in the interventions. Their patients receive additional assessments as needed, as well as care and treatment by specially trained teams of advanced registered nurse practitioners (ARNPs) and a social worker (SW). The ARNPs coordinate the implementation of intervention pathways, and are also available to provide episodic care by assisting physicians in the handling of urgent, unscheduled visits. ARNPs use the SW as a consultant and refer patients who need psychosocial services. Phone contact between the ARNPs and patients with chronic problems needing extra care and attention is highly encouraged.

Whereas chapters 2, 3, 4, and 5 focus heavily upon the use of nurses and nurse practitioners in consultation with physicians, the remaining set of chapters reveals the full diversity of roles and relationships demonstrated in the Generalist Physician Initiative. The use of physicians' assistants, social work/nurse teams, social workers, and paraprofessional staff are described in detail in chapters 6, 7, 8, and 9.

In Chapter 6, Anderson, Fortinsky, and Landefeld elaborate on how the Northeast Ohio Neighborhood Health Services, Case Western Reserve University School of Medicine, and University Hospitals of Cleveland, Ohio, developed Senior Health Connections. In this model, certified physician assistants (PAs) received three and one-half months of intense, advanced, highly individualized training in geriatrics, preventive care for the elderly, and gero-psychosocial issues of importance. Their training also included many field experiences with community agencies providing service to local seniors. The PAs (or senior care assistants, as they are known) work at two of the sites of Northeast Ohio Neighborhood Health Services, Inc., an urban community health center in Cleveland. Care of new problems, in collaboration with primary care physicians occurs when patients call in with new issues and are then seen, or when they "walk in" with new concerns. PAs visit hospitalized patients and arrange phone, office, or (occasionally) home follow-up. PAs are readily available to patients through voice mail.

Sommers and Randolph write in Chapter 7 about how California Pacific Medical Center in San Francisco developed Senior Care Connection (SCC), a 4-year project in three geographic sites in the Bay area. SCC makes each patient's primary care physician (PCP) the patient's "care manager." The PCP collaborates with a nurse and social worker team to provide primary care, augmented by a set of new services specifically geared to seniors with chronic illness and functional deficits. With the patients' consent, the nurse and social worker see patients in the office before, during, or after the physician visit and are in telephone contact at least every four to six weeks. The team makes home visits as necessary; visits hospitalized patients, and, if needed, assists in discharge planning and arranging home care services; works closely with patient, family members, and friends to organize a continuum of support; and makes referrals to community-based agencies.

In Chapter 8, Anker-Unnever reveals how the Coordinated Care Partnership developed by St. Joseph Healthcare System in Albuquerque, New Mexico, redesigned its model within a rapidly changing health care environment. St. Joseph Healthcare, a member of Catholic Health Initiatives, is a fully integrated health care system with three acute care hospitals, a rehabilitation hospital, and a physician network known as Med-Net. As a means to foster collaboration with primary care physicians in the process of caring for chronically ill elders, St. Joseph implemented an enhanced case management system in partnership with selected Med-Net physicians' practices. These offices serve as the patients' points of entry, from which case managers (nurses and social workers) provide services to patients. Case managers provide in-home assessment and care plan development in cooperation with patients, family, caregivers, and physicians. Specific in-home monitoring protocols have been developed in conjunction with physicians for each area of chronic care management. Integration of case management into physicians' practices requires fostering physicians' "ownership" of case management, including involvement in program design and decision making. Flexibility is a necessity. As demonstration projects must exist in the real world, this model reveals how adaptations are made to accommodate changes in organizations, physicians, practices, and patients.

Hornung, Brewer, and Stein provide an alternative model in Chapter 9. The South Carolina Department of Health and Environmental Control, located in Columbia, developed the Geriatric Rural Initiative Project. This model is designed to improve available health and medical care for rural elderly patients and to increase the professional and personal satisfaction that physicians derive from treating rural elderly persons. The model is built on the assumption that greater physician satisfaction will make practicing medicine more attractive, resulting in greater numbers of physicians who are willing to establish and maintain their practices in rural areas. The intervention sites include three physicians' practices in the upper Piedmont section of rural South Carolina, areas where services for the rural elderly are scarce and the recruitment and retention of physicians is difficult. The interventionists are paraprofessionals known as geriatric technicians, whose role is to improve care and service delivery.

In Chapter 10, Wasson and Jette present the Community Centers of Excellence for the Aging (CCEAs) concept developed by Dartmouth Medical School Center for the Aging in Hanover, New Hampshire. This intervention rests on the fundamental assumption that improved physician-patient communication is beneficial. This site developed and tested a method for assessing and managing elderly patients in busy community practice settings. CCEAs are the only models in the initiative that did not add collaborative personnel to the practices. Forty-five physicians in 22 practices (28 family practitioners and 17 internists) were recruited. All eligible patients are asked to complete a baseline survey about their health, previous medical care, and personal background. Comprehensive geriatric assessment (CGA), while benefiting selected subgroups, has been criticized because it is ill-defined, expensive, and targets few of the many elderly patients who need care. This model examines whether a standard strategy requiring fewer resources than CGA benefits elderly patients of primary care physicians. This model demonstrates that a standardized, easily replicable strategy, based on the proven principles of CGA yet requiring fewer resources, can be implemented in busy physicians' practices for the benefit of many geriatric patients.

Shearer, Simmons, Berkman, Gundrum, and White round out the presentation of models in Chapter 11. Huntington Memorial Hospital in Pasadena, California, pioneered the Senior Care Network Physician Partnership project. Funded for a 30-month period from February 1992 to August 1994, this project became the prototype that led to the full development of the Generalist Physician Initiative and the selection of nine more sites described in chapters 2 through 10. The Huntington project tested ways in which a non-medical, supportive partnership between physicians and a hospital-based, community-wide case management program could enhance the continuum of care and improve integration of service systems. This model provides rapid response for assessments, brief interventions, and linkages to home and community-based services through a social worker/liaison who is on call to physicians' offices.

The various models presented in chapters 2 through 11 have been developed to address the challenges of geriatric care discussed earlier in this chapter. The Huntington prototype described in Chapter 11 provided a seed from which the growth of diverse models could occur. Each model has distinctive characteristics that allow it to work within its unique environment. Yet there are overriding themes, as well as critical factors, that emerge across models. These themes and factors will be explored fully in Chapter 12 in an attempt to integrate what has been learned in the demonstration projects.

# References

Chrischilles, E.A., Segar, E.T. & Wallace, R.B. (1992). Self-reported adverse drug reactions and related resource use: A study of community-dwelling persons 65 years of age and older. *Annals of Internal Medicine, 117,* 634–640.

Davis, M.H. & O'Brien, E. (1996). Profile of persons with disabilities in Medicare and Medicaid. *Health Care Financing Review, 17*(4), 179–211.

Diabetes Complications and Control Trial Research Group. (1993). The effect of intensive treatment of diabetes on the development and progression of long-term complication in insulin-dependent diabetes mellitus. *New England Journal of Medicine, 329,* 977–986.

Engelhardt, J.B., Toseland, R.W., O'Donnell, J.C., Richie, J.T., Jue, D. & Banks, S. (1996). The effectiveness and efficiency of outpatient geriatric evaluation and management. *Journal of the American Geriatrics Society, 44,* 847–856.

Evans, D.A., Funkenstein, H.H., Albert, M.S., Scherr, P.A., Cook, N.R., Chown, M.J., Hebert, L.E., Hennekens, C.H. & Taylor, J.O. (1989). Prevalence of Alzheimer's disease in a community population of older persons higher than previously reported. *Journal of the American Medical Association, 262,* 2551–2556.

Fabacher, D., Josephson, K., Pietruszka, F., Linderborn, K., Morley, J.E. & Rubenstein, L.Z. (1994). An in-home preventive assessment program for independent older adults: A randomized controlled trial. *Journal of the American Geriatrics Society, 42,* 630–638.

Franks, P., Nutting, P.A. & Clancy, C.M. (1993). Health care reform, primary care, and the need for research. *Journal of the American Medical Association, 270,* 1449–1453.

Grisso, J.A., Kelsey, J.L., Strom, B.L, Chiu, G.Y., Maislin, G., O'Brien, L.A., Hoffman, S., Kaplan, F. & The Northeast Hip Fracture Study Group. (1991). Risk factors for falls as a cause of hip fracture in women. *New England Journal of Medicine, 324,* 1326–1331.

Grymonpre, R.E., Mitenko, P.A., Sitar, D.S., Aoki, F.Y. & Montgomery, P. R. (1988). Drug-associated hospital admissions in older medical patients. *Journal of the American Geriatrics Society, 36,* 1092–1098.

Health Care Financing Administration, U.S. Department of Health and Human Services. (1996). *Health Care Financing Review, Statistical Supplement, 1996.* Washington, DC: US Department of Health and Human Services.

Heffler, S.K., Donham, C.S., Won, D.K. & Sensenig, A.L. (1996). Hospital, employment, and price indicators for the health care industry: Fourth quarter 1995 and annual data for 1987–95. *Health Care Financing Review, 17*(4), 217–256.

Hendrickson, C., Lund, E. & Strømgård, E. (1984). Consequences of assessment and interaction among elderly people: Three-year randomized control trial. *British Medical Journal, 289,* 1522–1524.

Hypertension Detection and Follow-Up Cooperative Group. (1979). Five-year findings of the Hypertension Detection and Follow-Up Program: I. Reduction in mortality of persons with high blood pressure, including mild hypertension. *Journal of the American Medical Association, 242,* 2562–2571.

Institute of Medicine. (1996). *Primary care: America's health in a new era.* Washington, DC: National Academy Press, p. 1.

Levit, K.R., Lazenby, H.C., Sivarajan, L., Stewart, M.W., Braden, B.R., Cowan, C.A., Donham, C.S., Long, A.M., McDonnell, P.A., Sensenig, A.L., Stiller, J.M. & Won, D. K. (1996). National health expenditures, 1994. *Health Care Financing Review, 17*(3), 205–230.

Mark, D.M., Gottlieb, M.S., Zellner, B.B., Chetty, V.K. & Midtling, J.E. (1996). Medicare costs in urban areas and the supply of primary care physicians. *Journal of Family Practice, 43,* 33–39.

Melin, A.L., Wieland, D., Harker, J.O. & Bygren, L.O. (1995). Health outcomes of post-hospital in-home team care: Secondary analysis of a Swedish trial. *Journal of the American Geriatrics Society, 43,* 301–307.

Radecki, S.E., Kane, R.L., Solomon, D.H., Mendenhall, R.C. & Beck, J.C. (1988a). Do physicians spend less time with older patients? *Journal of the American Geriatrics Society, 36,* 713–718.

Radecki, S.E., Kane, R.L., Solomon, D.H., Mendenhall, R.C. & Beck, J.C. (1988b). Are physicians sensitive to the special problems of older patients? *Journal of the American Geriatrics Society, 36,* 719–725.

Ramsdell, J.W., Swart, J.A., Jackson, E. & Renvall, M. (1989). The yield of a home visit in the assessment of geriatric patients. *Journal of the American Geriatrics Society, 37,* 17–24.

Reuben, D.B. (1991). Geriatric syndromes. In J.C. Beck (Ed.), *Geriatrics review syllabus: A core curriculum in geriatric medicine. Book 1: Syllabus and questions* (Part 2, pp. 117–231). New York: American Geriatrics Society.

Rubenstein, L.Z., Stuck, A.E., Siu, A.L. & Wieland, D. (1991). Impacts of geriatric evaluation and management programs on defined outcomes: Overview of the evidence. *Journal of the American Geriatrics Society, 39*(Suppl.), 8S-16S.

Schneider, E.L. & Guralnik, J.M. (1990). The aging of America. Impact on health care costs. *Journal of the American Medical Association, 263,* 2335–2340.

Shua-Haim, J.R. & Gross, J.S. (1997). Osteoporosis: Preventing the "emphysema" of the bone. *Clinical Geriatrics, 5*(2), 54–67.

Sloane, P.D. (1991). Changes in ambulatory care with patient age: Is geriatric care qualitatively different? *Family Medicine, 23,* 40–43.

Stuck, A.E., Aronow, H.U., Steiner, A., Alessi, C.A., Büla, C.J., Gold, M.N., Yuhas, K.E., Nisenbaum, R., Rubenstein, L.Z. & Beck, J.C. (1995). A trial of annual in-home comprehensive geriatric assessments for elderly people living in the community. *New England Journal of Medicine, 333,* 1184–1189.

Toseland, R.W., O'Donnell, J.C., Engelhardt, J.B., Hendler, S.A., Richie, J.T. & Jue, D. (1996). Outpatient geriatric evaluation and management. Results of a randomized trial. *Medical Care, 34,* 624–640.

Wagner, E.H., Austin, B.T. & Von Korff, M. (1996). Organizing care for patients with chronic illness. *Milbank Quarterly, 74,* 511–544.

Weiss, L.J. & Blustein, J. (19 96). Faithful patients: The effect of long-term physician-patient relationships on the costs and use of health care by older Americans. *American Journal of Public Health, 86,* 1742–1747.

Wilcox, S.M., Himmelstein, D.U. & Woolhandler, S. (1994). Inappropriate drug prescribing for the community-dwelling elderly. *Journal of the American Medical Association, 272,* 292–296.

# CHAPTER 2

# Complementary Geriatric Practice Model

*Nancy A. Whitelaw, Mary Beth Tupper,*
*Alice Early, and Phyllis Collier*

The Henry Ford Health System (HFHS) is one of the nation's large comprehensive health systems. Begun in 1912, with the founding of Henry Ford Hospital, HFHS now includes a network of health promotion, diagnosis, treatment, research, education, medical equipment, and home health services as well as health care financing options. HFHS serves approximately 800,000 residents of southeastern Michigan through its six hospitals, 35 outpatient clinics, two nursing homes, hospice program, home health care agency, and other services and facilities. More than 1,000 physicians are on staff as members of the Henry Ford Medical Group, and HFHS is affiliated with another 1,700 private practice physicians.

Health Alliance Plan (HAP), the health plan component of HFHS, is Michigan's largest non-profit, mixed-model managed care plan. HAP offers a variety of insurance options, including the traditional health maintenance organization (HMO), a preferred provider organization (PPO), a Medicare risk program, a Medicare complementary program, and a Medicaid program.

As a major academic medical center, HFHS attracts some 850 physicians-in-training as well as students in nursing, social work, and allied health. It has educational affiliations with Case Western Reserve University School of Medicine, Michigan State University School of Osteopathic Medicine, Wayne State University, and Oakland University School of Nursing.

While HFHS offers training and research in specialty areas, it has strengthened and expanded the generalist physician role in the face of many challenges. For example, in the 1960s HFHS consisted of a large hospital and a 17-story clinic building in downtown Detroit. The changing social climate brought about a major population shift that resulted in dispersion of the hospital's patient base. In response, HFHS established ambulatory care "satellites" where patients were located—in urban, suburban, and rural sites—and staffed these satellites with general internists, pediatricians, and family practitioners.

Furthermore, HFHS's experience in managed care has strengthened generalist physician activities and brought attention to the need for high quality primary care. HFHS has approximately 400 generalist physicians on staff. Given the increasing scarcity of generalist physicians, particularly in the inner city (Pew Health Professions Commission, 1995), HFHS must actively seek ways to enrich the role and improve the productivity of generalist physicians.

The John A. Hartford Foundation Generalist Physician Initiative represented a new and important dimension in the efforts of HFHS to strengthen generalist physician capacity and effectiveness. This initiative provided an opportunity to simultaneously redefine the generalist physician's role in the care of elders and improve integration of care. Such endeavors are critical to health systems, as they seek ways to attract and retain generalist physicians while improving the quality of care in a cost-constrained environment.

As people live longer, chronic diseases emerge as the major cause of death and disability, resulting in much health care utilization and expense (Institute for Health and Aging, 1996). Successful treatment of previously fatal conditions has prolonged life expectancy, but has also increased the frequency and duration of chronic conditions and disability (Institute of Medicine, 1991). As with other systems, HFHS is currently confronting the challenges of serving an elderly population. Adults age 65 and over make more than 300,000 visits to our clinics and account for 40,000 discharges—one-third of all discharges—from our hospitals.

## Project Design

The Complementary Geriatric Practice model consists of generalist physicians and nurse practitioners working together in the ambulatory clinic setting to provide primary care for frail elderly patients. The model targets elderly patients who are most likely to experience improved quality of care and overall well-being from a team approach—for example, elderly patients considered at high risk for hospitalization, those with cognitive or mental status problems, and those near the end of life.

At HFHS, the intervention occurred at two clinics. These clinics were selected because primary care nurse practitioners were already on staff. Four "comparison" clinics, without nurse practitioners, were selected from among HFHS's other 33 outpatient clinics to provide comparison patients who were demographically similar to those in the intervention.

In the intervention model, depending on the patients' needs and the availability of the providers, patients are scheduled to see either the nurse practitioner or the physician for the first visit. This visit may be for a history and physical, or to address an acute health concern. At this visit, the team approach is explained. Many patients arrive unaware of nurse practitioners and their roles, but most leave the clinic accepting the nurse practitioners as primary care providers.

The providers then schedule return visits based on the nature of the problems identified. Individuals with undiagnosed or poorly controlled medical conditions are seen regularly by physicians, with the nurse practitioners consulted to assist in developing and implementing appropriate care plans. Individuals with stable chronic disease are followed primarily by the nurse practitioners after introductory visits with their physicians, with periodic physician visits thereafter to support therapeutic relationships. All patients see nurse practitioners for an annual health maintenance review. Thus, stable patients may see their nurse practitioners more often than they see their physicians, but there is a sharing of the patients' management plans by the nurse practitioner and physician teams.

The following case illustrates the core features of the Complementary Practice model. Mr. McDonald is an 86-year-old man with diabetes and hypertension who has been under the care of Dr. Jonas for the past six months. Mr. McDonald's blood sugar was high at his last two clinic appointments. Dr. Jonas discovers that Mr. McDonald eats pancakes with syrup every morning, has a couple of cookies with coffee for lunch, and eats dessert every evening while watching television. Dr. Jonas encourages Mr. McDonald to see Mrs. Simmons, the nurse practitioner, emphasizing that he values the nurse practitioner role. After Mrs. Simmons meets Mr. McDonald, she and Dr. Jonas discuss the case. As a team they determine that the nurse practitioner will provide primary care, teach and counsel regarding diabetes and hypertension, monitor compliance, conduct assessments, and consult with the physician regularly. The physician will supervise the medical plan and will become more directly involved if Mr. McDonald becomes acutely ill or develops other medical problems. Together, they discuss the plan with the patient. Like the vast majority of patients, Mr. McDonald is pleased with the plan and he feels he benefits from having a nurse practitioner as part of his care.

End-of-life issues are ever present in our geriatric practice. In the Complementary Practice model, both physicians and nurse practitioners routinely talk with patients about their expectations and preferences for care and decision making near the end of life. The nurse practitioner explores patient preferences and goals for care during the patient's annual health maintenance review, and during other visits when the opportunity arises. Labeled "advance care planning," summaries of these conversations are documented in the meeting notes, and the dates listed on the medical record. Ongoing and open communication of this nature builds rapport and offers guidance to clinicians and families during periods of crisis when active patient input into decision making may be severely limited or impossible. Such personal knowledge about the patient has advantages over advance directive documents—only a small proportion of individuals complete such documents, and the documents themselves may be too vague to be useful in specific circumstances.

Weekly or bi-weekly team meetings are a critical piece of the Complementary Practice model. Team meetings are used to create a coordinated care management plan for specific patients and to share skills and knowledge among team members. For example, at one meeting a provider described the difficulty of convincing family members that a patient was demonstrating symptoms of dementia. Another team member suggested that the provider ask the patient's permission to review the patient's checkbook with the family, to assess how well the patient was managing her finances. The checkbook was in such disarray that the patient's difficulty was immediately apparent. This simple approach helped the family members to recognize the problem and to work on a solution. In addition, all the team members had learned something new that would improve their practice.

Team meeting time must be protected actively from encroachment by paperwork, administrative duties, or clinic care. In our project, teams conduct meetings using a formal structure (e.g., pre-set agendas with specific time allocations and pre-assignment of leader, recorder, and timekeeper roles). This structure gives a focus to continuously improving team work, efficiency, and patient care. Of course, informal discussions and sharing of information also occur in hallways and exam rooms as part of a typical day's work.

We cannot overemphasize the importance of ongoing communication with mutual sharing of patient information. In patient care, there is constant change from stable to unstable conditions, anticipated responses to unanticipated responses, and typical to atypical symptoms. For the team members to maintain consistency and continuity in the patients' care plans and to provide the best care, they must share their questions, concerns, findings, and plans.

For example, one of our team practices included an elderly patient who had long used habit-forming medication. The nurse practitioner was verbally contracting with the patient to wean her off the medication. It appeared as though this strategy was working because, after several weeks, the patient stopped asking for refills. Much to the chagrin of the nurse practitioner, however, the patient had merely obtained the prescription from the physician. The physician did not think to discuss this with the nurse practitioner, even though the physician knew that the nurse practitioner was involved in the patient's care. As a result, the nurse practitioner's strategy was undermined, as was the team care approach. This problem was discussed at a team meeting so that all team members could work together to find ways to avoid future communication breakdowns. Such cycles of learning and improvement are a fundamental part of the Complementary Practice model.

# Patient Selection and Enrollment

Selecting patients to participate in the Complementary Practice model was a 2-stage process. Providers and researchers jointly decided that the model was best suited for frail patients, most particularly those at risk of hospitalization, those near the end of life, and those with mental health problems. Two sets of selection criteria were then operationalized with data from HFHS information systems so that a pool of appropriate patients could be identified.

First, patients had to meet all of the following four conditions:

- Were age 70 years and older
- Had not received primary care at both an intervention and a comparison clinic during the prior 12 months. This reduced the risk of contamination.

- Had had two or more primary care visits during the prior 12 months. This helped to ensure that patients were regular users of HFHS.
- Was not insured under a "risk" or HMO contract. Since type of insurance can influence utilization, we wanted to reduce the variety of acceptable insurance plans.

The second set of criteria was designed to identify the frail sub-population. For patients to be selected, they had to meet at least one of the following seven criteria:

- Hospitalization during the past two years
- Diagnoses of psychiatric or mental status problems
- Four or more primary care visits during the past 12 months
- High specialty care use (top 25% of outpatient charges for all elderly patients)
- Diagnoses of heart disease, stroke, or degenerative joint disease
- Two or more emergency room visits during the past 12 months
- Age 90 years and older

After selection criteria had been established, we divided the project population into five groups. Within each of the first four groups, we randomly selected patients to participate in the project.

After patients at the intervention sites were selected, clinic staff were notified so that they could invite patients to participate. Patients were "enrolled" at a clinic visit, when the nurse practitioner or physician explained the Complementary Practice model. At both intervention clinics, patients who had not been selected could be served by the Complementary Practice model based upon provider discretion, but these patients were not tracked for the evaluation.

Ultimately, 977 patients were included in the project. Their average age was 78 years, 50% were African-American, 58% were female, and 69% had at least an eighth-grade education. When the project began, 40% were living alone and 51% reported incomes below $12,000 annually. At the two intervention sites, 442 geriatric patients received the Complementary Practice model and were followed for a 12-month period or until death, while 535 patients from the four comparison clinics were followed for the same amount of time.

# Roles and Relationships

To meet the needs of this frail population, the basic Complementary Practice model consists of the nurse practitioner-physician team, working in an environment with other health professionals (e.g., social workers, clinic nurses, care managers, and home care nurses). In caring for a shared population of patients, each discipline contributes its expertise to the assessment and joint care planning of a given individual, and actively engages the patient and caregiver in the process.

At the start of the project, the roles of all providers were only vaguely defined. Over the course of the intervention period, more definition was brought to these roles, although they still evolve and vary somewhat by the unique skills, interests, and personalities of each provider.

## Nurse Practitioner

The expertise of the nurse practitioner complements that of the physician in managing complex geriatric patients. Issues relating to skin care, nutrition, medication management, elimination, mobility, and compliance with the care plan are the domain of the nurse practitioner. The nurse practitioner approaches the patient in a holistic manner due to both basic and advanced nursing preparation.

Nurse practitioners are especially skilled in assessment and care planning. After establishing a baseline, the nurse practitioners use tailored educational approaches to develop the knowledge and skills of the patients and/or caregivers so that they understand and can effectively carry out the individualized care plans. This is not accomplished in a single visit, but develops over time, with the nurse practitioners, physicians, and patients negotiating the priorities.

Nurse practitioners routinely assess the patients' understanding of an illness in terms of the patients' own health beliefs and behaviors. They work closely with the physicians to tailor the care plans to incorporate patient beliefs, goals, and behaviors, since these factors ultimately affect patient compliance and health outcomes.

For example, our nurse practitioners are often involved in the patients' medication regimens. The costs of medications can be truly prohibitive for the patients. When medications are prescribed without any inquiry into the patient's ability to pay, the plans may fail because the prescribed medications cannot be purchased. This care scenario is becoming more frequent as medication costs rise and patients' incomes remain stable or shrink. In other instances, patients reject the addition of new medications, expressing concern that they are already taking too many drugs. They may point to their ancestors who lived long, healthy lives without all of the current medical miracles. (If a patient expresses this concern, a new prescription will likely be placed in a drawer and ignored). Based upon our experience, patient noncompliance is not a simple, willful act of stubbornness or neglect but rather an expression of confusion, or disbelief, or rejection of a poorly explained management plan. To counter this, the nurse practitioners question the patients, review the current medication regimes, make inquiries related to patient reluctance to take new medications and reach medication plans that are acceptable to the patients.

When patients are no longer independent, the nurse practitioner works closely with caregivers to educate them and assist them in managing the patient. The patient's caregivers often express their fears, weariness, and frustrations in caring for elderly family members. In one instance, the wife of an elderly patient wept openly to the nurse practitioner while expressing shame over being tired of caring for her husband. The patient was interrupting her sleep during the night and was extremely dependent and demanding during the day. The wife was exhausted, depressed, and feeling guilty because she could no longer meet his needs. The nurse practitioner arranged for respite care on a regular basis for the caregiver, made certain that the wife's own health was attended to, and reassured the wife that she was not guilty of anything other than expressing basic human needs.

## Physician

In Complementary Practice, the physician is responsible for the medical plan of care for each patient and the diagnostic evaluation of new complex problems. The physician is the primary care provider for patients having complex or unstable medical conditions and coordinates subspecialty care for many of the team's shared patients. The physician is actively involved in decisions to admit patients to the hospital and in working with hospital staff and "rounders" on inpatient care and discharge plans. In addition, the physician consults with the nurse practitioner on those patients with stable chronic disease and minor acute problems.

## Patient and Caregiver

Key to the success of Complementary Practice is the active role of patients and their caregivers. As active partners, patients report new symptoms or exacerbation of chronic symptoms promptly. The team must engage patients and caregivers in the care planning process, encouraging them to voice concerns or objections whenever there is conflict so that an acceptable plan is developed. Included in the plan is a method for timely communication between patients and caregivers on the one hand, and providers on the other hand, so that changes in patient condition can be recognized and addressed appropriately.

# Implementation and Relationship Development

The urban intervention clinic is located in the heart of Detroit and serves only elderly patients. The clinic as a whole made the decision to take part in this project, so all four general internists participated. The suburban intervention site is a large, multi-specialty clinic west of Detroit. Two of the general internists with particularly large panels of elderly patients volunteered to participate.

There were three nurse practitioners at each clinic. Each one was trained either in adult or geriatric care, and each one had more than 10 years of experience with elderly patients. The Complementary Practice model was introduced into existing practices and schedules for both the physicians and the nurse practitioners. Caring for the 442 project patients was a small part of their overall responsibilities for several thousand older adults.

The two clinics have very different histories. The urban clinic had been using a team approach to provide health care for frail elders since 1987. When the Complementary Practice project began, it already had a staff of nurse practitioners, physicians, social workers, and nurses as well as other office personnel. The physicians and nurse practitioners provided services in the clinic, a nursing home, a senior housing site, and an inpatient unit.

Ten years ago, when the clinic was first starting, the nurse practitioners struggled to win the physicians' trust and respect. Consequently, not all physicians at the clinic embraced the team approach, and some only reluctantly shared the care of a few patients. But as these shared cases proved successful, the team approach grew, so that there was a positive feeling about collaboration when the Complementary Practice project began.

To implement the Complementary Practice model, the existing clinic team worked together to more clearly define roles, to tighten referral relationships, to grow as a team, and to better educate new providers on team processes. Team members reviewed existing practices in relation to the particular professional expertise within the group and how best to utilize that expertise. Better definition of the nurse practitioner's role and expertise increased patient referrals for nurse practitioner care. This team also adopted an improved team meeting agenda, stressing the importance of case study presentations, seeking assistance for difficult care management situations, and sharing team successes.

At the multi-specialty suburban clinic, the Complementary Practice model was implemented when a nurse-managed clinic was established within the larger clinic. The nurse practitioners collaborated with two internists who were willing to participate in the Complementary Practice model and share their existing elderly patients. Initially, the relationship between the physicians and nurse practitioners was extremely fragile since this approach was new for the physicians and, to a lesser extent, the nurse practitioners. The nurse practitioners, being relatively new to the clinic, also needed to develop relationships with other providers, administrators, support staff, and patients.

To facilitate patients' acceptance of the nurse practitioners, the physicians at the suburban clinic introduced their patients to the nurse practitioners' role and the team concept of care, giving reassurance that they would remain involved in their patients' care. In many instances, the nurse practitioners went directly to the physicians' offices and were personally introduced to the patients. These personal expressions of physician endorsement were appreciated by patients and fostered acceptance and then enthusiasm for the nurse practitioners' role. As the patients gave positive feedback to their physicians regarding their care from the nurse practitioners, the trust grew between the physicians and the nurse practitioners.

In the early months, processes of communication between physicians and nurse practitioners at the suburban clinic occurred in several ways, including face-to-face contact, written notes, telephone calls, and brief conferences at the end of each day. During these conferences, the physicians became more aware of the nurse practitioners' expertise and the nurse practitioners were able to experience a truly collaborative relationship with the physicians. Weekly team meetings, lasting from 60 to 90 minutes, provided an opportunity to discuss care plans in greater detail, to share provider skills, to address concerns with the team process, and to recognize new team successes. After a year, scheduled daily conferences were discontinued. Weekly meetings and ad hoc conferences proved adequate.

Relationships among providers within and across clinics were strengthened early in the project when they jointly developed care plan guides for the three target groups of elderly people—those with delirium, depression, or dementia, near the end of life, or at high risk for hospitalization. These care plans address the common geriatric issues of incontinence, weight loss, medications, caregiver burden, functional decline, cognitive decline, and patient autonomy. Working on these guides helped team members build trust and understanding, and provided an opportunity to discuss different approaches to care. The guides reflect the group's consensus about care planning and provide a template for individualized care plans. They are especially valuable in helping less experienced professionals and those not familiar with geriatric issues to join a Complementary Practice team.

Implementation of the Complementary Practice model evolved through three stages: wariness, acceptance, and enthusiasm. The collective process of defining roles and activities provides the foundation for developing a trusting relationship between physicians and nurse practitioners. While our experience and learning can help other teams get started, each new team must undergo its own process of developing trust, respect, and shared practice. At both clinics, there is unanimous agreement that team meetings are crucial to the development and maintenance of this model of care.

## Assessment and Care Planning

In our experience, assessment and care planning are the core of high-quality geriatric care, and a team approach is crucial to a successful assessment and care planning process. During the initial visit, the patient is interviewed and a history and physical exam is performed. Decisions are made about which assessments to perform and when. Specific health concerns and problems are discussed with the patient or caregiver and an initial plan of care is developed. At subsequent appointments, further assessments are conducted according to the need, and the care plan is revised based upon discussions involving the patient, caregiver, nurse practitioner, physician, and other involved health care providers.

The case of Mrs. Carney illustrates this process. Mrs. Carney has been receiving her health care at the clinic for the past six months. Mrs. Edwards, the nurse practitioner, and Dr. Matthews are her primary care team members. She usually drives herself to the clinic and comes alone. Today, Mrs. Carney is accompanied by her daughter, Emma, who has some specific concerns. Mrs. Carney has always been an impeccable housekeeper; however, Emma has noted that the house has not had much attention lately. There is clutter on the floors and dirty dishes in the sink. Mrs. Carney explains that she is tired of working and so she's been letting things go.

Emma is also concerned about her mother's "antisocial behavior." She usually plays bridge every Thursday but stopped going about a month ago. Her friends are concerned about why she has dropped out so suddenly.

Mrs. Edwards, the nurse practitioner, asks if she could do some specific assessments for depression and evaluate mental and functional status. Mrs. Edwards will evaluate Mrs. Carney's mental functioning by administering the Folstein Mini Mental Status Examination (Folstein, Folstein & McHugh, 1975). This tool is useful in evaluating for cognitive decline and memory loss. Mrs. Carney scored a 26 out of 30 on her examination, which is representative of a mild cognitive deficit.

It is important to screen Mrs. Carney's functional status in view of the changes noted by her daughter. The nurse practitioner uses the Henry Ford Functional Assessment Tool (Stoor, Johnson & Early, 1989) to obtain a comprehensive profile of how well Mrs. Carney is meeting her basic needs and taking care of herself. Mrs. Carney was independent in ADLs and IADLs at this point but her daughter was quick to point out that she was not as capable of doing the household chores as she had been. The Functional Abilities Screening Evaluation (FASE) Instrument (Russell, 1984) can also be used for screening functional status. However, when deficits are noted, a comprehensive functional assessment should be done.

Mrs. Carney's withdrawn and apathetic behaviors are possible symptoms of depression. The Geriatric Depression Scale (Yesavage, Brink, Rose, Lum et al., 1983) is specific to older adults and can help screen for depression. When this tool is administered, Mrs. Carney is determined to be clinically depressed.

Mrs. Carney, Emma, Mrs. Edwards, and Dr. Matthews arrange for a conference time to sit down and discuss the findings of these assessments and develop a plan of care. Mrs. Carney agrees to see a geriatric psychiatrist for further evaluation of her depression. She recognizes that her memory is becoming a bigger problem to her. Her daughter plans on daily contact with her mother to identify and address any problems early. Dr. Matthews discusses testing to further evaluate Mrs. Carney's memory loss. Mrs. Edwards will ask the social worker to contact Mrs. Carney about community resources. A follow-up appointment is made with Dr. Matthews to discuss the results of the new tests.

Our teams have found that basic nutrition must often be evaluated for geriatric patients, particularly those suffering from Alzheimer's disease. Frequently used is the Nutrition Initiatives Screening Tool (Greer, Margolis, Mitchell & Grunewald, 1992). When more detailed nutritional assessments are needed, the Level 1 and Level 2 Nutrition Screening Tools are available (Greer et al., 1992).

There are several other areas of assessment useful in working with the geriatric population to evaluate specific areas of concern. One is caregiver burden, which can be assessed using questions such as "Are you feeling overworked? Do you think that your health has declined?" Caregiving expertise is assessed through nurse practitioner and physician interactions with the patient and family. Teaching is done as specific needs are identified.

The care guides developed by the two clinics jointly early in the project identify specific critical assessments and interventions that can guide the care of a patient. For example, in assessing patients at the end of life, pain management is essential. Pain assessment tools and points to consider in assessing pain and the person's response to pain are incorporated into the guides. Non-drug modalities such as relaxation therapy, meditation, and guided imagery are outlined for pain management as well as very specific drug management of mild, moderate, and severe pain.

Safety is also a concern for geriatric patients. Teams evaluate driving ability in relation to functional level, cognitive abilities, and overall health. Bathroom, kitchen, and fire safety are assessed. There is particular concern for safeguarding the demented patient, such as putting double locks on the doors and removing knobs from stoves. Teaching and counseling are done when safety concerns are identified.

Medication use is a major problem among elderly persons and an emphasis is placed on evaluating medication knowledge and compliance. The nurse practitioners at the two intervention clinics designed a medication assessment questionnaire to evaluate patient knowledge and compliance.

Assessment of health maintenance, including health habits (i.e., exercise, sexual habits, sleep, and use of alcohol, drug, tobacco, seat belts, and firearms), preventive health practices, and screening tests are conducted initially by the nurse practitioner, and then on an annual basis. Teaching and counseling are provided in relation to health practices and staying healthy.

While the majority of the time the nurse practitioner completes these assessments, the physician is also trained to administer them. However, since so many of these assessments incorporate patient education in the intervention, the nurse practitioner is usually better trained to carry out this aspect of the care plan.

The frequency of any assessment is determined by the patient and the health care team. If a team member identifies a need for a specific assessment, it is conducted in a timely manner and findings are shared with other team members. The overall assessment process provides a holistic view of the patient and assists in identifying areas of concern for the health care team. Once a specific area of concern is identified, the care plan outlines recommended interventions.

Although care plan development is a team effort, the forum for team interaction varies. For complex and complicated patients, care plans are developed primarily at the monthly team meeting. Assessment findings are shared and the team develops a plan of care. For less complex patients, conferencing occurs between team members during and after a patient's appointment. The care plan is revised, amended, or supplemented on an ongoing basis. The patient and family are always actively engaged in the care planning process through discussions with them during and between appointments. Mutual goals are discussed and agreed upon by the patient before being incorporated into the care plan.

Documentation of the care plan is accomplished either through a dictated note for the medical record or in writing. Several approaches, including office dictation and formal and informal conferences, are used to monitor patient progress, communicate progress to other team members, and revise the plan of care.

## Evaluation and Lessons Learned

The success of the Complementary Practice model was judged by four criteria: sustainability over time, patient health and functional status, patient satisfaction, and health care utilization. Data on satisfaction and health and functional status were gathered through a mail survey distributed at enrollment and 18 months later. Utilization data were obtained from HFHS data bases for the 12 months following enrollment.

Judging by sustainability, the project has been a great success. The two intervention clinics continue the Complementary Practice model, and nurse practitioner-physician teams have been implemented at four other sites: a geriatric inpatient unit, a clinic in a retirement community, a nursing home, and a Program of All-Inclusive Care for the Elderly (PACE) replication site. Though there are struggles at the beginning, both physicians and nurse practitioners enthusiastically support the model after they have worked together for a year or so.

In addition, several HFHS general internal medicine clinics are exploring the feasibility of implementing the model. While physician and administrator reluctance continues at some clinics, the greatest barrier to starting more team care sites is the shortage of nurse practitioners with primary care expertise. To alleviate this problem, and to further enhance the work of our existing teams, HFHS is participating in a new John A. Hartford Foundation Initiative on Geriatric Interdisciplinary Team Training. Working with Wayne State University in Detroit and University Hospitals Health System, Case Western Reserve University, and The Benjamin Rose Institute in Cleveland, we are operating a program to train current and future physicians, nurse practitioners, social workers, pharmacists, administrators, and other members of the health care team to work together in geriatric teams.

At the end of the project, there were some significant differences in health and functional status between the intervention and comparison clinics. The suburban clinic significantly improved the patient's self-reported ability to perform activities of daily living and the patient's self-assessment of physical activity level compared to one year ago. The urban intervention clinic was disadvantaged from the start, because those patients were significantly older, poorer, more likely to be living alone, and more functionally deficient than the urban comparison patients. Despite these differences, at the end of the intervention, there were no longer significant differences in either instrumental activities of daily living or measures of general fitness.

Patient satisfaction was divided in two categories, ratings of satisfaction with different characteristics of the provider and clinic, and measures of the quality of patient-provider interaction. Since these types of measures tend to receive high scores, we looked at the impact of the Complementary Practice model on patients who had expressed some dissatisfaction at baseline. The urban intervention and comparison clinics showed no significant difference on improving these ratings except among patients 80 years or older. Across multiple measures, intervention patients 80 years and older reported significantly improved levels of satisfaction, compared to comparison patients. For the suburban patients, there were several measures of satisfaction that showed significant improvement, regardless of age, and all favored the intervention patients.

There were no sweeping differences in utilization between intervention and comparison patients. At the urban clinic, where the patients were older and more frail, the comparison group had significantly fewer admissions, but once admitted there was no difference in length of stay. At the suburban clinics, the comparison patients had significantly more specialty care, but shorter inpatient stays.

As we reflect on both our quantitative findings and personal experiences, we conclude that the Complementary Practice model is good for patients and providers. Patients appreciate the breadth of skills and knowledge that the team brings to their care; providers appreciate having someone to share the challenges of caring for these frail patients with complex needs.

The Complementary Practice model tries to create an organized interdependency among providers, and between providers and patients. But it can slip into chaos and redundancy if left unattended. Two issues need constant monitoring. Are roles and responsibilities understood by all providers and the patient? Are there effective ways to communicate changes in the patient's situation and changes in roles and responsibilities?

To address these issues takes time and dedication, and a change in practice patterns for both physicians and nurse practitioners. These changes come only after providers understand the skills and patient care preferences of each team member. We found that developing this understanding can be fostered through a variety of strategies: developing care guides for groups of patients, working together to formally define roles and relationships, holding regularly scheduled team meetings and patient care conferences, and engaging in team building exercises.

The support of system leaders and clinic administrators is crucial. We recommend that a strong project manager or director be assigned to help teams as they attempt to implement the Complementary Practice model. This person can motivate the teams, facilitate team meetings, give visibility to the team's accomplishments and challenges, and identify and help secure needed resources (e.g., computers, training, data).

Senior leadership needs to recognize that team building takes time and some of that time is taken from direct patient care. Even when leadership is supportive, administrators struggle with how to measure the productivity of teams, and how to justify the "expense" of team meetings and special training sessions. Our physicians and nurse practitioners live with the dual pressures of increasing patient satisfaction and teamwork on the one hand, and increasing productivity and lowering costs on the other hand. There is no easy resolution to this dilemma.

The Complementary Practice nurse practitioners have prepared a manual called "Sharing the Care: An Innovative Geriatric Team Model" that provides more detail on how to replicate our Complementary Practice model (Collier, Early, Tupper & Whitelaw, 1998).

# References

Collier, P., Early, A., Tupper, M. & Whitelaw, N. (1998). *Sharing the caring: An innovative geriatric team model*. Detroit: Henry Ford Health System.

Folstein, M.F., Folstein, S. & McHugh, P.R. (1975). Mini-mental state: A practical method for grading the cognitive state of patients for the clinician. *Journal of Psychiatric Research, 12*, 189–198.

Greer, F., Margolis, J., Mitchell, D. & Grunewald, M. (1992). *Nutrition intervention manual for professionals caring for older Americans*. Washington, DC: Nutrition Screening Initiative.

Institute for Health and Aging, University of California. (1996). *Chronic care in America: A 21st century challenge*. Princeton, NJ: The Robert Wood Johnson Foundation.

Institute of Medicine. (1991). *The second 50 years: Promoting health and preventing disability*. Washington, DC: National Academy Press.

Pew Health Professions Commission. (1995). *Critical challenges: Revitalizing the health professions of the twenty-first century*. San Francisco: Pew Health Commission.

Russell, D. (1984). *FASE instrument*. Ames, IA: College of Medicine and Graduate College of the University of Iowa.

Stoor, E., Johnson, T. & Early, A. (1989). *Henry Ford functional assessment tool*. Detroit: Henry Ford Medical Center for Seniors.

Yesavage, J.A., Brink, T.L., Rose, T.L., Lum, O., Huang, V., Adey, M. & Leirer, V.O. (1983). Development and validation of a geriatric depression screening scale: A preliminary report. *Journal of Psychiatric Research, 17*, 37–49.

# CHAPTER 3

# Collaborative Care Teams

*Cheryl Schraeder, Paul Shelton, Teri Britt,*
*Robert Turngren, and Ida Nagele*

What is a better way to coordinate medical, psychosocial, and environmental care than the ways we have done it in the past? How can patients and families play a central role in care management and evaluation? What alternative delivery models will assist primary care physicians to practice efficiently in providing high quality care across the spectrum of health services? These questions are asked every day in health care organizations. Creative solutions require a departure from traditional roles and delivery patterns (Senge, 1990). The literature suggests that multidisciplinary teams provide an effective mechanism for delivering quality geriatric care (Blumenthal, 1996; Greenfield, Kaplan, Ware, Yano & Frank, 1988; Hibbard & Nutting, 1991; Wagner, 1996; Wright, 1993). However, there are few models that have tested this approach to care delivery in the ambulatory setting. The purpose of this chapter is to describe an innovative approach to primary care, the Geriatric Collaborative Care model, which uses teams comprised of patients, physicians, and nurses working together to manage care across the continuum.

## Background

### The Carle Organizations

The Carle organizations (Carle Clinic Association, Carle Foundation, and Carle Foundation Hospital) serve as the regional medical center for more than eight million individuals residing in predominantly rural areas of central Illinois and western Indiana. Although Illinois has a sizable urban population base in the Chicago area, rural and sparsely populated areas characterize most of the state.

The Carle Foundation and Carle Clinic Association offer a full range of vertically integrated health care services. Carle Clinic Association is a multispecialty physician group practice located in Urbana, Illinois. The clinic serves approximately 2,000 patients daily, with more than 290 physicians practicing in 50 medical and surgical specialties and sub-specialties, including 120 primary care physicians and a large ambulatory nursing component.

Carle's delivery system provides primary care through its network of branch clinics, each staffed by physicians (adult medicine or family practice), nurse practitioners, and/or physician assistants. These clinics serve more than 24,000 elders. The main campus, located in Urbana, is the primary referral center and specialty care hub. The branch clinics enhance access to health services for patients in outlying communities. Each clinic uses local community services and networks with local practitioners to create smaller "hubs" of service within a 30-mile radius of the branch. Referrals come to Carle from a network of over 2,000 physicians, with more than 50% of patients coming from outside the Champaign-Urbana communities. The level of managed care penetration in this market is approximately 40%.

Carle Clinic provides a "real world" setting to demonstrate a generalist physician–based model for geriatric collaborative practice. The main clinic, with its large physician staff and ancillary departments, is linked to branch clinics that are typically smaller physician groups in rural settings. This arrangement provides the size and complexity required to deliver the scope and amount of care necessary for implementation of this model. Carle Clinic and its branches are considered representative of national group practices according to data from the Medical Group Management Association.

## Rationale for Project Development

Organizational success will not hinge on a single provider working autonomously, but rather on a mixture of providers working closely together as a team. Organizations must address the issue of having the right provider placement, intensity, and mix to meet complex patient needs over time. Carle envisioned starting team-based primary care by targeting at-risk elderly patients (Mauksch, 1981; Radecki & Cowell, 1990). It was advantageous for Carle to explore a new delivery model with the potential of proactively addressing challenges posed by geriatric primary care.

The Geriatric Collaborative Care model was presented to Carle administrative leadership as a strategic extension of prior models that would explore and develop a more systematic and coordinated way to achieve organizational goals (Schraeder, Britt & Shelton, 1995; Schraeder & Shelton, 1995; Schraeder, Shelton, Britt & Buttitta, 1996; Schraeder, Shelton, Dworak & Fraser, 1993). Geriatric Collaborative Care was a good match with Carle's organizational mandate to provide superior health care through a comprehensive regional network. The mission includes the following goals for elderly patients: (1) to ensure appropriate, timely access to care; (2) to be cost effective in managing high quality care; (3) to deliver coordinated services, including referral to community agencies; and (4) to maintain seniors in the most appropriate setting.

Several factors in Carle's organizational structure and health care marketplace provided a strong impetus for developing the geriatric collaborative model. These factors included: a steadily increasing number of elderly patients, a shift to a larger percentage of the elderly enrolled in managed care, the creation of new mechanisms to deliver primary care (with a focus on team care), and the redefinition of teams comprising different types of providers.

## The Intervention Sites

Primary care physicians in adult medicine and family practice were contacted to determine their interest in the model. A total of 53 physicians (33 family practice and 20 adult medicine physicians) from eight clinics agreed to participate. The clinic sites are located in rural counties and four cities (urban centers) with an average population of 100,000 persons. The sample was drawn to ensure representation of rural and urban practices. Therefore, the practices of internal medicine and family practice physicians were randomized separately and then combined to form a treatment group of 10 family practice and 9 adult medicine physicians, and a comparison group of 23 family practice and 11 adult medicine physicians. The comparison group received customary and usual care.

We implemented the model in four of Carle's multi-specialty group practice sites in Illinois: Bloomington, Danville, Mahomet, and Monticello. In May 1993, Bloomington and Danville were the urban sites, serving both the urban center and contiguous rural counties. Mahomet and Monticello are located in rural counties, serving their own communities and contiguous rural counties. The Geriatric Collaborative Care model, therefore, was based in both urban and rural environments.

# Geriatric Collaborative Care Model

## Model Description and Goals

The Geriatric Collaborative Care model (Figure 3.1) was designed to address Carle's overall mission and trends in elder care. Our goals were to (1) develop collaborative partnerships between physicians, nurse partners, and patients and families to more effectively deliver and manage care; (2) strengthen the primary care delivery system with targeted elderly patients to have an impact on selected outcomes; and (3) develop effective strategies for managing panels of elderly patients within an integrated health care system.

We chose to build the model with RNs as nurse partners because of their broad-based, clinically oriented education and experience. We felt their expertise would complement that of the family practice and internal medicine physician participants without duplication (a potential problem if nurse practitioners were chosen). We thought that clinical patient care issues would be the kernel around which collaboration was most easily layered, so RNs were chosen because they could provide direct patient care as well as participate in case management processes.

Geriatric Collaborative Care is an integrated approach to patient- and family-centered primary care. It links primary care physicians, nurse partners, and patients and families across the continuum of care. Pertinent medical, nursing, and patient and family information is synthesized for better care management, planning, decision making, and coordination. The physician shares diagnostic and medical management information while the nurse partner is responsible for a comprehensive nursing assessment, monitoring, support, and health education and promotion within the patient's own community. The patient and family are central to the model. The patient brings experience, knowledge, and self-care strategies to the team. The team works together to ensure the provision of cost-effective services and the appropriate level of care by

- Arranging and coordinating services
- Reassessing the patient and family as needed
- Joint care planning
- Providing care at the appropriate site by the appropriate provider
- Proactively monitoring and evaluating health status, life changes, and adherence to care recommendations.

**FIGURE 3.1**

Geriatric Collaborative Care Management Model

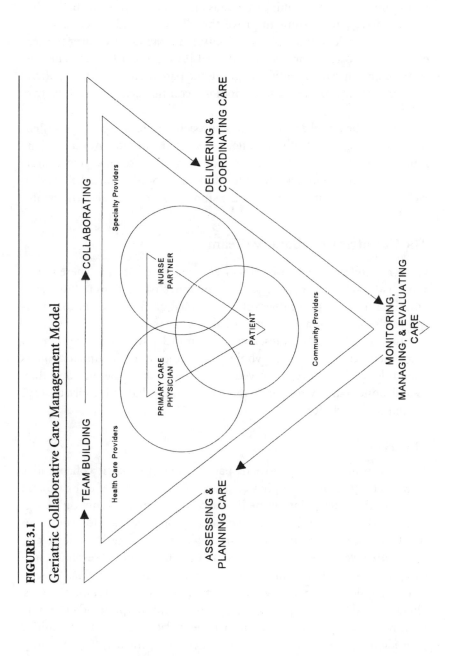

This approach gives patients a more significant and active role in the management of their health care needs and services. It is our belief that collaborative partnerships improve the efficiency and effectiveness of health care services, enhance accessibility, maintain quality, lower the cost of care, and foster improved patient and provider satisfaction. The creation of appropriate incentives aligning the patient, nurse partner, physician, and other providers also promotes a commitment to cost-effective, quality care.

The model emphasizes a team approach and encompasses a system of patient targeting and screening, assessment, monitoring, care planning, service provision and coordination, ongoing care management, follow-up, patient advocacy, and education. The process of collaboration yields a product that is more than the sum of the individual participants.

## The Geriatric Collaborative Team

Geriatric Collaborative Care teams were established at sites where physicians had established patient panels. The nurse partners were hired specifically for the collaborative role. The collaborative care approach required a reorientation on the part of all members.

Individual roles are presented here in order to describe what each team member brings to the whole. These roles must be understood as team roles because they are played out as interlocking pieces rather than "stand alone" parts. We separate them here, somewhat artificially, to serve the purpose of clarity.

### Physicians

Nineteen primary care physicians participated in geriatric collaborative teams. The primary care physician provided skilled medical care and served as the entry point for medical access. This involved not only diagnostic and treatment skills, but coordinating medical care to avoid fragmentation or duplication. The physician also served as team leader, facilitating effective and efficient medical management through evaluation of care processes and coordination of care in a variety of settings. This required physicians to relate with team members in non-traditional ways, characterized by interdependent cooperation and accepting others' input, with more equitable distribution of patient data collection and unified goal identification and achievement (Shelton, Schraeder, Britt & Kirby, 1994).

From the beginning, the physicians were generally enthusiastic about the potential the model held in terms of optimal management for their panels of elderly patients. They were receptive to new ideas for practice pattern enhancement. It took time for teamwork and innovation to be effective. At first teamwork felt clumsy and more like extra work rather than improved productivity. But as time went by, and the team had opportunities to interact regarding patient care issues, the collaborative relationship developed. Practice patterns changed gradually as the nurse partners became more integrated into the office practices and as the team could identify program "success stories." The physicians welcomed pertinent data about psychosocial, environmental, and financial issues provided by the nurse partners. They were typically optimistic and encouraging about how the model could be further refined to meet patient needs, and were often the first to point out improvements in their productivity and patient satisfaction attributable to the model.

### Nurse Partners

There were originally six nurse partners in the model, covering the four project sites. Nurse partners were RNs with community health, ambulatory care, or general medical-surgical backgrounds. The nurse partner role was different from an office or home health nurse. Home health nurses assess patients' medical needs and deliver care in the home, referring to social and community agencies as appropriate. The nurse partner combined the local proximity of the office nurse role with the home-based nursing processes used by home health nurses.

Nurse partners learned their role within the specific cultures of the work environment, team member personalities, and how patient care was delivered. It was critical that the nurse partner was aware of the day-to-day operations of the clinic so that the new model could enhance, rather than duplicate or threaten, established operations. The challenge was for the nurse partner to create a role that worked to fill the gaps and improve quality of patient care through collaborative practice.

The nurse partner role evolved around two aspects of care delivery: the direct provision of primary care in collaboration with physicians, and coordination of care, or case management. Nurse partners integrated objective and subjective data from medical records, physician reports, office staff comments, family, and patient reports to build an initial assessment and care plan. Assessments took place in the home or in the office, depending on patient need. Proactive telephone monitoring occurred on a regular basis and patients were reassessed every six months or as necessary. Continual and open communication between team members was a hallmark of the geriatric collaborative model and took place in formal meetings, informal conversations in the office, and with written notes and voice mail.

Nurse partners also provided direct hands-on care, coordinated service delivery, evaluated patient progress, promoted health maintenance strategies, and advocated for patients. A primary task of the model was bridging the gap between home, clinic, and hospital. The nurse partner often saw hospitalized patients and worked with discharge planners and home care nurses to ensure the most appropriate level of care after discharge. The model emphasized ongoing patient monitoring rather than a focus on specific diseases or acute episodes of illness.

## Case Assistants

There were four case assistants who provided clerical and operational support for the collaborative teams. Case assistants were required to have computer and phone skills and the ability to communicate effectively with physicians, office staff, patients, community providers, and the nurse partner. The case assistant role included assisting the team with non-clinical portions of patient interviewing, enrollment, and monitoring activities. This role was important in increasing efficiency by allowing clinical personnel to focus on clinical issues instead of clerical functions. Case assistants maintained data files, compiled reports, and checked hospital records for admissions and discharges so that the nurse partner and physician would be notified.

Case assistants were often the first persons patients spoke with after being referred to the program, so they had to be able to articulate the program's aims and participants' roles clearly and to answer a variety of questions. They received calls from patients experiencing health problems and conveyed this information to the nurse partner or to an office nurse if the nurse partner was unavailable. Strong written and verbal communication skills were essential. The role also demanded earning the trust of office staff so that when patients came to the office or called, the case assistants were first notified, and in turn the nurse partners received the information. Case assistants learned to use Carle's mainframe computer and to screen clinic and hospital schedules and admission lists. They worked closely with the nurse partners to monitor patient progress toward care plan goals, track patients through the care continuum, and maintain confidential and complete patient records. Case assistants also supplied data and patient lists for reports.

## Patients

Patients and their families were at the center of the model and were vital players in ensuring excellent health care. The patients' role was to provide accurate information to their health care team and to notify them of any changes in health status or life situation. The patients prioritized their health problems and selected interventions with assistance of the other team members. In the model, the patients were the primary problem solvers who reviewed alternatives and were the final decision makers in the process of care. Patients and families made adaptations in lifestyle patterns to accommodate necessary health interventions and recommendations made by the team. The patient identified and communicated signs, symptoms, health issues, constraints to change, as well as psychosocial and financial issues impacting health.

Patients also had to relearn how their care was accessed, structured, and delivered. This required a concerted effort from the collaborative team to encourage trust and develop rapport, as well as to engage patients as active participants in their health care. A major consideration was how to make this change least imposing on patients while at the same time empowering them to play a more active role in their health care.

## Patient Selection and Enrollment

Eligible Carle patients were assigned to the intervention and comparison groups of the Geriatric Collaborative Care model. This occurred in several stages. Participating physician practice sites were first randomized into intervention and comparison groups. This strategy was chosen to maintain consistency in practice patterns and to facilitate the implementation and development of the model.

Patients enrolled in the model were selected if they met four criteria: (1) elderly (65 years of age and older) patients of primary care physicians (family practice or adult medicine) who were participating in the intervention group; (2) residents of the catchment area; (3) at risk of hospitalization and/or nursing home admission as determined by their primary care physicians; and (4) likely to benefit from geriatric collaborative practice.

Several steps were taken to identify potential participants. Individual patients were initially identified through Carle's automated claims tracking system by primary care physician, age, clinic location, and number of physician visits in the past year. Those lists were then reviewed by the patient's primary care physician or office nurse for possible benefit from geriatric collaboration. Those individuals selected by their primary care physicians were contacted by mail to participate in the project. All individuals who returned a completed screening questionnaire, provided informed consent, and met the above criteria were eligible for the project.

## Patient Characteristics

Patient demographics and health conditions for both the intervention and comparison groups are listed in Table 3.1. A total of 758 patients were served. The ages of intervention participants ranged from 55 to 97 years, with a mean age of 76. Seventy-one percent of the intervention group were female, 52% were high school graduates, and over half (61%) had incomes of less that $20,000 per year. When rating their own health, 64% of both groups reported very good or good. Of the intervention group, 24% reported their health as fair and 6% as poor. The most frequently reported medical diagnoses were arthritis, heart disease, hypertension, and hearing difficulties.

Assessment data collected from patients in the intervention group at program entry revealed that the top seven active health problem areas were neuromusculoskeletal function, circulation, nutrition, vision, pain, emotional stability, and health care supervision. This second set of health problem areas may be a reflection of how specific medical conditions impact a patient's lifestyle.

# Geriatric Collaborative Care: Clinical Processes

The four clinical processes described below transpired in the context of formal meetings between physician and nurse partner, informal conversations in clinic hallways, phone calls, and written messages. As teamwork evolved, each team found its own most streamlined and effective means of communicating. This varied greatly by site. Most processes are enacted by all team members in conjunction with the others. Individual roles vary depending on expertise and specific patient and family needs.

## Screening and Assessment

In this model, the physician conducts medical examinations and review of systems, identifies risk factors and needs for diagnostic tests and procedures, makes pertinent diagnoses, determines the need for referral to other providers, and plans follow-up. The nurse partner completes the nursing

**TABLE 3.1**

Geriatric Collaborative Care Patient Demographics
and Health Conditions

| (N=758) | Intervention Group | Comparison Group |
|---|---|---|
| | N=440 | N=318 |
| **Gender** | | |
| male | 29% | 27% |
| female | 71% | 73% |
| **Age in years (Mean)** | 76 | 75 |
| **Ethnicity** | | |
| white | 97% | 96% |
| other | 3% | 4% |
| **Marital status** | | |
| married | 48% | 51% |
| widowed | 42% | 40% |
| divorced/separated | 6% | 3% |
| single | 4% | 6% |
| **Educational background** | | |
| not high school grad | 35% | 25% |
| high school/some college | 52% | 55% |
| college graduate | 13% | 20% |
| **Household income per year** | | |
| less than $20,000 | 61% | 54% |
| $20,000–$39,000 | 31% | 31% |
| over $40,000 | 8% | 15% |
| **General health (self-rated)** | | |
| excellent | 6% | 10% |
| very good | 25% | 32% |
| good | 39% | 32% |
| fair | 24% | 21% |
| poor | 6% | 5% |
| **Current health conditions*** | | |
| arthritis | 75% | 72% |
| heart disease | 28% | 24% |
| hypertension | 58% | 54% |
| hearing difficulties | 43% | 34% |
| stroke | 14% | 10% |
| vision difficulties | 26% | 24% |
| diabetes | 23% | 18% |
| COPD/asthma | 22% | 18% |

*Percentages do not add to 100% due to multiple patient conditions.

assessment across psychosocial, physical, environmental, and preventive
and health maintenance domains. Patients participate in the assessment by
supplying complete information about past and present history, and by de-
scribing and prioritizing their health status across domains. Patients assist
team members in understanding individual social and environmental
health norms and well-being during the home/office visit. Each of these
perspectives is blended to form a comprehensive plan of care.

The physician and nurse also review the medication regimen with
the patient. The team focuses on the patient's response, including barriers
and facilitators to properly taking medication. This occurs during office
visits, home visits, and phone calls.

Over time, team members collaborate to incorporate medical, nursing, and patient-specific information into a meaningful plan of care that
accurately reflects the patient's medical diagnosis, individual needs, preferences, and lifestyle. Through the comprehensive and ongoing assessment process, the team detects potential and actual threats to health and
well-being, evaluates care being provided, and identifies areas for health
promotion. The patient alerts the team at early onset of symptoms or
with concern for maintenance of health status.

For example, at the in-home assessment the nurse partner might find
that the patient's environment is not well lit and poses a high risk for falls.
The physician may have noted that the patient has osteoporosis and arthritis, so a fall could be quite harmful. The patient may have also voiced
fear of falling due to decreased mobility. These pieces of information
would be incorporated into the care plan. The team would then work together to summarize the findings from medical, nursing, and patient and
family self-assessment perspectives.

## Care Planning

The physician and nurse develop a comprehensive plan of care with the
patient and family that includes goals relating to medical diagnoses, as
well as problems identified and prioritized during the assessments. Team
members plan and implement interventions, identifying strategies for
optimal adherence to the plan of care. The nurse partner reviews physician recommendations and educates the patient and family as needed.
The team continually evaluates the feasibility of the care plan and assesses
patient understanding of the plan.

The physician prescribes medications, treatments, and procedures as
needed and recommends a schedule for follow-up. The nurse partner coor-

dinates and communicates with all referral sources as necessary, and relays pertinent information to the physician. The patient and family identify actions they want to take toward meeting their identified health goals. Team members are sensitive to payment sources and insurance limitations. They plan services that are satisfactory and within reasonable financial limits. The team supports informed decision making by the patient and family.

Returning to the example just cited, the patient who is at risk of falling would agree to replace old light bulbs with higher intensity light and to eliminate throw rugs. The physician would treat osteoporosis and arthritis with medications, and the nurse partner would make another home visit and reinforce the medication teaching plan. What results is an integrated plan of care where all the components fit together and all participants understand strategies, interventions, responsibilities, and goals of care. Review and evaluation mechanisms would be put in place for monitoring the plan of care.

## Providing Medical and Nursing Care

In addressing the medical and nursing needs of patients, the physician and nurse provide preventive and health maintenance care across the health care continuum and over time. It is hoped that the patient will follow accepted, feasible, evidence-based protocols recommended by the team, or let the team know if the recommendations are not acceptable. In this model, the team provides services across home, clinic, community, hospital, and nursing home settings. They deliver physical, psychosocial, and environmental care. Team members advocate for the patient, make appropriate referrals, and educate patients and families about health and lifestyle related issues. They review and monitor treatment protocols of specialists and other community providers, and encourage the patient and family to participate in implementation of care strategies as able. As a result, the patient and family participate in and adhere to the plan of team care to achieve maintained or increased independence, health, and quality of life. Throughout this process, patient comfort and dignity remain paramount.

## Referring to Appropriate Providers

At this stage, the physician refers to medical or other specialists. The team serves as the point of access for additional services, including other health care providers and community services. Team members ensure follow-up on referrals and communicate this information to each other.

The nurse partner and physician identify available community resources and advocate for development of new services when appropriate.
The team interprets health services data to help manage utilization. The
team encourages the patient to coordinate services independently, and
advocates to ensure the patient receives necessary services. It is expected
that the patient and family actively participate in decision making.
Through the referral process the result is that patients have access to appropriate providers and services. In addition, care is coordinated without
gaps or duplication. With the support of the team, the patient and family
are more skilled in decision making regarding health services. The team,
therefore, becomes better able to plan, provide, coordinate, and evaluate
services effectively.

# Model Application: Case Studies

The following three case studies are illustrative of the geriatric collaborative practice model. They are presented in order to bring to life the clinical processes discussed above.

### Case Study 1

A 76-year-old white female, Mrs. C., who lives with her granddaughter, is
in poor health. Her medical diagnoses include peripheral vascular disease, diabetes mellitus, congestive heart failure, depression, diabetic retin-
opathy, arthritis, and a history of gastrointestinal bleeding. Although
legally blind, she is able to complete all activities of daily living independently, but needs some assistance with money management, routine
housework, laundry, and meal preparation. She is frequently upset by ongoing family conflicts.

In July, the nurse partner made a home visit to Mrs. C. in conjunction with the physician's request for medication changes and instructions.
Mrs. C. reported that she was not feeling well and was sleeping poorly
due to an increase in family conflicts. The nurse partner encouraged her
to identify strategies she had used to cope with family conflict in the past,
and listened closely to her response. The nurse partner then provided
education regarding the patient's medications and gave support and reassurance about the family situation.

The next day, the nurse partner made a follow-up home visit and
found Mrs. C. very weak and feeling worse. The physical exam revealed a

worsening of her respiratory and circulatory status, and some indication of possible gastrointestinal bleeding. The nurse partner notified the physician of the assessment and he ordered medication changes and an office visit later in the week. She showed no improvement. Mrs. C. was instructed to go to the local hospital where she received a transfusion of two units of packed cells and was discharged per her primary physician's orders. The adjustments in her medications, early intervention, and close monitoring contributed to a smooth recovery.

At her two-week follow-up visit Mrs. C. had no signs of congestive heart failure and was taking her medication as ordered. The short-term worsening of her chronic condition had been well-managed, and she returned to her baseline level of functioning. The nurse partner coordinated with family members to help provide companionship and light housekeeping as well as monitoring her condition and any changes in signs and symptoms. Mrs. C. is seen weekly by the local home health agency for congestive heart failure monitoring, skin breakdown, syringe refills, medication box refills, and monthly laboratory tests.

Through follow-up at home of medication changes and instructions, patient teaching, ongoing assessments, and communication between physician, nurse partner, patient, and other providers, Mrs. C.'s chronic illnesses are being managed effectively with a mix of services that allows her to stay in her home environment. Exacerbation of congestive heart failure and gastrointestinal bleeding were managed without a prolonged inpatient hospitalization. She now appears to be coping better with family issues as evidenced by decreased complaints, better sleeping, and more pleasant interactions with her family members.

## Case Study 2

An 81-year-old widowed female, Mrs. M., lives alone. She is able to accomplish all activities of daily living and instrumental activities of daily living without assistance except heavy chores and home maintenance. Her medical diagnoses include urinary incontinence, high levels of lipids (fats) in her blood, and osteoarthritis.

Mrs. M. phoned the nurse partner to report a sudden onset of dizziness and inability to walk. Mrs. M. said she was extremely frightened and was not going to leave her chair until the nurse partner arrived. The nurse partner made a home visit and assessed the patient's complaints of slight headache with sharp pains on the right side of her head. Neurological checks were normal. The nurse partner phoned the clinic and scheduled an appointment for Mrs. M., phoned the family to transport the patient, and voice-mailed the physician with the assessment and plan for an appointment. Subsequently, Mrs. M.'s family members designed a plan that she could activate if the symptoms should happen again. Mrs. M. was found to have an inner-ear infection that was treated successfully with antibiotics.

A home visit by her nurse partner and an office visit led to prompt and appropriate outpatient treatment for a problem that, if the patient's anxiety level had escalated, might have resulted in an ambulance ride to the emergency room. The nurse partner's role in making a home visit greatly assisted Mrs. M. in meeting her needs simply and promptly.

## Case Study 3

An 89-year-old widowed man, Mr. D., is living alone in his single-family home. He needs maximum assistance with all instrumental activities of daily living and some assistance with all activities of daily living, with the exception of eating, toileting, and walking. His diagnoses include prostate cancer, squamous cell cancer, hypertension, hypothyroidism, congestive heart failure, and cerebral vascular accident (stroke) with cognitive impairment. He appears to be managing the psychosocial aspects of his care quite well. He keeps in contact with his family and friends through frequent phone calls and visits. His daughter, who lives close by, serves as his primary caregiver.

Mr. D. was brought into the physician's office by his daughter when she noticed her father had lower leg and ankle edema and shortness of breath. The physician determined that Mr. D. had exacerbation of his congestive heart failure and recommended hospitalization. He declined and asked to go home. The physician called the nurse partner into the office and it was determined that Mr. D. would return home with an adjustment in his medications. The nurse partner was to make a home visit the next day and Mr. D. was to return to the physician's office in one week. At the home visit the next day Mr. D. was considerably better, with decreased swelling and shortness of breath. His daughter was instructed how to monitor weight and swelling and to call if her father's shortness of breath, swelling, or weight increased. A follow-up call by the nurse partner indicated continued improvement in his status. The follow-up visit to the physician the following week found Mr. D.'s congestive heart failure resolved; he was to continue on the increased medications as ordered.

About a week later, however, the nurse partner received a phone call from Mr. D.'s daughter saying that her father was tired and weak. The nurse partner made a home visit and found his blood pressure below normal; it also dropped significantly when he stood. The nurse partner consulted with the physician and medication changes were made. A subsequent follow-up home visit by the nurse partner indicated that Mr. D. was tolerating the medication changes without difficulty.

A collaborating team managed Mr. D.'s congestive heart failure at home and prevented an inpatient hospital stay, and through proactive monitoring and continued communication between team members avoided further patient complications. This case example illustrates the important role played by a patient's family when they are active team members.

# Lessons Learned

We have learned that a collaborative and integrated approach is extremely important in geriatric care. In our experience, planning care in isolation from other disciplines is duplicative, costly, and simply does not work for the good of the patient. When patients and providers collaborate, communicate openly, and work on mutual goals, care is streamlined and costs can be successfully managed. Lessons learned can be divided into three categories: organizational, clinical, and team building.

## Organizational Lessons

Before implementing a new model of care, the concept has to be introduced and described in a systematic manner. It is important for the overall purpose, goals, and direction to come from top administration and to be communicated in a variety of ways. Reinforcement of the ideas and progress of the transition should be communicated on a continual basis. This can be accomplished through provider meetings, newsletters from the CEO, and formal and informal training efforts. In addition, the medical leaders of the organization have to make a concerted effort to meet with providers and provider groups to introduce and reinforce collaborative care on a regular basis. Physicians and nurse partners that are successful collaborative team members are the best advocates for the process and can be instrumental in influencing colleagues who are struggling with the process or are just starting out.

Assembling a multidisciplinary team comprised of primary care physicians, nurse partners, and patients is not enough to make collaboration work effectively. Office nurses and support staff are integral to making the process work. They have great influence in day-to-day patient care operations. In their roles as gatekeepers, they must believe that collaboration is an effective and efficient way to deliver care. If they do not, they can direct patients away from the geriatric team in a variety of ways. On the other hand, they may be advocates by reinforcing the concept with patients, directing patients to the nurse partners, facilitating office and working space arrangements, and assisting in communicating with physicians in a constructive and timely manner.

Primary care is a natural place to initiate the model because of the variety and complexity of patient panels and sufficient numbers to support the collaborative model. For the best chance of success, it is helpful to start with a small, focused, well-defined patient population. Once collaboration is established and functioning smoothly, expansion to other at-risk populations or other types of care (e.g., emergency room, specialty care, intensive care) is appropriate.

We have found that implementing team care makes providers think about how they were trained. Autonomy and independent practice have traditionally been highly valued in medicine and nursing. However, some aspects of autonomous practice need to be modified for team care to be effective. Management must discern when to take an active role in facilitating team building and when to take a "hands off" approach.

We have demonstrated that geriatric collaborative practice can be valuable in managing health service utilization, patient and provider satisfaction, and physician productivity. These results take time to be achieved. Success depends on the maturation of team processes, enrollment stability, and increased patient participation in the model.

## Clinical Lessons

We found that it was important to develop or adopt specific criteria for enrolling and screening patients for eligibility for team care. Once patients are involved in team care it is important to standardize assessment tools, patient care letters, educational materials, and summaries that incorporate medical, nursing, and other provider information that can be synthesized for better communication. Standardization of clinical practice patterns should also occur. Particularly important is developing standard mechanisms to track patients through different levels of care. For example, it is necessary to know when patients are regularly scheduled for routine office visits, or when patients have visited the emergency room or been hospitalized.

Early clinical success with complex patient situations helps foster collaborative team building. The learning that comes from working together in clinical problem solving is rewarding. It provides a foundation for developing trust, confidence in professional skills and competencies, and situational leadership skills. When the nurse partners gain the trust of patients quickly, then patients often discuss the positive impressions with their physicians. This helps the physicians gain confidence in the nurse partners' abilities.

We learned that the team's awareness of self-management skills provides the foundation for initial patient involvement and commitment to the collaborative process. We discovered that providers are not traditionally trained to conceptualize the patient as central to clinical decision making. Clinicians in care teams learned to acknowledge that patients are quite capable of synthesizing information, and have the power to make their own care decisions.

Team members also learned that patients cannot always adhere to a plan of care. Instead of seeing this as a deficiency on the part of the patient, the team needs to adjust the plan of care to fit the patients' situations and their priorities. This allows the team to focus on why people cannot comply, whether for personal, financial, or lifestyle-related reasons. Subsequently the team can support behavioral management as well as encourage, monitor and provide feedback.

Related to behavioral management is the intervention of patient education. We learned that patient education requires constant reinforcement, follow-up, and re-evaluation. Patient education should be based on sound and consistent materials. It must be guided by the patient's priorities.

In addition, it is important for the team to find out how many other providers are involved with a patient's care and in what ways. This prevents duplication or gaps of care. More times than not the primary care physician is not fully aware of the extent of involvement by other providers. Understanding the web of providers is critical in managing care.

## Team Building Lessons

At Carle, nurse partners work with four to five physicians and have patient panels of 150 or more. Each patient has a different disease and lifestyle constellation. This results in a multitude of complex relationships for team members to navigate. Negotiating functional communication patterns with multiple physicians and patients requires high levels of flexibility and sensitivity to individual needs.

Geriatric Collaborative Care involves team members encountering a broad range of clients with multiple health issues. Sometimes situations arise that are beyond the skills or competencies of the providers. It is crucial for team members to acknowledge when they don't know what to do and to seek help.

Collaboration is a developmental process. As a process it has different levels of team member interaction. At first, collaboration is characterized by the physician, nurse partner, and patient working in the same environment. Each team member functions somewhat independently, with little meaningful communication regarding problem solving. Communication centers on minimal sharing of facts regarding discipline-specific information. At this stage, patient involvement is low at best, except for those patients who are assertive in making their wishes and conditions known.

As collaboration develops, the physician and nurse partner get comfortable with each other's roles, responsibilities, and professional skills. The team begins to translate information into different ways of managing patient care. However, patient involvement in the care process remains minimal. Next, teams begin to progress from autonomous patient care management to more joint decision making, sometimes involving the patient and family and their preferences. However, this still involves more communication occurring between the physician and nurse than with the patient.

True collaboration is reached when there is more equitable distribution of decision making, power, and feedback among all team members. Patient self-management abilities and preferences are paramount. At this point, the physician and nurse know and accept each other's capabilities and limitations. Patients may then develop a high level of confidence and trust in the combined abilities of the team members, be highly satisfied with the care received, and learn new self-management skills that contribute to enhanced quality of life.

## Summary

Research into effective health service delivery models that span the continuum of care must begin with attention to pragmatic issues related to health care redesign, financial management, and the demographics of an aging population. The Geriatric Collaborative Care model has demonstrated an effective and efficient approach to achieve and monitor quality outcomes while benefiting patients as well as health care professionals. For patients, the collaborative approach has been meaningful, especially in times of impaired health, altered levels of functioning, or hospitalization. Knowing that they have knowledgeable advocates within the health care system can be a great source of relief and comfort. The teamwork, shared vision, and communication so vital to the success of the model have become areas of professional reward and growth for the health care providers involved. A statement by a primary care physician who participated in the project sums up the positive impacts of the model on patient care:

> First, the basic premise of a collaborative nurse to improve efficiency and effectiveness of delivery of care to the elderly is an excellent concept and one that has proved to be quite useful to us thus far. I feel that this concept of collaboration and its implementation in our practice has not only reduced cost of care to these various patients, but has greatly increased the level of patient satisfaction. I firmly believe that the collaborative practice model is the wave of the future for rural medicine and indeed for primary care medicine in general.

# References

Blumenthal, D. (1996). The origins of the quality-of-care debate. *New England Journal of Medicine, 335*, 1146–1149.

Greenfield, S., Kaplan, S.H., Ware, J.E., Yano, E.M. & Frank, H.J.L. (1988). Patients' participation in medical care: Effects on blood sugar control and quality of life in diabetes. *Journal of General Internal Medicine, 3*, 448–457.

Hibbard, H. & Nutting, P.A. (1991). Research in primary care: A national priority. In H. Hibbard, P.A. Nutting & M.L. Grady (Eds.), *Primary care research: Theory and methods* (pp. 1–4) (AHCPR Publication No. 91–0011). Washington, DC: U.S. Government Printing Office.

Mauksch, I.G. (1981). Nurse-physician collaboration: A changing relationship. *The Journal of Nursing Administration, 11*, 35–38.

Radecki, S.E. & Cowell, W.G. (1990). Health promotion for elderly patients. *Family Medicine, 22*, 299–302.

Schraeder, C., Shelton, P., Dworak, D. & Fraser, C. (1993). Alzheimer's disease: Case management in a rural setting. *Journal of Case Management, 2*(1), 26–31.

Schraeder, C., Britt, T. & Shelton, P. (1995). Creating collaborative processes in primary care. *Primary Practice News, 2*(4), 3–5.

Schraeder, C. & Shelton, P. (1995). The Carle Clinic Association. In C. Evashwick (Ed.), *The continuum of long-term care: An integrated systems approach* (pp. 347–355). Albany, NY: Delmar Publishers.

Schraeder, C., Shelton, P., Britt, T. & Buttitta, K. (1996). Case management in a capitated system: The Community Nursing Organization. *Journal of Case Management, 5*, 58–64.

Senge, P.M. (1990). *The fifth discipline: The art and practice of the learning organization.* New York: Doubleday/Currency.

Shelton, P., Schraeder, C., Britt, T. & Kirby, R. (1994). A generalist physician-based model for a rural geriatric collaborative practice. *Journal of Case Management, 3*, 98–104.

Wagner, E.H. (1996). The promise and performance of HMOs in improving outcomes in older adults. *Journal of the American Geriatrics Society, 44*, 1251–1257.

Wright, R.A. (1993). Community-oriented primary care: The cornerstone of health care reform. *Journal of the American Medical Association, 269*, 2544–2547.

# CHAPTER 4

# Advanced Practice Nurses as System-Wide Case Managers for Internists
*Linda J. Battaglini and A. Judith Czerenda*

United Health Services is a comprehensive health care delivery system formed in 1981 from the merger of two municipal hospitals and a community teaching hospital in Broome County, New York. This area has an urban core comprised of the "Triple Cities" of Binghamton, Endicott, and Johnson City, surrounded by rural communities. The area was a manufacturing center until suffering a significant employment decline after a peak in 1988.

Though United Health Services comprised all of the major components of the health care continuum when the project began, trying to get even two of these services to create a seamless transition process for the patient was a daunting task. A completely different strategy was needed to create a truly integrated health care delivery system.

The System Case Management project was designed in 1993 to test the integration and customization of the delivery system at the individual patient level. United Health Services anticipated that integration would yield greater patient satisfaction, more efficient and cost-effective institutional services, and better patient monitoring and prevention of deterioration. United Health Services had used case management in many settings, with limited goals; what had not been tested was the integration of the entire delivery system.

The primary care physician's office was chosen as the location of the service, because the patient looks to this physician as the chief decision maker about care. To facilitate care coordination and delivery system integration, the Patient Care Coordinator (PCC) position was added to the primary care office. Advanced practice nurses were recruited as PCCs to serve elderly patients in a collaborative practice with five internists.

# Background

United Health Services operates 539 acute care beds, and a geriatric campus with a capacity to serve 450 clients with congregate housing, assisted living, skilled nursing, and long-term home care. In addition, United Health Services maintains a rural hospital, a home care company, and a system-affiliated medical practice with 120 physicians. This system serves a population of approximately 300,000 people in the south-central tier of New York and the northeastern tier of Pennsylvania.

The United Health Services service area has a growing base of retirees. Those over 65 comprised 15% of the population in 1990 and are projected to reach 17.1% of the population by the year 2000, compared to an expected 12.5% national average. The area is also relatively homogeneous with respect to race, with less than a 5% minority population in 1990, compared with a 20% national average.

Physician practices in the region are in transition. Before the start of this project there was only one large group practice of approximately 35 primary care and specialty physicians. United Health Services acquired this practice in 1991 and combined it with its teaching hospital faculty physicians into a single physician corporation called United Medical Associates (UMA). During the course of the project, both United Health Services and Our Lady of Lourdes, a Binghamton hospital that is part of the Daughters of Charity System, pursued aggressive physician acquisition strategies, continuing the process of practice acquisition and primary care site development. By the end of the project, UMA had grown to a practice of 120 physicians.

United Health Services currently dominates the market with a 65% inpatient market share, and Our Lady of Lourdes is an active competitor. Competition from large systems on the outskirts of the region (the Guthrie, Bassett, and Geisinger systems), is threatening the specialty services offered by local physicians and hospitals. United Health Services has been advocating cooperation with Lourdes to avoid duplication and achieve greater quality and integration to keep patients within the community. This effort has not proved fruitful and the two are maintaining their separate roles.

Managed care is in the early stages of development in this community, although its presence is increasing. The UMA practice began the project with fewer than 5% of revenues from managed care, and by the completion of the project this had increased to approximately 27%.

Medicare managed care had not been marketed in this area by the end of the project period. The System Case Management project was designed to help prepare the United Health Services system to manage the cost and quality of care across the entire health care continuum, within managed care risk-sharing incentives. The grant funding allowed the organization to test the model for its ability to reduce service costs, to improve the quality of care as measured by patient satisfaction, and to improve physician satisfaction and productivity.

The introduction of advanced practice nurses into the primary care setting is not new. Nurse practitioners have been primary care providers since the mid-1960s (Mezey, 1993).

> Primary care remains a major practice opportunity for advanced practice nurses. The drive to provide services in the least expensive setting, services which promote health and prevent more costly episodes of illness and services to populations who continue to be underserved makes primary care an attractive practice option. (McGivern, 1993, p. 20)

Advanced practice is defined by the National Council of State Boards of Nursing (McGivern, 1993) as:

> the advanced practice of nursing by nurse practitioners, nurse anesthetists, nurse midwives, and clinical nurse specialists, based on the following: knowledge and skills required in basic nursing education; licensure as a registered nurse; graduate degree and experience in the designated area of practice which includes advanced nursing theory; substantial knowledge of physical and psychological assessment; appropriate interventions and management of health care status. The skills and abilities essential for the advanced practice role within an identified specialty area include: providing patient/client and community education; promoting stress prevention and management; encouraging self help; subscribing to caring; advocacy; accountability, accessibility; and collaboration with other health and community professionals. (p. 5)

The Triple Cities area was endowed with a large number of clinical nurse specialists. Therefore, it was logical to use these advanced practice nurses in our project.

## Project Design

A patient survey conducted in 1990 by United Health Services revealed that patients expected primary care physicians to be actively involved in medical decision making and care coordination. The physicians interviewed for the System Case Management project expressed frustration at their inability to meet patient expectations. Time constraints and their limited knowledge of the full range of social and medical services available in the community prevented them from meeting even a fraction of patients' needs.

The purpose of the project was to design and test a new provider position—the Patient Care Coordinator (PCC). Based in primary care physicians' offices, advanced practice nurses (clinical nurse specialists, nurse practitioners, and other master's-level nurses) worked in a collaborative, supportive role with the physicians, while coordinating and monitoring patient care across the health care and social services continuum. The PCCs emphasized health education and prevention in their practices, made home visits when needed, and coordinated care across inpatient and outpatient settings.

Ten physicians were selected to participate in the project. Five were chosen to partner with PCCs and five were used as comparison practices. The demonstration-group physicians were chosen from a pool of general internists who had practices with a significant portion of elderly patients, were interested in incorporating advanced practice nurses into their practices, and felt comfortable with the clinical goals of the project. The original plan was to select a mixed group of family practitioners and internists for the demonstration group. The family practitioners interviewed in the selection process, however, felt that they had been trained to do care coordination and did not feel a strong need for additional support of their patients. In contrast, the internists expressed frustration with trying to manage the course of care and welcomed the potential for additional expertise. The comparison group physicians were chosen to match the mix in the demonstration group, with four in a general internist practice and one in a mixed general and sub-specialty practice.

The System Case Management Model partnered PCCs with five United Medical Associates (UMA) internists from two offices operated by the practice. This allowed a clustering of two physicians and two part-time PCCs at one site, and three physicians and one full-time and one part-time PCC at the other site. The comparison group physicians were also practicing at two separate offices, two at one site and three at another. The demonstration practices differed in that the two-physician suburban office was completely converted to the System Case Management model of practice, while the three physicians at the other office were a subset of a much larger group and were not exclusively sharing resources with each other.

Patients were selected from the active caseloads of the physicians' practices. Once identified and enrolled, patients in both the intervention and comparison practices were contacted by telephone for an initial baseline survey interview by an evaluation team led by faculty from the Cornell University Sloan School of Organization and Management. All enrolled patients were followed for one full year following their initial baseline interviews. Three follow-up telephone questionnaires were administered at 4-month intervals with the patient or patient surrogate. Questionnaires focused on general health status, functional status, health services utilization, and satisfaction with services provided in the physician's office. Utilization data were also collected from hospital and outpatient records. The principal variables were measures of: (1) the patient's health status at baseline, (2) changes in health status during the project, (3) changes in the satisfaction of each patient over the project period, (4) the role of the patient in making medical decisions at baseline, and (5) end-of-project health services utilization.

The project also included an information system component intended to capture ongoing care planning activities and patient monitoring. This was linked with the hospital's clinical information to improve communication between the hospital and the physicians.

During the project year 535 patients were enrolled. Seventy-nine patients (15%) dropped out or were excluded because of death, relocation, incomplete data, and refusals after initial contact. At the end of the project 222 patients remained enrolled in the demonstration group, and 234 were enrolled in the control group.

# Roles and Relationships

## Description of the Patient Care Coordinators (PCCs)

Service delivery was based on the traditional case management process of assessing patient needs, planning necessary services, intervening to facilitate patient-centered goals, coordinating services with interventions, monitoring the efficacy of services and interventions, and reassessing the need for changes and modifications on a continuous basis. Capitalizing on the multi-faceted roles of the advanced practice nurse, PCCs also provided education and counseling services and direct hands-on provision of care through health assessments and nursing interventions.

Collaborative practice has been shown to improve patient outcomes, job satisfaction for nursing professionals, and quality of care at lower costs (Kerfoot, 1989). Advanced practice nurses were used in this model because of their ability to deliver hands-on primary care and also provide education and liaison with patients' families and a vast array of health and community agencies (National Council of State Boards for Nursing, 1992). Master's-level preparation also helped to ensure acceptance of this new role. Although most of them had never worked directly with advanced practice nurses, physicians recognized the nurses' education and professional ability.

The PCCs were required to have advanced health assessment skills, and three of four PCCs initially hired were nurse practitioners. The PCCs, however, did not function as nurse practitioners; that is, they did not see patients for the diagnosis and treatment of medical problems and generate fee-for-service revenue. This was at first difficult for the physicians and nurses to understand. Though the PCCs who were nurse practitioners could, in theory, have combined this role with the care coordination role, there was concern that the model would be severely compromised if these two roles were combined. If there had been any tendency to give primacy to the revenue-producing nurse-practitioner role, the time available for care coordination, home visits, and collaboration with community agencies and other providers would have been substantially reduced.

## Selection of PCCs

Each of the PCCs was hired based on knowledge of primary care and geriatrics, experience in multiple settings along the continuum of care, and potential for unique contributions to System Case Management. Two of the PCCs were geriatric specialists and educators. One of the remaining had dual specialties in women's health and mental health, and the other in home care and acute care.

Project physicians participated in PCC selection. Each physician interviewed a small pool of candidates and final assignment was based in part on their recommendations. This process allowed the physicians to establish early rapport with the PCCs and reinforced the importance of the team approach. Documentation of this process in the form of candidate assessments provided some insight into the kind of PCC educational preparation, work experience, and personality traits desired by physicians for this role. Their responses reinforced the appropriateness of using advanced practice nurses.

The advanced practice orientation of the nurses, combined with their diverse backgrounds and expertise, formed the basis for a PCC professional practice group. The PCCs regularly met with each other to share ideas and new patient intervention strategies. They provided consultation to each other, practice physicians, and office staff.

## PCC Training

The PCC training program focused on a variety of educational needs. The PCCs who were hired had sound foundations in geriatrics, but lacked case management experience. There were case management elements in various UHS units, but the project caused UHS to view case management education in a more integrated, system-wide manner. This training program communicated United Health Services' goal of delivering a "seamless" continuum of care to any patient using the United Health Services system. It also built cohesiveness among those doing case management in the United Health Services system.

All United Health Services case management staff, including the PCCs, were required to attend this core training program as well as training for their specific positions. The curriculum included philosophy and practice of case management at United Health Services; health care delivery issues, including access, cost, and quality; a general overview of case management, including history, definitions, and "turf issues"; case management standards and certification; the case management process; a patient's perspective of case management; the change process; health care financing and patient advocacy; coalitions, networks, and alliances; documentation issues and strategies; continuous quality improvement; and stress management (Czerenda & Best, 1994).

Each PCC received a System Case Management orientation manual. The manual included an extensive collection of case management and geriatric-related articles, forms, and policies and procedures. A library, established in the System Case Management central office, became a valuable United Health Services system resource for case management and geriatrics information.

Continuing education was also provided through PCC attendance at local, state, and national conferences and meetings. In addition, the PCCs spent a great deal of time visiting community agencies and becoming familiar with available services and staff. A monthly brown-bag lunch program evolved from the need to continue case management education as a system-wide function. It was designed to keep all interested abreast of new case management practices in the community and within United Health Services. This program was very successful in attracting United Health Services staff as well as community agency case managers. It helped to maintain an open dialogue within the United Health Services system and with others in the community. System Case Management staff were involved in presentations and the project's central office coordinator assumed responsibility for organizing these programs.

## Guiding Principles

A set of guiding principles was developed for the project to define the nurses' practice as PCCs. These principles defined some of the limits of the PCC's role while taking into account that, for a limited period of time, the PCC might have to provide intense support until gaps in the delivery system could be filled. In order to make the best use of their expertise and to promote patient and family skill-building and autonomy, the PCCs were expected to provide services that would function as described in Table 4–1.

## PCC Roles and Duties

Patients and family members were seen by the PCC during regular office visits, in the home, hospital, or other health or social care facility. The level of service provision that a patient received was based upon need. For patients who were essentially well, but had some health risk factors that could result in future illness, interventions were limited to providing risk-reduction strategies such as changes in diet or exercise patterns or referring the patient to a health promotion program. The PCCs were able to assist directly patients with borderline hypertension or diabetes to control their conditions. They provided the needed monitoring, support, and reinforcement that helped the patient to effectively integrate diet and exercise into permanent lifestyle changes. Other patients required more complex interventions, including initiation and coordination of at-home

**TABLE 4.1**

System Case Management (SCM) Guiding Principles
for Patient Care Coordinators' Case Management Practice

1. Promote patient and/or family independence.
2. Enhance patient and/or family member knowledge bases through education and role modeling.
3. Provide SCM services to patients and/or family members only when they are unavailable to them elsewhere.
4. Provide "care facilitation" rather than "care taking."
5. Limit duplication or overlap of services with other community providers.
6. Utilize all family and friend support alternatives before instituting formal services.
7. Utilize all community-based services before initiating institutional services.
8. Reduce or discontinue SCM services as soon as other systems are in place.
9. Provide advocacy services only until the patient or family/friends can assume the advocacy role modeled by the PCC.

services, and family education and support assistance directly through System Case Management or other community providers. Typical coordination of care in complex cases might involve the initiation and monitoring of wound care and intravenous therapy after hospital discharge. For example, close monitoring, with the home care nurse, of a patient's exacerbation of symptoms of congestive heart failure or cardiopulmonary disease, would enable the PCC to facilitate needed medication changes or schedule an urgent office visit.

The PCC acted as a conduit for information between the patient and his or her family, other care providers, and the physician to streamline service provision and act as an advocate and advisor when dealing with health care providers and payers. The PCCs interviewed the patients, usually at the required pre-operative history and physical by the primary physicians one week before surgery. Rehabilitation plans after hip or knee replacements or cataract surgery were the chief procedures which activated an in-depth PCC review to determine if the patient was fully aware of and agreeable to the post-procedure plans. At times, alternative rehabilitation plans were put in place utilizing formal and informal support services.

The PCCs' broad knowledge of medical and psychosocial aspects of care, coupled with their working partnerships with the primary care physicians, placed them in a unique position to expedite care across the health care continuum. The PCCs worked extensively with the families of Alzheimer's patients to assist them in their struggle to delay institutionalization. Providing the caregivers with timely access to a PCC prevented catastrophic episodes when new disruptive behaviors surfaced (e.g., incontinence, agitation, sleep disorders). The PCC interventions included medication management, behavioral strategies, emotional support, referrals to community resources such as social day care or support groups, and assistance with long-term planning for financial issues.

The PCC was able to facilitate the linking functions of the system by anticipating the patient, family, and system needs. This added to the system efficiency and well-being of the patient. Institutionalization, short- or long-term, is an emotionally laden topic and difficult for all concerned. Information on and discussions about levels of care and reimbursement issues became part of the long-term planning that was initiated for all frail elders and their families.

The goal was to care for the patient at the most appropriate level using the most appropriate caregivers. Patients and families also benefited from the education they received from the PCC, which they could use to better direct and facilitate future care.

## Relationship Development

Matching PCCs to physicians was accomplished using information gathered at meetings and the PCC interviews. The identification of each provider's philosophy of care was useful in making a successful match. No problems arose regarding the matching of PCCs and physicians.

Communication between demonstration physicians and their PCC partners was not systematic. Impromptu hallway chats and informal discussions coupled with notes stuck to charts and brief joint patient visits all contributed to the communication process. Each physician/PCC partnership developed its own unique style and tempo for communication. In one circumstance, the PCC helped the physician organize his flow of mail and other messages to create more opportunities for communication and build a working relationship. This role helped create mutual trust, and even though it was not defined as part of the PCC's function, contributed to the success of the partnership.

The weekly office staff meetings to review patient care plan prog-ress envisioned in the original plan never materialized, largely because of the rigorous demands of the busy practices. When the physicians came to rely on the knowledge and expertise of the PCCs, and when the PCCs felt more confident in their own roles, practice boundaries were established that facilitated easy access between the PCCs and the physi-cians. For example, changes in a patient's medication or dosage were initially made only with prior approval from physicians. Over time, as the PCCs became more comfortable with the physicians' practice pat-terns, medication changes were initiated before the physicians were in-formed.

Health promotion forms, as well as problem and medication sum-mary lists, facilitated communication among providers and staff, as did the SCM patient identification system. The physicians and staff became accustomed to this identification and communication system and used it to quickly obtain case management information.

When project physicians were queried about what patient issues they most relied on the PCCs to help manage, their responses included health risk, service needs, mental health status, medical programs, and compli-ance with treatment plans. Medication management was referenced as a health risk factor, health education need, and compliance problem—it clearly was a factor that triggered many of the referrals to the PCC ser-vices. This is an indication of the roles assumed by the PCCs, and how the physicians developed confidence in their ability to manage advanced clinical services.

## Patient Selection and Enrollment

Referrals to the project were made by patients, family members, health and social care agency representatives, primary care or specialist physi-cians, or medical office staff. The project targeted persons age 60 and older that physicians felt could benefit from care coordination. If they agreed to participate, patients were selected as part of the evaluation pro-tocol. A broad range of patients was included in the program, from those with complex chronic problems, to those at risk of having significant problems, to those needing only routine medical care. The variable of risk was stratified at patient entry through the use of a 16-factor screening tool, described in Table 4.2 (on page 76).

## TABLE 4.2

### Sixteen-Point Patient Assessment Criteria Screen

| | LEVEL 1 | LEVEL 2 | LEVEL 3 | LEVEL 4 |
|---|---|---|---|---|
| **MEDICAL** | | | | |
| **Health risk factors** | routine health monitoring | acute or chronic problems with *no* other problems | acute problems causing other problems | chronic problems causing debilitation |
| **Prognosis for current illness** | no disability expected | at some risk for disability | sudden onset with moderate–major disability risk | chronic condition, disability expected |
| **Patient compliance** | compliant with treatment plan | mostly compliant | episodic non-compliance | non-compliant |
| **Patient self-assessment** | cooperative and realistic | cooperative, but unrealistic regarding abilities and needs | uncooperative and unrealistic | unable to comprehend need for treatment |
| **Mental status** | no impairment | at risk for impairment | minimal impairment | severe impairment |
| **Service needs** | physician's office | outpatient/ambulatory or inpatient short term | inpatient short-term and/or moderately complex | inpatient long-term and/or complex |
| **EDUCATIONAL** | | | | |
| **Need for health education** | patient educated | could benefit from wellness education or behavior modification | needs medical self-management training | unable to be educated |
| **PERSONAL SUPPORT** | | | | |
| **ADL Status** | independent | risk of dependence | some assistance needed | totally dependent |
| **Living environment** | appropriate | may become inappropriate | environment needs some modification | inappropriate |
| **Family involvement** | involved and supportive | available, but unable/unwilling to give support | no family available | involved, but uncooperative or unrealistic |
| **Decision making** | able to make decisions | could become unable | unable–has decision maker | unable–has no decision maker |
| **Agency supports** | no social services required | informal supports | required and available | required and unavailable |
| **WORK** | | | | |
| **Vocational activity** | no change in activity level | short-term and/or minimal change | change and help required | disabled, ongoing assistance |
| **FINANCES** | | | | |
| **Financial status** | sufficient | could become insufficient | limited sufficiency | insufficient |
| **Reimbursement management** | none required | may be required | episodic requirement | required |
| **RISK** | | | | |
| **Risk management** | none required | risk of legal involvement | episodic legal involvement | major legal entanglements |

The patient's status in each of the 16 categories was solicited from the patient and/or family by the PCC through an interview conducted during an office visit, telephone call, or home visit. The patient assessment criteria form was developed by United Health Services staff during the project planning process. It was modeled after a tool developed by the social work staff and was augmented by adding references to financial and legal issues that occur when doing community-based case management. This assessment tool was evaluated by an independent researcher and found to be a reliable and valid measure of patient health.

The screen responses were tallied, a numerical score determined, and a level of care assigned. The levels were 1 through 4, with 1 indicating minimum need for System Case Management services and 4 the greatest need for services. The levels of acuity derived from the screening tool were also used to measure the PCC's caseload so a balance of lower- and higher-intensity need patients could be maintained.

Patients were informed about the service and asked about interest in participation in the project when making appointments or seeing physicians. It was more difficult to recruit enrollees for the control group, who were essentially being asked to answer the survey questions without receiving any new services. Patients who were more acutely ill and frail were less interested in participating, leading to the lower intensity of the control group.

The demonstration group had more limitations in activities and significantly more days in bed during the baseline period than did the control group. They also had a higher use rate for emergency room services and hospital nights. Both groups were more satisfied with the services of the physician's office, and more willing to try a new physician. The demonstration group had a higher proportion of females, was slightly older, and had lower levels of education—factors for which a significant difference existed between the two groups.

The factors for which there was no significant difference between the two groups included utilization of physician visits, rehabilitation services, home care services, and counseling services after adjusting for health status. Both groups had similar perceptions of the quality of care, confidence in the physician, and frustration about receiving needed services. Patients were also similar with respect to marital status, household income, Medicaid eligibility, supplemental insurance, and role in decision making.

The full-time PCC's caseload was approximately 75 patients. Since this was a demonstration project and the PCCs spent a significant amount of time in development work, it is estimated that a standard, full-time active caseload would be approximately 100 patients.

Throughout the project, the PCCs were asked by physicians to provide care coordination to non-project patients—those not participating in the survey process. Each PCC's caseload included a small percentage of these persons. Often, requests were limited to providing information or referrals to patients and family members; however, a few situations were much more involved. These patients were not included in the evaluation because they were either new to the practice and had missed the enrollment period, had not experienced significant issues during the enrollment, or were younger than the project criteria allowed.

## Assessment and Care Planning

After identifying the appropriateness of a patient for the project, a comprehensive assessment form adapted from a tool used by Connecticut Community Care, Inc. in Bristol, Connecticut, was completed by the PCC. This tool was used if it was determined that a detailed analysis of some aspect of the patient's status needed to be conducted before a plan of care was developed. This usually occurred when the patient had multiple care coordination issues or complex health or social care concerns. Completion of the comprehensive assessment provided the PCC with an in-depth review of all aspects of the patient's biopsychosocial status, including past and present medical diagnoses, therapeutic interventions, levels of activities of daily living (ADLs), and independent activities of daily living (IADLs). An assessment of the patient's environmental and support system was included, as well as an optional financial status review.

This comprehensive assessment form was completed soon after the initial referral; however, a change in a patient's condition or health status necessitated reassessment to more fully identify changing needs that required new services. The PCC also had the option to complete only those portions of the assessment that were relevant to System Case Management services. For example, this may have occurred when there was an outside case manager who had primary responsibility for the patient during a course of home care or rehabilitation. The patient and/or family had the right to refuse to answer any of the questions on the comprehensive assessment form; however, completion of the 16-point screen was necessary to receive System Case Management services. Physicians generally were not involved in this stage of care planning, and were informed as needed of any conditions or situations that affected the plan of care.

The PCC developed a problem list that reflected the needs and issues of the patient. This list was shared with the primary care physician to solicit input regarding medical diagnoses, diagnostic procedures, and treatment regimes. Outstanding data or information not yet available to substantiate a diagnosis or need were documented on the problem list as "incomplete data base"—a reminder that there were still outstanding issues to be resolved. The problem list was placed on the medical record and served as a patient communication tool for medical office personnel and as a framework for the development of the plan of care.

The provision of System Case Management services to patients was based on a collaborative process between the PCC, primary physician, patient, family, and/or their service providers that resulted in the creation of a document called the plan of care. The plan of care comprehensively addressed each problem individually by outlining specific health, educational, and psychosocial goals in well-defined and measurable ways.

Interventions to assist the patient in achieving those goals were incorporated into the plan with specific information, such as names of services, providers, and time schedules when available. The plan of care was reviewed with the primary physician and developed in cooperation with the patient and/or family. The plan of care was a working document and was, therefore, subject to frequent changes as patient needs dictated. All proposed changes were discussed with the patient and involved caregivers, and acceptance of the plan of care was the ultimate responsibility of the patient or her or his surrogate.

The care of each patient was open to a review by the patient, family, physician, PCC, and other appropriate involved caregivers. The purpose of this review was to assess the patient's receptiveness to care and the adequacy of the services provided. If an informal review was not adequate, a case conference may have been requested by anyone involved in the patient's care. It was usually the PCC who set up the case conference and facilitated the agenda. A case conference may have been needed prior to the initiation of the care plan; during the course of care delivery, if the patient or family were not satisfied with the provision of care, if the patient was not responding to the care plan as anticipated, or if there was a significant deterioration in the patient's condition; or prior to termination of one or more services. At the conclusion of the conference, a summary outlining the care plan changes was documented in the patient's medical record.

# Evaluation Results

The results of the quantitative and qualitative evaluation studies confirm that the System Care Management model achieved most of the project's goals and objectives. The qualitative research team observed the services and interviewed the PCCs, the physicians, and some patients. Their evaluation indicated that the PCCs did their jobs by (1) bringing information together from fragmented sources and devising solutions which supported patients' goals for health, functioning, and comfort; (2) articulating a plan of care which joined or connected different parts of the patient's health care and social support system and by keeping these constituents together through unexpected contingencies over time; and (3) persuading the patient and family and other health professionals to take action to improve their care (Stein & Anderson, 1994).

The final results of the quantitative evaluation showed that, by the last survey period, the demonstration group patients were 43% less likely to use the hospital and 44% less likely to use the emergency room than patients in the control group. The absolute cost of medical care for the demonstration group was lower than the control group by $220,214 for the 220 patients who completed the study. If the fourth period's use rates are annualized, the savings for the demonstration group would be $596,211. These savings are offset by an ongoing operating cost of $246,789. While discrete measures of health status did not significantly improve, patients in the demonstration group reported that they felt healthier than they had a year earlier (Kuder, 1996).

Physicians in the demonstration group were significantly and positively affected by having the PCCs' support in caring for elderly patients. They reported more satisfaction with caring for older persons and more satisfaction with their practices than control physicians reported. They also reported feeling less rushed (and more productive) in serving patients than the control group.

Demonstration group patients were pleased with the services delivered and had a higher degree of loyalty to their physicians as a result of this service. They also expressed increased levels of confidence in the physicians' ability to help them in managing their health service needs.

# Lessons Learned

Eight important lessons learned in operating and evaluating this service should help others considering how to meet the need for greater consistency in the patient care process and greater control over the costs of care. Some lessons were recognized early in the project, while others became apparent only in the post-grant period as the service continued to adapt to evolving conditions.

First, using advanced practice nurses who were qualified to review medication management and reactions and recommend changes to physicians greatly facilitated timely resolution of patients' medication problems, and minimized the physician time involved.

Second, the ongoing collegial relationship between the nurse and the physician became an important element in a quick resolution to problems for the patient and family. This relationship was strong because the nurse was in the practice office every day. She was available to patients who were seeing the physician and often was included in the patient's visit with the physician. Both the physician and the patient viewed her as an important part of the effort to define and resolve problems.

Third, a single contact point was important for the patient and family for dealing with a broad range of medical, social, and mental health issues, all related and with the potential for impact on the stability of the patient's independence. Issues of pre-admission education and planning, discharge planning, home care management, medication management, and emergency services could be coordinated through the familiar PCC. This created efficiency for the clinicians and for the family.

Fourth, integration of the System Case Management service with the rest of the delivery system through education and ongoing case study forums helped to define case management as a way of using various professions to practice in various settings, with similar goals for the patient.

Fifth, because the patient and physician still had the option of using providers outside of the United Health Services network, it was difficult to collect complete system-wide cost information and therefore difficult to determine true system-wide costs. Software information systems are needed that can be tailored to this kind of service. The package used was adequate for collecting data on patients and services delivered, but did not provide the management reporting capability to monitor productivity, or the integration with the hospital's systems that would improve the communication with the other providers in the system.

Sixth, Medicare risk sharing/global capitation payment is needed to support care management with a system-wide scope. It is the Medicare population who most need care coordination and management of chronic and acute illnesses. Most of the savings identified from this service accrue to the payer (i.e., reduced hospital, nursing home, and emergency room use). It is the primary care practice, however, that bears the cost of the service. Physicians who want to make this kind of care coordination available to their patients need to negotiate a risk-sharing or a service cost-sharing deal with Medicare, Medicaid, or a managed care payer.

Seventh, targeting certain types of patients would produce greater cost savings and greater increases in patient satisfaction. Sub-group analysis showed that those in poorer health or those whose health deteriorated during the study were more likely to show reduced utilization and cost profiles due to the intervention. In addition, patients who had a more participating style expressed greater satisfaction with the service.

Eighth, expanding the primary care practice to include psychosocial aspects of the patient's situation was an important factor in preventing deterioration and institutionalization. As stated in the project's qualitative evaluation,

> the PCCs are dealing with chronic illness in a system designed to deal with acute care. The current system can deal with big events with acute short-term consequences, but it is not designed to take care of the small events that have big consequences over time. Some of the interventions by the PCCs don't sound or appear dramatic, but they have important consequences for the patient and family. The education and experience of the nurses provide a large repertoire of possible ways to address the key problems and sentinel events in the course of a chronic illness. Interpreting information to and from the patient and physician helps the patient to make informed decisions about the care plan proposed, and to understand how their behavior will contribute to its success. (Stein & Anderson, 1994, p. 30)

The service has created a new way of doing business for the internists in the United Medical Associates practice. It has become integral to the delivery and management of primary care services, and the question of its ability to pay for itself seems to have a lower priority. System Case Management has helped the practice by re-introducing the nursing coordination role that was lost as care shifted from inpatient to ambulatory settings. Both physicians and office staff are now strong supporters of the service.

The System Case Management service has continued with operational funding by United Health Services, including support from the physicians' practices. PCCs now serve the patients of all internists at the two project sites. The service is focused on patients with the most complex needs, including those under age 60, although most of the patients are older. The process of routine monitoring of lower acuity patients has been discontinued in the interest of maximizing the impact of the intervention. United Health Services has been negotiating with its managed care partner, which is developing a Medicare managed care product, about how to make best use of this service.

## Summary

United Health Services' System Case Management project has shown that adding a skilled nurse clinician to the primary care team which is responsible for making the delivery system work for the patient produces both cost and quality improvements. The service reduced inpatient and emergency room use by over 43%, improved physician productivity and satisfaction with serving the elderly, and improved patient satisfaction. This is a service that can create clinical integration of the delivery system through the PCCs' coordination of services across the continuum of care. It enables the patient and family to effectively secure services when needed, and to easily adapt the care plan as conditions change.

## References

Czerenda, A.J. & Best, L. (1994). Tying it all together: Integrating a hospital-based health care system through case management education. *Journal of Case Management, 3*(4), 69–73.

Kerfoot, K. (1989). Nursing management considerations. *Nursing Economics, 7*, 335–338.

Kuder, J. (1996, July 9). *Supplement to a quantitative evaluation of UHS System Case Management.* Paper presented at the Association for Health Services Research Conference, Atlanta, GA.

McGivern, D. (1993). The evolution of advanced nursing practice. In M. Mezey and D. McGivern (Eds.), *Nurses, nurse practitioners* (pp. 3–30). New York: Springer.

Mezey, M. (1993). Preparation for advanced practice. In M. Mezey and D. McGivern (Eds.), *Nurses, nurse practitioners* (pp. 31–58). New York: Springer.

National Council of State Boards for Nursing. (1992). *Position paper on the licensure of advanced practice nursing.* Unpublished manuscript.

Stein, L.K. & Anderson, A. (1994). *The patient care coordinator: Defining a new model of care.* Unpublished report. Binghamton, NY: SUNY HSC, Clinical Campus.

# CHAPTER 5

# A Collaborative Model with Nurse Practitioners and Social Workers

*Gloria B. Weinberg*

The older patient often faces overwhelming barriers when trying to obtain comprehensive medical care. Primary care providers frequently face similar obstacles when trying to deliver and coordinate care. In this chapter, the focus is on how our project was designed to increase access to, and delivery of, comprehensive geriatric medical and social care, while enhancing satisfaction of both patients and providers. In addition, the characteristics of patients most likely to benefit from this type of comprehensive intervention are profiled.

## Background

Mount Sinai Medical Center was the recipient of a John A. Hartford Foundation grant entitled "Intervention Pathways to Integrated Care" (IPIC) beginning in 1993 and ending in 1997. The center is a 707-bed acute-care teaching hospital located in Miami Beach, Florida, and it is an ideal site for a program intended to increase and improve primary geriatric care by physicians practicing general internal medicine (internists). Miami Beach has one of the largest concentrations of elderly in the country; 31.2% of the population is over age 65. This is in sharp contrast to Dade County, in which Miami Beach is located, with 14% over age 65, and to Florida as a whole, with 18% over age 65 (U.S. Department of Commerce, 1990).

Mount Sinai Medical Center has approximately 25,000 inpatient admissions per year, 52% of which involve patients over age 65. Patients over the age of 75 account for 62% of these geriatric admissions. The payer mix for hospitalized patients over the age of 65 is as follows: 0.5% commercial insurance, 1.5% self payment, 3% Medicaid, 73% Medicare, and 22% managed care contracts. Outpatient visits number approximately 150,000 per year. Persons over age 65 account for 43% of these ambulatory visits, and more than half of these visits (54%) are made by patients over 75 years of age.

More than 50 provider groups (128 physicians in 56 offices) have practices within an office building on the campus of the medical center. Most office practices actively participate in primary care internal medicine and geriatrics; approximately 50% of the physicians practicing primary care are trained not only in internal medicine, but in a medical sub-specialty (e.g., cardiology).

## Project Rationale

At Mount Sinai Medical Center, the typical internist's patient population is 50 to 60% geriatric. As managed care increases its market share, and reimbursement from all payers declines, our center's internists are under increasing pressure to see more patients per office session. The majority of health care plans in south Florida do not recognize geriatrics as a sub-specialty and do not provide either increased time or reimbursement per geriatric patient visit. Internists are also expected to gatekeep so that patients do not overuse specialists, and to coordinate care, both time-consuming activities, especially for the geriatric population.

The center's sub-specialists are listed as primary care internists and/ or sub-specialists on various managed care rosters; thus, sub-specialty practices reflect a mixture of primary care internal medicine and sub-specialty patients. These sub-specialists, just as internists, are often placed in the role of gatekeeper and coordinator for their primary care patients, approximately 50% of whom are older persons.

The practice of primary care geriatrics by internists and sub-specialists is of concern for several reasons. Most internists and sub-specialists have never received training in geriatric assessment and treatment, and are unaware of the special needs of the aging population. Even when adequately prepared educationally, physicians may not allot the time necessary to complete comprehensive medical, cognitive, psychosocial, and functional assessments because they are not appropriately reimbursed.

The additional medical and social needs of geriatric patients may lead to physician frustration and decreased satisfaction with geriatric primary care practice, further decreasing enthusiasm and desire to care for this population. Of additional concern is literature suggesting that overall care provided by sub-specialists is more intensive and expensive than that provided by internists (Payne, Lyons & Neuhaus, 1984). Geriatric inpatient care by specialists may also prove to be more expensive but no more effective (MacLean, 1993).

Given these concerns, Mount Sinai Medical Center was interested in implementing a program designed to improve the quality and accessibility of geriatric care. Our institution was also interested in determining the overall effectiveness of geriatric assessment and comprehensive care. Geriatric evaluation and management (GEM) programs have been studied extensively in both inpatient and outpatient settings. Analyses have shown reduction in mortality for inpatient, consultation, and home programs, but not consistently for ambulatory programs (Rubenstein, Stuck, Siu & Wieland, 1991; Epstein et al., 1990). Entry criteria (i.e., specific medical and/or social conditions presented for acceptance into programs), assessment instruments, and interventions have not been standardized among programs. We hoped our program would provide an opportunity to further study the effectiveness of ambulatory (outpatient) GEM programs and determine the most useful and cost effective ones. Results would assist not only in determining which programs would be maintained and/or expanded at our medical center, but possibly affect program planning in other institutions nationwide.

## Project Design

As we planned IPIC and reviewed the extensive literature on GEM units and geriatric care delivery by various primary care providers, we asked many questions. Central to our intervention was whether physicians would accept and work in a collaborative manner with Advanced Registered Nurse Practitioners (ARNPs) and a social worker (SW), and even report more professional satisfaction in the process. ARNPs are RNs with at least one year of formal training in a nursing clinical specialty area with specialized practitioner skills—geriatric medicine is one such specialty. Thus, a geriatric ARNP is well trained to perform thorough assessments of elderly persons. ARNPs practice within protocol guidelines (in both physicians' offices and/or institutions) and are eligible for Medicaid, Medicare, and third-party reimbursement. SWs licensed in Florida are trained to assess psychosocial situations and provide a variety of services, including counseling. We believed that providing physicians with ARNP and SW support would enable delivery of affordable comprehensive geriatric care, and promote both physician and patient satisfaction.

In addition, we asked other questions that focused on providing primary care with older persons. Is health care truly improved by interventions that enable comprehensive care? Which interventions are most effective? Will the program be cost-effective? Will implementation of the program in other communities be possible? Can profiles be generated that will describe the patient population benefiting the most? How will all of these endpoints (and others) be measured? Based on these questions, three broad sets of goals were developed (see Table 5.1).

**TABLE 5.1**

**Intervention Pathways to Integrated Care (IPIC) Project Goals**

| Focus | Goals |
| --- | --- |
| Patient Care | Improve outcomes |
| | Improve satisfaction with care |
| Physician | Promote satisfaction with practice |
| | Promote teamwork, thereby enabling delivery of comprehensive geriatric care |
| Public Policy | Demonstrate cost-effectiveness |
| | Develop a patient profile describing the types of patients most likely to benefit from comprehensive intervention |
| | Determine which assessment instruments are helpful in selecting the patient population most likely to benefit |
| | Develop a mechanism to handle complex patients |
| | Analyze differences in primary care provided by internists and sub-specialists |

## Selecting and Orienting Physicians' Practices

Physicians' offices were screened for appropriate patient populations, consisting of at least 50% geriatric patients. Sub-specialty physicians were included if half of their practice time was spent in the delivery of primary care. In order to maximize efficiency and access for project personnel, physicians with offices on the Mount Sinai campus were selected for participation. Twelve physicians were included in the project design. Six were primary care general internists, and six were sub-specialists (five cardiologists, one endocrinologist). Three internists and three sub-specialists were placed in each intervention and non-intervention group. Fifty patients from each physician office were enrolled, representing a total of six hundred patients.

The practices of the 12 participating physicians were quite busy, with physicians caring for a combination of inpatients and outpatients. Most of the physicians had approximately five hospitalized patients whom they saw prior to starting office hours. During a typical office workday each physician saw 12 to 25 patients, depending on the mix of new and follow-up visits and on their sub-specialty. Most of the physicians worked 12- to 14-hour days. All of the physicians believed that one of their patient care goals was to provide comprehensive and thorough care to their geriatric patients, and they agreed that time and expertise were essential to accomplishing this goal.

The principal investigator, a physician, provided the project orientation for each physician. The role of the ARNP as a collaborator in patient care was stressed. The physicians' office staffs underwent an in-service briefing, coordinated by IPIC's project director. All staff were educated about enrollment criteria and were encouraged to refer patients to the project. IPIC staff stressed the need to contact the ARNP (not the physician) with calls from project patients, and explained and reinforced the various methods of communication available to be used between ARNP, SW, and physician. Project staff also emphasized the importance of scheduling appointment times that were mutually convenient for the patient, ARNP, and physician. After the initial formal meeting was held, informal meetings were often conducted and frequent phone contact was made to reinforce the project procedures.

## Selected Roles for Collaboration

In our project, three Advanced Registered Nurse Practitioners (ARNPs) and one MSW-level Social Worker (SW) were selected. As part of the project, they were trained to provide assistance needed by internists to help minimize the barriers to delivery of comprehensive geriatric care.

Mount Sinai Medical Center has employed ARNPs for many years in specific hospital areas such as the employee health center, emergency department, outpatient services, anesthesia/pre-operative area, industrial and occupational medicine sites, and for employee screening services for Miami Beach and Dade County. Many physicians in the institution were, therefore, familiar and comfortable with ARNPs and their credentialing process. Studies have shown that ARNPs can provide, at lower cost and with equivalent quality, the majority of primary care and other services currently provided by physicians (Prescott, 1994). Additionally, ARNPs often provide more health promotion activities and are able to spend more time with patients (Brown & Grimes, 1993). Thus, it was posited that ARNPs trained in comprehensive geriatric assessment would be an excellent and accepted addition to the IPIC teams.

The department of social work plays an active role at Mount Sinai Medical Center, with almost every geriatric patient receiving an evaluation upon admission to the hospital. Physicians frequently call upon social workers to assist, not only with discharge planning, but with various aspects of in-home assessment and care. Most of the social work staff at Mount Sinai are licensed clinical social workers, and are very skilled in advising patients and families about living wills and surrogate care, as well as conducting group therapy and individual counseling. Thus, it was believed that this expanded social work role would be an asset for our program and would readily be accepted by physicians.

## Training

A 3-month training program for the project's ARNPs combined didactic and practice-based experiences. Participants included the principal investigator and two internists (all board certified in geriatrics), a neuropsychologist, a rehabilitation specialist, a dietician, and a pharmacologist. Topics covered in the ARNP training program included:

- Introduction to Geriatrics and the Physiology of Aging
- Maintenance Health Care for the Geriatric Population
- Preventive Health Care
- Psychosocial Aspects of Aging
- Cognitive Functioning
- Anxiety/Depression in the Older Population
- Proper Utilization of Medications
- Psychosocial Assessment

- Advance Directives
- Training in the Use of Geriatric Assessment Instruments
- Geriatric Rehabilitation
- Assessment of Sensory Impairment

"Hands-on" comprehensive assessment of the geriatric patient was accomplished in an ambulatory geriatric clinic, with treatment and follow-up planning stressed. ARNPs were instructed in the use of the patient measurement instruments. A rotation in the Memory Disorder Unit familiarized the ARNPs with the instruments used in the assessment of cognitively impaired and/or depressed patients.

The project's SW underwent a 1-month training program. Topics covered included:

- Psychosocial Aspects of Aging
- Anxiety/Depression in the Older Population
- Death and Dying
- Advance Directives, Surrogate Health Care, and Other Legal Issues
- Availability of Geriatric Community Services
- Communication and Interviewing Skills with Geriatric Patients and Families
- Training in the Use of Geriatric Assessment Instruments in the Areas of Depression and Anxiety

The SW spent time with a geriatric social worker in the geriatric outpatient clinic, concentrating on assessment of psychosocial needs and availability of resources, training in administration and interpretation of more comprehensive assessments for depression and anxiety when initial testing indicated further evaluation was needed, and training in the assessment of the cognitively impaired patient in the Memory Disorder Unit.

Whenever possible, the ARNPs and SW were trained together. For example, there was considerable cross-training in instrument use by the ARNPs and SW, enabling them to help each other complete patient assessments within the prescribed times. Indeed, tools originally believed to be in the domain of the ARNP or SW frequently were administered by the other. This was especially true in the assessment of depression. For example, if a patient had a high score on the Beck Depression Inventory (Beck, Ward & Mendelson, 1961), the SW often administered the Hamilton Depression Scale (Hamilton, 1960) during his initial interview, rather than have the patient wait for a follow-up visit with the ARNP. If a patient had difficulty completing the take-home battery of tests given by the ARNP, and the SW was making a home visit, he often helped the patient complete them. Some patients had frequent medical appointments, while others saw the SW for ongoing group therapy or individual counseling. Whenever possible, the professional that had an appointment with the patient administered the assessments at appropriate times.

## Patient Selection and Enrollment

Outpatient comprehensive interventions have not consistently shown reductions in morbidity, mortality, and cost as have inpatient programs (Williams, Williams, Zimmer, Hall & Podgorski, 1987). Given the small number of patients hospitalized, an effective ambulatory program would have significant national impact. As there are no standardized criteria for enrollment in outpatient programs, a combination of selection criteria involving age, medical conditions, social factors, and functional status was established for our project by IPIC staff.

Patients were referred by office staff and physicians. The ARNPs reviewed the patients' records to determine eligibility. To be included, patients had to meet the following five criteria:

- be age 70 or over
- be a resident of Dade County for a majority of the year
- be an English or Spanish speaker
- be a patient of the practice for at least three months
- have one or more, but no more than four, medical or social problems (e.g., mild dementia, incontinence, depression, recent stroke, or low income, recent bereavement, living alone).

Patients with more than four active conditions were excluded from the project, as it was believed that they probably would not gain maximum benefit from this type of comprehensive intervention due to the serious nature and/or complexity of their extensive medical or social conditions. On occasion, however, the ARNP and physician presented a patient with multiple problems believed not to be severely ill, and therefore able to benefit from the project. These patients were enrolled and provisions were made to determine if outcomes would be any different from those of the other project patients.

Patients were not included in the project if they were terminally ill, had severe dementia, cardiopulmonary disease resistant to medical management, significant substance abuse, delirium or psychosis, or were facing an imminent move to an adult congregate living facility or a nursing home. Finally, patients were not included if they had already participated in an inpatient rehabilitation program that determined that they had reached maximum rehabilitation.

Because only 50 patients were enrolled from each office, physicians often asked IPIC staff to see other patients, both within and below the specified age range, whom they believed would benefit from a comprehensive approach to care. However, the enrollment criteria described above were strictly followed, and only project patients were seen.

There were no significant differences in the sociodemographic and economic profiles in our intervention and non-intervention patients. Comparison of internist and sub-specialist groups also revealed no significant differences.

Our patients' sociodemographic profile is summarized in Table 5.2.

---

**TABLE 5.2**

**IPIC Patient Sociodemographic Profile (N=246)**

| Age (years) | | Country of birth | % |
|---|---|---|---|
| (mean) | 79.98 | US | 63.8 |
| (range) | 68–98 | Poland | 5.3 |
| | | Germany | 4.1 |
| **Gender** | % | Cuba | 3.7 |
| female | 64.0 | Russia | 3.3 |
| male | 36.0 | unknown | 10.6 |
| | | other | 9.2 |
| **Religion** | | | |
| Jewish | 74.7 | **First language** | |
| Catholic | 13.6 | English | 91.9 |
| Protestant | 4.5 | Spanish | 5.5 |
| other | 4.1 | other | 2.5 |
| not applicable | 3.1 | | |
| | | **Advance directives** | |
| **Living arrangements** | | none | 50.0 |
| apartment | 56.2 | combination | |
| condominium | 21.3 | (living will, | |
| house | 15.7 | health care sur- | |
| hotel | 2.1 | rogate, power | |
| low-income housing | 1.7 | of attorney) | 50.0 |
| other | 3.0 | **Use of community** | |
| | | **services** | |
| alone | 50.0 | none | 77.6 |
| with spouse | 39.0 | private duty | 11.2 |
| with significant other | 5.0 | home health | 3.4 |
| with children | 3.0 | other | 7.8 |
| other | 3.0 | | |

Percentages may not add to 100% due to rounding.

---

## Assessment and Care Planning

Patient assessments, conducted in the physicians' offices by the ARNPs, were very comprehensive. Patients' records were reviewed for thoroughness of medical, social, demographic, and psychological information. In the office setting, the ARNPs updated records and administered instruments to all project patients that assessed cognition, activities of daily living, functional abilities, and gait and balance. These included the Folstein Mini-Mental Status Examination (Folstein, Folstein & McHugh, 1975), Record of Independent Living (Weintraub, Barataz, & Mesulam, 1982), Index of Activities of Daily Living (Katz, Ford & Moskowitz, 1963), Index of Instrumental Activities of Daily Living (Lawton & Brody, 1969), and the Tinetti Gait and Balance Evaluation (Tinetti, 1986). The ARNP usually completed these assessments by extending the time of one or two routine office visits; on occasion, the patient had an additional office appointment scheduled in order to finish the assessments.

All patients were requested to complete additional instruments at home. These included the Beck Depression Inventory (Beck, Ward & Mendelson, 1961), Clinical Anxiety Scale (Westhuis & Thyer, 1986), Geriatric Depression Scale (Yesavage & Brink, 1983), Multidimensional Health Locus of Control (Wallston, Wallston & DeVellis, 1978), Internal Control Index (Duttweiler, 1984), Provision of Social Relations (Turner, Frankel & Levin, 1983), Life Satisfaction Index-Z (Neugarten, Havighurst & Tobin, 1961), Satisfaction with Life Scale (Dienter, Emmons, Larsen & Griffin, 1985), Impact of Event Scale (Horowitz, Wilner & Alvarez, 1979), and the COOP (Nelson, Wasson, Johnson & Hayes, 1996). If a patient had difficulty completing the home assessments, the ARNP or SW assisted by phone, or, if necessary, made a home visit. The instruments used in the initial assessment were repeated at 9- and 18-month intervals for all patients.

For intervention patients only, the ARNP performed or completed all the preventive and maintenance health items not completed by the internist. Psychosocial, hearing, gait, skin cancer, and oral exams, mammograms, pneumonia vaccine, and rectal examinations were positively facilitated by the presence of ARNPs. For example, only 10.1% of patients had psychosocial data bases at the time of initial assessment. ARNPs completed this assessment in 93.3% of patients by the 18-month follow-up visit. No patients had received objective assessments of cognitive abilities, function, depression/anxiety, life satisfaction, or control indices prior to involvement of ARNP staff.

The SW scheduled visits with intervention patients only. The majority of visits occurred in either the physician's or SW's office, depending on
patient convenience and space availability. Occasionally, a patient was
fearful of meeting with the SW, found it difficult to make the trip to the
hospital, or was in need of a home visit to assess social or medical needs
(as judged by the ARNP's initial evaluation). The SW then scheduled a
home visit to complete the evaluation. During the initial SW meeting,
economic status, need for surrogate health care and living will and guard-
ianship determinations, evaluation of risk for elder abuse and neglect,
and need for social and community support were assessed. Patients at
risk for depression received further diagnostic testing, were referred for
treatment and/or counseling, and were invited to join the project's support group. Some patients received ongoing individual counseling by the
project's SW. Home safety was assessed, and referrals were made to occupational therapy as necessary.

There were a total of 4,466 documented phone contacts between the
project's clinical staff and intervention patients. The average amount of
time per call was seven minutes, for a total time commitment of 613
hours during the project period. Phone contact was initiated by both patients and project staff for a variety of reasons such as diagnostic test reporting (e.g., blood, x-rays), medication adjustments and advice, management of medical problems handled without an office visit (e.g., upper
respiratory infection, change in insulin dosing), transportation arrangements, durable equipment needs, scheduling of appointments, and assistance with completion of questionnaires. Calls made to physicians were
routed to the ARNPs, who decided on a treatment plan. Phone contact by
patients with chronic problems needing extra care and attention was encouraged by the ARNPs. All interventions were documented, and physicians were kept informed of these encounters by phone and/or fax.

A total of 131 home visits by clinical staff were documented. The average visit lasted one hour, and involved three-quarters of an hour of
transportation time. Home visits were performed for a variety of reasons
including completion of study assessments, home safety checks, assessment of social situations, delivery of medical care, and follow-up of
medical and rehabilitative care. On occasion, patients were unable to
travel to their physicians' offices because of illness, and refused to contact
emergency services. Assessment at home by the ARNP expedited care,
usually by the ARNP arranging emergency transport and admission to
the hospital.

Scheduled visits with intervention patients over the 18-month study

time averaged 6.5 visits per patient with the ARNP, and 3 visits per patient with the SW. The range varied widely, with some study patients having as few as 2 or as many as 18 contacts with their ARNP. Similarly, the
SW saw some patients only once during the project period, and others as
often as 10 times (e.g., when ongoing counseling was required).

## Relationship Development Among Collaborators

Project staff worked cooperatively, sharing information daily. Common
office space facilitated this regular exchange. Screening and interview
data were discussed, and follow-up care was arranged by either the ARNP
or SW.

Weekly team meetings with project staff (ARNPs, SW, project director, and principal investigator) were held. Difficult patient problems were
discussed, and modifications of plans were sometimes suggested via this
multidisciplinary approach. The changes were presented to the primary
physician for approval prior to implementation.

ARNP-physician contact was ongoing, developing, and changing differently within each intervention office practice. In the state of Florida,
ARNPs practice under developed protocols. These protocols must provide for general supervision by a physician; supervision is defined as the
ability to communicate or maintain contact on site or by telephone.
ARNPs may work in independent office settings or they may be salaried
employees of institutions, caring for patients with varying levels of independence and supervision. In the latter situation, billing may then be
submitted under the ARNP or supervising physician, with reimbursement going to the institution. At Mount Sinai medical center, ARNPs are
hospital employees, practicing either independently via detailed protocols, or under varying levels of physician supervision. The ARNPs and
SW in this project were medical center employees, supported by grant
funds. However, patients seen were patients within specific physician's offices, and the patients identified the internist or sub-specialist as their primary physician. The physicians wanted to bill for every patient visit as a
physician-patient encounter. Thus, every ARNP-patient interaction had
to be supervised and countersigned by the physician.

In addition to administering the program's assessment instruments,
ARNPs participated in ongoing care of intervention patients. Phone calls
were routed to the ARNPs, follow-up visits were scheduled whenever

possible with the ARNPs, and ARNPs were contacted to provide urgent or unscheduled care. Some physicians made contact with every patient at the time of each ARNP-patient encounter. The intensity of contact varied, ranging from re-examination of every patient, to a directed examination, or only a conversation. These physicians reviewed and implemented care plans and countersigned records during, or immediately after, each contact. Other physicians made contact with each patient, but permitted the ARNP to implement care plans independently; those records were reviewed and co-signed subsequently. On occasion, ARNPs saw patients and implemented care plans independently. Physicians were made aware of those encounters via written communication, faxed summary sheets, and/or chart notes, all of which were countersigned.

Most physicians supervised the ARNPs with a combination of methods. For example, if the ARNP was assessing gait and balance, an area that the physician usually was not very familiar with, the ARNP often worked independently. The same type of independent practice occurred often when the ARNP was completing health maintenance items (e.g., Pap smears, breast examinations), or assessing cognitive function, depression, or functional status. Assessments that were more complicated medically (e.g., congestive heart failure), usually resulted in more direct physician supervision. The process resulted in slightly different procedures in each intervention office, enabling each physician to maintain the level of contact with each patient with which he or she was comfortable. Overall, the expertise of each team member was utilized appropriately, and decision making and patient care were usually accomplished jointly.

Physicians were appreciative and accepting of the comprehensive assessments the ARNPs and SW performed. ARNPs completed portions of the physical examination not previously performed and provided follow-up of referrals made; they coordinated care between various services, and worked closely with the SW. Physicians were pleased to have ARNP assistance when intervention patients needed urgent visits, and they were relieved to have issues of surrogate health care and living wills discussed by the SW. The physicians realized that many important, time-consuming, but non-reimbursable aspects of geriatric care were being completed by IPIC personnel.

The ARNPs understood and appreciated the intervention physicians' desires to maintain personal contact with their patients; many patients had been cared for by the physicians for many years and had close, personal relationships. They were aware that the intervention was limited to 18 months, at which time all care would revert back to the physicians.

The ARNPs were also sensitive to the financial pressures of practice, and worked easily within the supervisory parameters requested by the physicians. In turn, the physicians were supportive of the ARNPs, encouraging long-time patients to see the ARNPs and complete the rather extensive assessments. Most of the physicians were eager to share medical knowledge, and were accepting of the ARNPs' areas of geriatric expertise. As the program progressed, the ARNPs' role in comprehensive assessment and integration of care was further appreciated. Practice patterns became more collaborative, with each team member's expertise used to full advantage.

## Evaluation

Project evaluation revealed that ARNPs greatly enhanced psychosocial, hearing, gait, and skin cancer assessments, and increased mammogram use, pneumonia vaccine administration, and performance of rectal examinations. There were no significant differences noted between the practice patterns of the internists and subspecialists.

There was a significant increase over time in the total number of medications ordered in both the intervention and non-intervention patients. At baseline, patients received 4.91 medications (with a range of 0 to 14); at the end of the study, the average number of medications was 5.5 (with a range of 0 to 18).

There was no change in reported general health, cognitive status, ADLs, IADLs, life satisfaction or depression with time or the intervention. Although the number of medications increased with time, there was no significant effect or interaction noted due to the intervention.

Intervention and non-intervention patients had no significant differences with regard to responses on the patient satisfaction questionnaire. Currently available instruments are inadequate as they are unable to account for changes in life status (e.g., new economic problems, death of significant other), nor can they assess many positive aspects of the intervention on individual patients' care. For example, one elderly patient was noted to have worsening kidney function. The ARNP discussed this with the physician, who believed no further action was necessary. The ARNP informally consulted a nephrologist who suggested further testing; the ARNP persuaded the study physician to proceed with testing. As a result, a reversible cause of the dysfunction was discovered. Dialysis was probably prevented by the ARNP's intervention. The patient was unaware of the importance of the ARNP's involvement, and his satisfaction question-naire could not reflect this positive outcome. Many patients added narra-tive comments on their questionnaires, indicating their satisfaction with IPIC's intervention. For example, one patient wrote, "This is the care and concern that all us senior citizens need. How lucky I was to have had her. They're better than some members of my family."

Physician responses regarding satisfaction did not differ significantly at baseline and follow-up. As with the patient questionnaires, the satisfac-tion instrument for physicians could not assess the impact of many fac-tors other than the intervention (e.g., financial pressures due to managed care, increasing office expenses, additional time-consuming paper work). In addition, the assessment instrument measured overall effect, making analysis of an effect involving only a small proportion of patients within the practice impossible. Written comments from physicians were, how-ever, very positive. Responses to the question, "If this program were to be terminated and your practice returned to how it had operated before the program, how would you react?" included:

- Upset. I would feel more pressure and responsibility on my shoul-ders.
- My patients would be lost/depressed.
- I would miss the psychological advantage that I have somebody to help me.
- I would consider having an ARNP working in my office.

Our small sample size limited statistical analyses, thus the clinical sig-nificance of findings must be cautiously interpreted. There is no doubt that our intervention patients received more comprehensive medical and psychosocial evaluations. The effect on outcome, however, remains unde-termined. The complexities of individual medical and social problems, as well as differences in number and types of interventions employed, pre-vented equalization of patients for analysis purposes. Essentially, every patient was an individual whose condition was unique.

Our goals included increasing patient satisfaction with medical care, and physician satisfaction with the delivery of comprehensive geriatric care. Patient and physician satisfaction with the intervention could not be adequately assessed using available instruments. Written comments by both patients and physicians helped us realize that improved measures of patient and physician satisfaction should be developed, as positive results could contribute to the viability of comprehensive programs nationwide.

Our project staff have developed such an instrument, and are in the process of administering it to our patients and physicians.

IPIC is extending for an additional nine months through a continuation grant. Current non-intervention patients will enter the intervention process, patients from additional physician practices will be added, and current intervention patients will continue in the project. The assessment components will be significantly decreased as the measures have not been found to predict patient outcome, and the intervention does not affect the scores obtained. Exams will be limited to the Beck Depression Inventory, the Folstein Mini-Mental Status Examination, the Internal Control Index, the Index of Activities of Daily Living, the Index of Instrumental Activities of Daily Living, and the Tinetti Gait and Balance Evaluation. Other measures may be added pending final analyses. The reduction in data collection will enable the ARNPs and SW to serve more patients, as well as increase their availability for physicians and patients. The decreased demands on the patients' time should minimize attrition during the second phase of the project. Streamlining the assessment will enable the ARNPs and SW to have the time necessary to assess and manage the multiple psychosocial and functional problems so important to the successful management of frail elderly persons.

# Lessons Learned

Projects involving patient care, especially in a changing medical and economic environment, face unanticipated problems. In implementing our project, we learned a great deal about project design, process, and the development of roles and relationships.

## Project Design Lessons

Twelve physicians' offices were recruited for our project. During the project, two non-intervention sub-specialist physicians left the practice of medicine; one (a cardiologist) retired and one (an endocrinologist) entered the managed care industry as a consultant. One intervention internist became medically disabled. Most of the cardiologist's patients transferred their care to a new cardiologist, and the project was maintained in his office. Some patients, however, transferred their care to a cardiologist who was one of our intervention sub-specialists. He was helpful and assisted in keeping his newly acquired non-intervention patients in the study. The endocrinologist's patients went to a variety of offices for their care. Through the efforts of our SW, ARNP, and project director, most of the patients continued to be followed in their new offices. Fortunately, this was a non-intervention group of patients who were not receiving on-going care by project staff. The intervention internist's patients were absorbed by another physician in the existing group who was interested in the project and worked well with the ARNP. It is not possible to assess the impact of these changes on patient outcome or satisfaction with care.

We anticipated a total of 600 patients for baseline evaluation. This was adequate to analyze differences between intervention and non-intervention groups, and to compare practice patterns between internists and sub-specialists. An overall attrition rate of 25% was expected due to death, relocation, and failure to comply with follow-up visits. The projected remaining 450 patients were considered an effective sample size to conduct the analyses proposed. However, there was considerable unexpected attrition in both patient groups, with 57% of enrollees not completing the project. Of interest were the unexpectedly high numbers of patients who refused to complete the questionnaires (10.5%), and the surprising number who could not be located during the project period (8.8%). The decreased number of intervention patients resulted in difficulty with overall data analysis, and the higher attrition rate in the non-intervention group (63% vs. 51%) made comparisons between groups difficult to interpret. Overall, a larger sample size would have enabled more meaningful longitudinal analyses. Perhaps a more comprehensive explanation of the time commitment expected by the patients would have enabled project staff to select patients more likely to complete the project.

## Process Lessons

Originally, ARNPs were to have specific times scheduled in each physician's office for follow-up visits of intervention patients. However, in practice, ARNPs were contacted on an as-needed basis by physicians' office staff, and the ARNPs frequently rearranged their schedules to accommodate patients' needs.

Regularly scheduled multidisciplinary conferences between physicians, ARNPs, and the SW were included in the project design; however, they never occurred. Most physicians preferred to discuss each patient individually with the ARNP at the time of the supervised patient encounter. Following phone and home contacts, written communication was the preferred method of contact. Physicians were not willing to dedicate a block of time for multidisciplinary meetings, although they appreciated suggestions made after the project team's weekly conference.

As designed, a senior supervisory ARNP was to guide the other ARNPs through the process; however, this proved unnecessary. Each ARNP adapted individually and became responsible for each physician's office practice.

Phone contact and home visits accounted for approximately 850 hours of ARNP and SW time. Although we anticipated frequent phone and home intervention for medical and social assistance, this extensive amount was not foreseen. The ARNPs and SW realized early in the study that many patients were unable to complete, without assistance, the assessment tools distributed; this accounted for a significant amount of the phone and home contact (approximately 20% and 40% respectively). We learned that determining in advance the time and assistance needed to complete instruments would have been helpful, and for future projects this should be ascertained to plan for staffing needs.

## Role and Relationship Lessons

The degree of practice autonomy ARNPs were permitted varied from physician to physician. The types of communication preferred differed between office practices as well. In all settings, the successful integration of ARNPs into the physicians' practices depended on ARNP flexibility in patient care, scheduling, and adapting to individual physician and office practice modes.

During the project, it was realized that one physician was unwilling or unable to relinquish any meaningful patient care responsibility to the ARNP. Examinations were consistently reviewed in depth, and all decision making remained in his domain. Although this physician permitted more ARNP autonomy in geriatric assessment, dietary and social interventions, the ARNP never really achieved collaborative practice in this office. On the other hand, a few physicians encouraged very independent functioning, sometimes resulting in ARNP discomfort due to lack of supervision. At these times, the ARNPs consulted with the principal investigator regarding patient care. The practice patterns noted did not correlate to sub-specialty training, or whether the physicians were in hospital-based or independently owned private practice. It would be valuable to have a screening tool to help delineate physician practice patterns, as the goal was collaborative practice rather than independent or "physician-extender" practice styles.

IPIC staff believed that generalists and specialists practicing geriatric primary care would appreciate the ancillary support received through this project. The project's physicians were offered the opportunity to contribute to the cost of their practitioners in order to sustain the program. Three intervention physicians have offered salary support for the ARNPs working in their offices. They have indicated that the ARNP will continue to provide comprehensive geriatric care, but will also need to be involved with delivery of primary care to non-geriatric patients. Thus, there appears to be some commitment to geriatric assessment and collaborative care, but economics may well determine the strength of this commitment.

Mount Sinai is planning to expand the ARNP role in its hospital-based internal medicine and sub-specialty practices. The hospital-based cardiology offices have already acquired two ARNPs to assist with delivery of primary care by cardiologists who prefer to practice cardiology exclusively. The medical center views ARNP services as being a cost-effective way to care for patients, especially those enrolled in managed care. Physicians are pleased to have assistance in primary care delivery, and in the completion of tasks they consider time-consuming and non-reimbursable (e.g., completion of nursing home forms, prescription renewals). It is clear that we have been successful in integrating ARNP practice into both the private and hospital sectors, although in the latter the role will be primarily as a physician extender.

# Summary

IPIC was designed to promote comprehensive geriatric primary care in internist offices. Nurse practitioners and a social worker worked in a collaborative manner with physicians to promote comprehensive and integrated geriatric care, improve outcomes and satisfaction for elderly patients, and increase physician satisfaction. Additional goals included generation of a patient profile that could help determine what patient population would benefit most from this type of intervention, and what assessment measures could help professionals target patients most likely to benefit.

Geriatric care provided by physicians who had ARNP and SW assistance was shown to be more comprehensive. Successful integration of ancillary professionals into physician offices occurred, and ARNPs were hired and incorporated into several additional practices at the medical center. Both patients and physicians expressed satisfaction with the program in written statements.

The elimination of many time-consuming assessment measures that did not discriminate in the ambulatory population represented in this study will enable ARNPs to be more efficient and directed in their care of geriatric patients in the future. Our project demonstrated the need for continued clinical research. For example, a large epidemiologic study would help identify the medical and social factors important in the selection of patients most likely to benefit from intensive interventions. A large study would also ensure accurate statistical analyses of outcomes. The continuation of these types of programs is dependent upon recognition of their importance by physicians and health care policy officials, proof of efficacy in the ambulatory setting, and fiscal considerations.

# References

Beck, A.T., Ward, C.H. & Mendelson, M. (1961). An inventory for measuring depression. *Archives of General Psychiatry, 4,* 53–63.

Brown, S. & Grimes, D. (1993). *Nurse practitioners and certified nurse midwives: A meta-analysis of studies on nurses in primary care roles.* Washington, DC: American Nurses Association.

Dienter, E., Emmons, R.A., Larsen, R.J. & Griffin, S. (1985). The satisfaction with life scale. *Journal of Personality Assessment, 49,* 71–75.

Duttweiler, P. (1984). The Internal Control Index: A newly developed measure of locus of control. *Educational and Psychological Measurement, 44,* 209–221.

Epstein, A.M., Hall, J.A., Fretwell, M., Feldstein, M., DeCiantis, M.L. & Tognetti, J. (1990). Consultative geriatric assessment for ambulatory patients: A randomized trial in a health maintenance organization. *Journal of the American Medical Association, 263,* 538–544.

Folstein, M.F., Folstein, S.E. & McHugh, P.R. (1975). Mini-mental state: A practical method for grading the cognitive state of patients for the clinician. *Journal of Psychiatric Research, 12,* 189–198.

Hamilton, H. (1960). A rating scale for depression. *Journal of Neurology, Neurosurgery, Psychiatry, 23,* 56.

Horowitz, M.J., Wilner, N. & Alvarez, W. (1979). Impact of event scale: A measure of subjective stress. *Psychological Medicine, 41,* 209–218.

Katz, S., Ford, A.B. & Moskowitz, R.W. (1963). Studies of illness in the aged: The index of ADL. *Journal of the American Medical Association, 185,* 914–919.

Lawton, M.P. & Brody, E.M. (1969). Assessment of older people: Self maintaining and instrumental activities of daily living. *The Gerontologist, 9,* 179–186.

MacLean, D.S. (1993). Outcome and cost of family physicians' care. Pilot study of three diagnosis-related groups in elderly inpatients. *Journal of the American Board of Family Practice, 6*(6), 588–593.

Nelson, E.C., Wasson, J.H., Johnson, D. & Hays, R. (1996). Dartmouth COOP Functional Assessment Charts. In B. Spilker (Ed.), *Brief measures for clinical practice book: Quality of life and pharmoeconomics in clinical trials* (2nd ed.). Philadelphia: Lippincott-Raven Publishers.

Neugarten, B.L., Havighurst, R.J. & Tobin, S.S. (1961). The measurement of life satisfaction. *Journal of Gerontology, 16,* 134–143.

Payne, B.C., Lyons, T.F. & Neuhaus, E. (1984). Relationships of physician characteristics to performance quality and improvement. *Health Services Research 19,* 307–332.

Prescott, P.A. (1994). Cost-effective primary care providers: An important component of health care reform. *International Journal of Technology Assessment in Health Care, 10*(2), 249–257.

Rubenstein, L.A., Stuck, A.E., Siu, A.L. & Wieland, D. (1991). Impacts of geriatric evaluation and management programs on defined outcomes: Overview of the evidence. *Journal of the American Geriatrics Society, 39* (Suppl.), 8S-16S.

Tinetti, M. (1986). Performance-oriented assessment of mobility problems in elderly patients. *Journal of the American Geriatrics Society, 34,* 119–126.

Turner, R.J., Frankel, B.G. & Levin, D.M. (1983). Social support: Conceptualization, measurement, and implications for mental health. *Research in Community and Mental Health, 3,* 67–111.

U.S. Department of Commerce. (1990). Census of Population, 1990. Washington, DC: General Printing Office.

Wallston, K.A., Wallston, B.S. & DeVellis, R. (1978). Development of the Multidimensional Health Locus of Control (MHLC) Scales. *Health Education Monographs, 6,* 160–170.

Weintraub, S., Barataz, R. & Mesulam, M. (1982). Daily living activities in the assessment of dementia. In S. Cirkin, K. Davis, K. Cravdem, E. Usdin & J. Wurtman (Eds.), *Alzheimer's Disease: A report of progression in research* (pp. 189–192). New York: Raven Press.

Westhuis, D. & Thyer, B.A. (1986). Development and validation of the Clinical Anxiety Scale: A rapid assessment instrument for empirical practice. Unpublished manuscript, University of Georgia, School of Social Work, Athens, GA.

Williams, M.E., Williams, T.F., Zimmer, J.G., Hall, W.J. & Podgorski, C.A. (1987). How does the team approach to outpatient geriatric evaluation compare with traditional care: A report of a randomized controlled trial. *Journal of the American Geriatrics Society, 3,* 1071–1078.

Yesavage, J.A. & Brink, T.L. (1983). Development and validation of the Geriatric Depression Screening Scale: A preliminary report. *Journal of Psychiatric Research, 17,* 437–449.

# CHAPTER 6

# Physician Assistants in Urban Neighborhood Health Centers

*Philip A. Anderson, Richard H. Fortinsky, and C. Seth Landefeld*

## Background

Senior Health Connections, a project implemented at Northeast Ohio Neighborhood Health Services, Inc. (NEON), aimed to improve the health care of frail urban elders by providing a new colleague for their community health center generalist physicians—the gerontologic physician assistant.

NEON is a federally supported (Title 330) independent non-profit community health center providing health care for residents of relatively impoverished areas of the east side of Cleveland for over 30 years. At the start of Senior Health Connections in 1994, NEON had five sites for care delivery, and annually provided care to over 1,500 patients age 70 or over (the target population for our project). Along with NEON, cooperating partners for Senior Health Connections included the Division of General Internal Medicine and Health Care Research at Case Western Reserve University School of Medicine and University Hospitals of Cleveland. The division is part of an academic department of medicine and has staff with skills and resources in geriatrics, education, and health care research. One member of the division had been a physician and assistant medical director at NEON in the past.

NEON's essential mission is the provision of excellent health care to its community; research and education have not been priorities. However, during the decade before Senior Health Connections started, several cooperative patient care projects were initiated between NEON and University Hospitals of Cleveland, in which NEON physicians usually admitted and cared for their patients in the same way that other community physicians did. These initiatives, including joint operation of several primary care clinics involving resident physicians, helped clarify that participation of the health centers in education could be consistent with excellent care and facilitate later staff recruitment, and that participation in research could lead to improved patient care.

Although NEON received some federal funding as a community health center, other sources made up a large part of the budget. In 1987, NEON had started a Medicaid HMO, and at the time Senior Health Connections began, it was considering starting or participating in a Medicare program in which they would receive a month's capitation payment rather than fee for service. Although Medicare capitation was not yet significant in the local market, it was expected to grow rapidly.

NEON sites usually contained two to five primary care physicians (internists and a few family physicians) caring for adults, and several sites used physician assistants (most often for urgent care visits). Pediatricians, obstetricians, and ancillary services such as nutrition counseling, podiatry, and optometry were available, but social service support was very limited. Each site had a nurse and a number of medical assistants. Patients were generally poor and primarily African-American; few had insurance other than Medicare or Medicaid.

## Project Design

The premise for Senior Health Connections was that any strategy to help generalist physicians provide better care for elders needed to directly assist and support physicians in providing excellent care for their patients. We believed that most physicians would welcome such a program. At the same time, we recognized that the demands on primary care physicians, especially in a community health center environment with limited resources, were high and constantly increasing. A program that required physicians to do more work, no matter how wonderful for patients and the health system, would be difficult to establish and especially difficult to maintain. In addition, we were eager to develop a project that would have a reasonable chance of continuing after grant funding ended. This meant that it would need to be financially viable (either in a fee-for-service or capitation environment) and institutionally acceptable. Finally, we recognized that different physicians, because of their varying backgrounds and experience, would welcome different kinds of help. Some would most appreciate help with routine preventive care, others with complex psychosocial problems, and others with managing geriatric syndromes that had not been part of their education and training. The answer to these needs, we thought, could be adding physician assistants with geriatric training to the community health center staff.

Several authors have encouraged using physician assistants in geriatric settings (Bottom, 1988; Cawley, Ott & DeAtley, 1983; Romeis, Schey, Marion & Keith, 1985), but little has actually been reported on such use. Physician assistants were chosen for Senior Health Connections for three reasons. First, Ohio permitted physician assistants to bill for office visits, which we hoped would improve the prospects for long-term financial viability of the project. Second, we wanted to propose a distinct approach to the Hartford Foundation, and we were not aware of other projects proposing a physician assistant model. Finally, we wanted a project that would be perceived as helpful by the existing physicians at the community health centers, who were generally receptive to a program to help provide excellent care for the elderly.

Although Ohio had a relatively restrictive practice environment for physician assistants and nurse practitioners, billing for office visits done by physician assistants was allowed if a physician provided simultaneous oversight. We felt that this would enhance the possibility that Senior Health Connections would remain economically viable for the health centers when foundation funding ended. If the local Medicare market moved more strongly toward managed care, we believed that research data about the effect of the project on patient care outcomes would provide economic justification for the program to continue. Thus we were hopeful that the project would persist if successful, regardless of how quickly capitation enveloped the local Medicare population.

We were also aware that the Hartford Foundation was interested in a number of variations on the theme of assistance for the generalist physician in the care of frail elders. The foundation encouraged not only our choice of physician assistants as the focus of the project, but also our proposed basis at an urban community health center.

Finally, we were aware that the physicians in our sites would likely accept a new program more readily if it involved new participants who were professionally accustomed to working closely with physicians, and under their direction. We expected that our physician assistants would have substantially more knowledge in some geriatric fields than many of the physicians with whom they would be working, and that this knowledge could be transmitted and put into use relatively easily.

The project, therefore, consisted of three essential parts: (1) recruiting and training two physician assistants in geriatrics, (2) integrating them into the daily practice at two of the NEON sites so that they could assist the physicians and improve care for elderly patients, (3) and studying the results of the project on patient care outcomes, and patient and physician satisfaction.

The design of the outcome study compared patient care results at two community health center sites, where the Senior Health Connections project was instituted, with two similar control sites. The four sites with room for a physician assistant were divided into pairs by size, and one of each pair was randomly picked as a site for Senior Health Connections. Names of study patients were obtained from a billing list of all patients age 70 and over who had been seen at the health center sites during a 12-month period shortly before the project started. The patients on the list at the two intervention sites and the two control sites were interviewed in detail over the telephone after receiving an introductory letter from the health center's medical director. For evaluation, a similar but longer interview was completed after Senior Health Connections had been in operation for a year; office chart abstractions were also done before and after the first year of the project. The outcome results of the project are based on patients with complete interviews and chart abstractions, and who indicated in their first interview that they usually received their medical care at the community health centers (some individuals only got dental care or sporadic care at the health centers, and received most of their health care elsewhere).

# Roles and Relationships

## Physician Assistant Recruitment and Training

Candidates for the two physician assistant positions were recruited by advertisements in local papers, by a mailing to all physician assistants in the region from the mailing list of the American Association of Physician Assistants, and by contact with physician assistant leadership at the local physician assistant training program. About ten candidates were interviewed; both physician assistants hired were women. One of those hired already worked at NEON (in pediatrics) and one was working at a local hospital. One was African-American, a potential advantage in a project serving primarily African-American patients.

Aspects of the positions that were attractive to applicants were the extensive additional training offered and the excitement of participating in a novel project. Impediments to recruitment included the neighborhood of the sites, uncertainty about long-term funding for the positions, and the possible need for home visits in some of the neighborhoods. We looked for candidates with clinical experience, the ability to work well with patients and colleagues, independence and motivation, and a desire to learn and willingness to embrace a learner-centered approach.

Once hired, the physician assistants underwent a 3.5-month training program grounded on three principles. First, the knowledge, skills, and attitudes required were based on specific needs of the elderly community health center patients identified through patient telephone interviews as well as meetings with community health center physicians and medical director. Second, principles of adult learning (Knowles, 1990) were used in training. We assumed that physician assistants would enter the training phase with substantial knowledge and skills that could in many cases be translated to the geriatric setting, would want to learn things that would be relevant to their job, would want to practice their new learning promptly, and could learn as self-directed individuals or as a team if the correct resources were provided. Third, we used existing geriatric education sessions where appropriate. We arranged for the Case Western Reserve Geriatric Education Center, based at the Fairhill Institute for Aging, to organize and conduct much of the training. Although the physician assistant training programs from which they graduated devoted only a minimal portion of the 2-year curriculum to geriatrics, our physician assistants had worked with a range of elders in most of their previous jobs. We hoped to provide knowledge, skills, and attitudes in four areas: (1) caring for patients with common geriatric syndromes and illnesses, (2) providing age-appropriate preventive care, (3) understanding the social situation of poor urban elders and the variety of community agencies available to support them, and (4) sharpening communication skills needed for optimal interaction with elders. In addition, we hoped to facilitate development of good relations between physician assistants and physicians by using the community health centers as clinical sites one day a week during the training. We reasoned that on-site experience would help physician assistants know what they would need to learn, practice what they were learning, and give the physicians time to become familiar with their strengths and practice styles.

The actual components of the training included one day each week for six weeks of didactic lectures and discussions (open to the physician assistant community and attended by about 10 other physician assistants), taught by project investigators and members of the local geriatrics faculty. Topics covered during these sessions are listed in Table 6.1.

The physician assistants also did independent readings with weekly discussion and case discussions with the principal investigator, who had expertise in geriatric medicine. The training also included participation in a number of geriatric seminars for various health professionals. For example, a 2-day conference on geriatrics for physical therapists provided an excellent survey of geriatrics issues, and a chance to understand what physical therapists could and could not provide for elders. A special 3-day course in communication skills with older patients taught by national faculty from the American Academy on Physician and Patient was attended by 15 people, including physician assistants involved with the project, other local physician assistants, and physicians from the community health center. The training also involved visits and clinical experience at many sites, including geriatric inpatient and outpatient settings, long-term care sites, hospices, geriatric primary care practices, and a large number of social service agencies serving elders.

The content of the training was also coordinated with the three primary goals of the project: increased preventive care, care of acute new or worsening problems, and follow-up after hospitalization. The physician assistants kept daily logs to record activities and what they had learned. The training continued after the official start of the program, with biweekly tutorials offered by the principal investigator (who was also available by pager throughout the project for consultation). These sessions covered topics and cases that the physician assistants had faced recently, as well as issues that came up in developing relations with the community health center physicians. For example, one physician assistant had seen a patient who came in with new abdominal pain. He had had colon cancer the year before, and testing revealed that he now had metastatic cancer. The difficulty was that the patient's physician was reluctant to provide any narcotic pain medicine, which the physician assistant felt was needed. The suggestion that he be referred to an oncologist at the University Cancer Center was agreeable to both and resolved the conflict.

## The Physician Assistant Role in Community Health Centers

The role of the gerontologic physician assistant in the community health centers was new and included three primary tasks. The first task for the physician assistants was to call patients who had not been in recently to en-

**TABLE 6.1**

## Senior Health Connections Didactic Session Topics

**Topics and issues in geriatric care for physician assistants**
Coming of age in America: What does that mean for you?
Functional assessment of elderly persons
Cognitive impairment and neurological disorders in later life
Psychological problems in later life
Issues in family caregiving
Communicating with older adults

**Medical and social care of older adults**
Assessing the geriatric patient
Drug use in the elderly population
Psychosocial assessment of the geriatric patient
Functional assessment of the geriatric patient
Community resources for older people

**Cognitive functioning and sensory loss**
Psychosocial issues in caring for someone with cognitive impairment
Panel of families facing memory loss
Alzheimer's Disease Support Center on Free-Net
Differential diagnosis and medical management of dementia
Managing difficult behaviors in dementia
Ethical issues in dementia care

**Health promotion and disease prevention**
Health screening and prevention in the elderly population
Health screening strategies: To use or not to use
Alcoholism and elders
Alcoholism Services of Cleveland
Fall assessment in elders

**Managing chronic conditions in elders**
Why geriatric medicine?
Medical management of chronic conditions
Health communication in aging
Psychosocial issues in chronic illness
Family decision making in later life

**Transition care: Moving through the care continuum**
Transitional care: Planning beyond acute care
Geriatric day care
Assisted living programs
What is new in institutional long-term care
Community-based long-term care

**Ethical and social policy issues in geriatric health care**
Maltreatment of old people
Palliative/hospice care for elderly persons
Ethical issues in end-of-life decision making
Policy issues in aging for the twenty-first century

courage and arrange preventive care and a geriatric assessment. The patients, if willing, would come to the community health center for an extensive geriatric assessment (see the Assessment and Care Planning section of this chapter) by the physician assistant. For example, a 75-year-old woman who came to the office with muscle spasms that turned out to be trivial was encouraged to have a more general assessment, to encourage prevention and functional assessment and investigate the possibility that her presenting complaint hinted some other difficulty. Her history was notable for hypertension, a stroke 13 years ago, anemia, and a hemicolectomy for a benign tumor 9 years previously. Not only were her physical exam and labs largely normal, it turned out that she had excellent functional status, and an involved and caring son to provide social support. For this patient, further evaluation was not needed, but mammography, fecal occult blood testing, continued control of hypertension, and immunizations were provided.

The second task was seeing elders with acute new or worsening problems for immediate appointments. This physician assistant role evolved over time. In the early part of the project, older patients usually called their primary care physician, who arranged for the physician assistant to see the patient promptly if their schedules were full. As the physician assistants got to know more of the patients, patients would call them directly. Because some patients found the telephone appointment system confusing, the physician assistants often made appointments directly, although they also had regular appointment slots in the center system. For example, a 78-year-old man seen by the physician assistant for routine care six months earlier, when relatively well, called the physician assistant for a sick visit. He now came to the community health center with shortness of breath, coughing, and fatigue. Evaluation in the office by the physician assistant revealed bronchi and pulmonary infiltrates, and after discussion with the physician, he was admitted to the hospital.

A third task for the physician assistants was to contact patients who were hospitalized, either in the hospital (by phone or occasional hospital visit) or shortly after discharge, to assess their status and make sure follow-up was arranged for the patients. Although most older patients of the community health center were hospitalized under the care of one of the center's physicians, it was often not the primary care physician. As such, identifying when older patients from a particular site were in the hospital was not always easy. This problem was especially acute early in the project when fewer patients knew about the physician assistants. The physician assistants advised patients to let them know if they were in the hospital, and had a phone mail system that was available 24 hours a day.

An example of post-hospital care was the case of the 78-year-old man found to have metastatic cancer. He had been getting help at home from his children, who were taking turns missing work to care for him during the brief period of his illness. Talking to the patient in the hospital, the physician assistant realized that the children would not be able to continue missing work, and learned that they would not be able to afford, nor did they desire, nursing home placement. The physician assistant worked with the patient and family to arrange a visiting nurse, a nurse's aide, meal delivery, and housekeeping support, as well as follow-up medical care. The physician assistant also arranged transportation to the cancer center for treatments, as well as providing support for the patient's children. Discussions of hospice planning also were initiated by the physician assistant.

Although it was recognized from the beginning that some home visits would be valuable, we did not include home visits as more than a possible option in the physician assistant job description because of the concern that requiring home visits in inner-city neighborhoods would make recruiting difficult. During the first few months of the project, both physician assistants became convinced of the potential value of home visits in certain cases. Safety concerns remained, however. About the same time, both physician assistants began taking students from the local physician assistant training program for 1-month clinical rotations. With the ability to travel in pairs, both physician assistants felt more comfortable beginning home visits. Once started, the value to patients and physicians and the satisfaction for the physician assistants and their students were great.

A striking example of the value of home visits occurred when a woman in her late 80s called her physician assistant in desperation when her terminally ill husband took a marked turn for the worse. Although there was no hope for cure, and both husband and his wife had desired that he stay at home to die, the reality was overwhelming for his wife. The physician assistant was able to go to the home and spend the afternoon with the couple while he died, sparing him a distressing trip to the hospital and supporting her through a most difficult experience.

In other cases, home visits revealed only partially suspected problems in function, confused compliance, or absent social support. Home visits were usually costly in terms of time and could not be billed. On the other hand, home visits were valued by patients, rewarding to the physician assistants, and cited by physicians as an advantage of the project. Nonetheless, the office base for physician assistants remained essential. Not only did the physician assistants see most of their patients there, but all of their contacts with physicians occurred there. Additionally, only office-based visits could lead to reimbursement.

The initial plan for supervision was for the assistant medical director at each site to supervise the physician assistants. The assistant medical director was one of the generalist physicians and provided primary care except for one half-day a week of "administrative time." However, the community health center revised its administrative structure just as the project began, eliminating the position of assistant medical director at each site. This occurred at the same time that two of the physicians at each of the physician assistant sites happened to depart to other jobs. As a result, supervision of the physician assistants remained with the project director, who, although he had worked as a physician at the community health center in the past, was not directly involved in health center operations. This was not an ideal arrangement, because the generalist physicians sometimes felt that the physician assistants worked for someone else, rather than for them.

In spite of the arrival of several new physicians just as the project started, and the supervision issue mentioned above, the rapport between physician assistants and physicians was generally good. Some minor tensions were recognized and resolved, and by the end of the first year all physicians working with the physician assistants gave positive opinions about the program. One physician said it was the best thing at the health center since he had been there.

## Relationship Development with Physicians

Each physician assistant worked with all the internists and family physicians at their site (three at one site and four at the other). The relationship between each physician assistant and physicians improved during the first year. The physician assistants discussed each patient visit with one of the physicians in person. There were no regular staff meetings or physician-physician assistant meetings because of organizational financial concerns that precluded meeting time apart from patient care. Thus, most contacts between physician assistants and physicians occurred in the office or hallway (each physician assistant had an office and exam room in the area also used by the physicians). From the qualitative interviews held with each physician after the first year of the project, clearly one of the most appreciated roles of the physician assistants was their ability to do detailed assessments of patients with complex psychosocial problems and to arrange support from community agencies. For example, the state program to provide additional in-home support to elders who would otherwise enter nursing homes ("Passport") typically required a very complex application process and hours on the phone for each patient, but could provide wonderful support once it was started. Since the physicians had indicated before the physician assistant training program that this sort of support was a major need, we were careful to include it in the physician assistant training. For some patients with significant illness and social needs, the physician assistants were able to provide a unique mixture of skills. But at another setting, with strong social service support, physician assistants would probably have spent more time providing other services. Although the use of flexible job descriptions without rigid roles for the physician assistants may have caused some initial difficulties, it meant that the physician assistants could adapt to provide for the particular needs of those physicians with whom they were working.

# Patients

### Patients Eligible to See Physician Assistants

Senior Health Connections was available to all patients age 70 and over who used the two community health center sites with gerontologic physician assistants. There was no enrollment or selection. The project did not limit itself to certain groups of patients because it had something to offer all elders—from preventive care for those with no health problems to detailed assessment and management for those close to nursing home placement. This meant that some eligible patients had no contact with the physician assistants, either because the patients only wanted to see their regular physician or did not visit the center.

### Patients Selected for Our Outcome Study

Our study group included all those patients over 70 years from the billing list who met three criteria: (1) they had completed telephone interviews before and after the first year of Senior Health Connections, (2) they had completed chart reviews before and after the first year of the project, and (3) they had identified the community health center as the primary source of health care. There were 292 such patients in the two control sites, and 289 in the two Senior Health Connection comparison sites. All demographic and outcome information was obtained by trained telephone interviewers and chart abstracters. Assessment tools used by the physician assistants as part of their care were not used, since they were not available for patients from control sites.

The demographic characteristics of the patients are detailed in Table 6.2. These patients tended to be aged, poor, and African-American, but as a group they had relatively good functional status and low

**TABLE 6.2**

**Senior Health Connections Demographic Characteristics of Patients (N=581)**

| | Intervention Site Group (N=289) | Control Site Group (N=292) | | Intervention Site Group (N=289) | Control Site Group (N=292) |
|---|---|---|---|---|---|
| | Years | Years | **Health status** | % | % |
| **Age** | 79 (±6) | 79 (±5) | excellent | 8 | 7 |
| | | | very good | 18 | 22 |
| | % | % | good | 33 | 32 |
| **Sex** | | | fair | 34 | 33 |
| male | 22 | 21 | poor | 7 | 6 |
| female | 78 | 79 | | | |
| | | | **ADLs performed** | | |
| **Race*** | | | fewer than 5 | 9 | 8 |
| African-American | 96 | 82 | 5 | 91 | 92 |
| white | 2 | 17 | | Mean | Mean |
| other | 2 | 1 | **Number of IADLs** | 6.2 | 6.2 |
| **Marital status** | | | | | |
| married | 20 | 16 | **Illnesses** | % | % |
| widowed | 61 | 62 | hypertension | 56 | 64 |
| divorced | 11 | 14 | diabetes | 18 | 19 |
| single | 8 | 8 | congestive heart | | |
| | | | failure (CHF) | 12 | 11 |
| **Living situation** | | | chronic lung disease | 6 | 9 |
| alone | 49 | 58 | | Score | Score |
| with spouse | 18 | 15 | **Charlson Comorbid-** | | |
| with child | 17 | 14 | **ity Index†** | 0.8±1.2 | 0.8±1.2 |
| other | 16 | 13 | | | |
| | | | **Mental Status** | | |
| | | | **Score Errors‡** | 1.3±1.1 | 1.6±1.2 |

*Differences between intervention and control sites in percent of African Americans and white patients is statistically significant. This was the result of only one site having a population with more than 3% white. Intervention and usual care sites were not significantly different in any other characteristics.

†Charlson Comorbidity Index (Charlson, Pompei, Ales, & MacKenzie, 1987) assigns 1 each for myocardial infarct, congestive heart failure, peripheral vascular disease, cerebrovascular disease, dementia, chronic pulmonary disease, ulcer disease, mild liver disease, and diabetes; 2 each for hemiplagin, moderate or severe renal disease, diabetes with end organ damage, any tumor, leukemia, and lymphoma; 3 for moderate or severe liver disease; and 6 for metastatic solid tumor.

‡Pfeiffer, 1975.

comorbidity scores. A majority reported health as "good" or "very good." Only 9% were dependent in any personal activity of daily living (washing, eating, dressing, transferring, toileting), although 27% reported some problems with urinary continence. Patient characteristics were not different between the control sites and the intervention sites, except that a higher proportion was white at the control sites. Only one site had more than a small proportion of patients who were not African-American, therefore an uneven randomization by race could not be avoided.

### Patients Actually Seen by the Physician Assistants

Each physician assistant was given the list of patients over 70 from her site, with the name, clinic number, and phone number and was directed to call those patients who had not been seen recently at the health centers. The physician assistants also saw patients not on this list—new to the health centers, or not seen during the sample period—if they visited the health centers. In addition, physician assistants occasionally saw younger patients when the smooth operation of the community health center required it—when a physician was sick or large numbers of same-day appointments were required. Although not directly serving the needs of the elder patients, this was viewed as part of the other mission of the project—to be helpful to the generalist physicians. Of the elder patients on the original list, the physician assistants had no interaction with about one-third, limited telephone interaction with about one-third, and substantial interaction with the remaining one-third.

## Assessment and Care Planning

The physician assistants had a large library of assessment tools, ranging from the traditional medical history and physical with a geriatric orientation to instruments for assessing functional status in activities of daily living (Katz, Ford, Moskowitz, Jackson & Jaffe, 1963), instrumental activities of daily living (Lawton & Brody, 1969), depression (Yesavage et al., 1983), dementia (Folstein, Folstein & McHugh, 1988), and current family and community resources. However, they did not use all instruments with all patients. Since they were seeing a range of patients and problems, physician assistants used assessment tools that were appropriate to particular patients, based on the information from their initial medical and social histories. For patients with significant difficulties, this often meant an extensive evaluation that could take several hours. Plans based on detailed assessments were normally discussed with the physician and integrated into the regular medical record, but completed assessment instruments were usually kept in separate file folders by the physician assistant. Based on interviews with the physicians, these detailed assessments were particularly valued, especially because other social service and nursing resources were very limited in the community health center.

In summary, Senior Health Connections used specific assessment tools as needed but generally worked within the structure and records of the primary care office to avoid adding new systems and tasks for the generalist physicians.

# Evaluation

## Patient Outcomes

Our primary evaluation of the effect of Senior Health Connections on patient outcomes relied on data from the telephone interviews and chart abstracts done before the project began and again after the first year. The results described here are from the 581 patients (289 in Senior Health Connections sites and 292 in control sites) for whom all four data sources were completed, and who also reported during their first interviews that they usually got their care at the community health center. Patients reported satisfaction to be high before the project started and no significant changes were observed during the grant period.

In brief, there was no significant change in the proportion of patients at either Senior Health Connections or control sites who received preventive procedures such as mammograms, flu shots, or fecal occult blood tests. There was a general increase in the number of patients reporting prevention counseling and risk assessment at all sites, and this increase was significantly greater for some types of counseling at the Senior Health Connections sites. There was no reported change in perceived access to care at any sites except for a statistically insignificant increase in telephone access at the Senior Health Connections sites. For both preventive care and access, baseline rates were quite high, a situation that may have made improvements difficult to achieve.

Intervention patients made an average of 5.4 office visits to control sites the year prior to the project compared with 4.4 office visits to Senior

Health Connections sites. During the first year of Senior Health Connections, the average number of office visits went up 0.1 at the control sites, but increased 0.7 at the Senior Health Connections sites (p=0.02). The number of emergency room visits was slightly but not significantly lower among patients of the Senior Health Connections sites (116) compared with those of the control sites (139) during the first project year.

In the year prior to Senior Health Connections, 16% of those patients at the control sites and 15% of patients at Senior Health Connections sites were hospitalized. During the intervention year, 20% of control patients were hospitalized compared to 17% of intervention patients.

## Physician Outcomes

Physician satisfaction with Senior Health Connections, based on qualitative interviews with involved physicians, was high. Although some physicians found the roles and supervision of the physician assistants poorly defined at first, they all appreciated the help that physician assistants were able to provide in caring for frail elderly persons. The physicians valued the physician assistants' professionalism, interpersonal skills, time spent with patients, problem solving abilities, and service coordination. Further, physicians felt that their clinical assessments were reliable.

## Institutional Outcomes

During and as a result of Senior Health Connections, a significant bond developed between NEON (the community health center) and the local physician assistant training program at a nearby community college, so that each month two physician assistant students did a clinical rotation with the project's physician assistants. Although this was officially their medicine rotation, it gave them much geriatric experience, so the number of physician assistants being trained with geriatric experience increased markedly. In addition, it increased the number of physician assistants who felt comfortable working in the community health center environment, and who might work there in the future.

NEON valued Senior Health Connections enough to continue it after the original grant ended. One of the physician assistants left to work at the local physician assistant training program full time, but the other agreed to work at both sites. NEON was able to obtain a grant from the Cleveland Foundation to help support the transition period. Experience with the program was also useful as NEON decided to enter the Medicare capitation market in a relationship with a local insurance company. A little less than two years later, however, a financial crisis forced NEON to close one site completely and lay off all mid-level providers, including the remaining Senior Health Connections physicians assistant.

# Lessons Learned

Physician assistants with geriatric training were able to fit into the ongoing operations of a busy community health center, and to provide care that satisfied patients and physicians. Any novel project will, however, provide learning opportunities, and we learned lessons in a number of domains that we believe might be of value to anyone working on a similar project.

## Fiscal Issues

While supported by the grant, the physician assistants did not have enough patient visits to support their full salaries in a fee-for-service setting. This probably reflects the complex needs in this population, as well as start-up inefficiencies. The ability of physician assistants to bill under Medicare is an important issue that is also related to state laws under which physician assistants are allowed to practice with physician supervision. We were careful to hire certified physician assistants, which is crucial under Ohio law, although it turned out that the Medicare reimbursement to NEON was done under a special formula that makes financial analysis of this project very difficult. As NEON became more involved in a capitated system, the ability of the physician assistants to reduce re-hospitalizations would have helped make the Senior Health Connections self-supporting. Unfortunately, other significant financial issues affecting the ability of the urban community health centers to provide care to impoverished inner-city citizens also have affected the long-term viability of Senior Health Connections.

## Duration of Assessment

We assessed the effects of Senior Health Connections after the first year of the intervention. We now believe that the benefits of the project might have been more clear if we had made the assessment after two years. Comments, both by physicians and by patients during the second telephone interview, suggested that acceptance of the physician assistants and their ability to improve care were still increasing as the project entered its second year.

## Physician Assistant Training

We were thankful that we had scheduled six months to prepare our training for the physician assistants. Although a standard geriatric curriculum might have been easier to organize, we believe our attention to learning the particular needs of the physicians in the health centers (e.g., the emphasis on social service coordination) and to facilitating the sharing of pre-existing knowledge and skills of the physician assistants we hired (e.g., familiarity with the specific cultural needs of the target population in one, and knowledge of routine hospital operations and discharge procedures in the other), enabled our training to be more efficient and more powerful. We also believe our assignment of the physician assistants to their future sites one day a week during the training period was especially valuable.

## Roles and Relationships

The flexibility and lack of strict structure in the physician assistant roles were both problematic and valuable. Initially, there was some confusion because physicians were not quite sure what the physician assistants would be doing. But as a result, physician assistants could be responsive to the needs of the specific physicians and patients with whom they worked. The teaching relationship with physician assistant students, mentioned earlier in this chapter, was the sort of unplanned but very creative and valuable addition (envisioned and developed by one of the physician assistants with approval of NEON leadership) made possible by the flexible role. It not only made possible the home visits, but helped the physician assistants contact more patients, exposed a significant cohort of physician assistant students to an excellent geriatric experience and a satisfying community-based practice, and enhanced the wider reputation of the community health center.

The relationship between the project and research leadership, based at Case Western Reserve University School of Medicine and University Hospitals of Cleveland, and the community organization where the physician assistants practiced, Northeast Ohio Neighborhood Health Services, worked well but required attention, especially when leadership changes occurred. Sensitivity to and respect for the differing organizational goals and styles on both sides was especially helpful. Skillful input from foundation program officers was also notably valuable in this arena.

## Summary

Senior Health Connections trained physician assistants for three and one-half months, and then successfully integrated them into generalist physician practices at two sites of an urban community health care center. Although unable in one year to improve on already high use of preventive procedures, physician assistants did raise the rate of preventive counseling, and maintained high access and patient satisfaction. The program was associated with a reduction in re-hospitalizations. In spite of the financial stresses of providing care for an impoverished population during a period of reduced federal and state support, the community health center continued the program for almost two years in spite of the loss of one of the physician assistants. As a practical method to aid generalist physicians in their care of elders, the Senior Health Connections model should be evaluated in additional settings.

## References

Bottom, W.D. (1988). Geriatric medicine in the United States: New roles for physician assistant. *Journal of Community Health, 13*, 95–103.

Cawley, J.F., Ott, J.E. & DeAtley, C.A. (1983). The future for physician assistants. *Annals of Internal Medicine, 98*, 993–997.

Charlson, M.E., Pompei, P., Ales, K.L. & MacKenzie, C.R. (1987). A new method of classifying prognostic comorbidity in longitudinal studies: Development and validation. *Journal of Chronic Disease, 40*, 373–383.

Folstein, M.F., Folstein, S.E. & McHugh, P.R. (1975). "Mini-mental state": A practical method for grading the cognitive state of patients for the clinician. *Journal of Psychiatric Research, 12*, 189–198.

Katz, S., Ford, A.B., Moskowitz, R.W., Jackson, B.A. & Jaffe, M.W. (1963). The Index of ADL: A standardized measure of biological and psychosocial function. *Journal of the American Medical Association, 185*, 914–919.

Knowles, M. (1990). *The adult learner: A neglected species.* Houston: Gulf Publishing.

Lawton, M.P. & Brody, E.M. (1969). Assessment of older people: Self-maintaining and instrumental activities of daily living. *The Gerontologist, 9*, 179–186.

Pfeiffer, E. (1975). A short portable mental status questionnaire for the assessment of organic brain deficit in elderly patients. *Journal of the American Geriatrics Society, 23*, 433–441.

Romeis, J.C., Schey, H.M., Marion, G.S. & Keith, J.F. (1985). Extending the extenders: Compromise for the geriatric specialization–manpower debate. *Journal of the American Geriatrics Society*, *33*, 559–565.

Yesavage J.A., Brink, T.L., Rose T.L., Lum, O., Huang, V., Adey, M. & Leirer, V.O. (1983). Development and validation of a geriatric depression screening scale: A preliminary report. *Journal of Psychiatric Research*, *17*, 37–49.

# CHAPTER 7

# Primary Care Physician, Nurse, and Social Work Collaboration in the Care of Community-Dwelling, Chronically Ill Elders

*Lucia Sommers and Janeane Randolph*

Inspired by McWhinney (1972), Kleinman (1978), Engel (1977) and others, about two decades ago leaders in primary care medicine began advocating for a biopsychosocial approach to care. More recently, a "relationship-centered" model of health and disease has emerged, in which patients' psychosocial, functional, and biomedical conditions have been integrated into a care model consonant with patient and family values and preferences (Pew-Fetzer Task Force, 1994). This revitalized model of care has potential to restore the long-held belief that physicians' healing role resides in the doctor-patient relationship and in the fiduciary bond that physicians, as a result of managed care, are called upon to vigorously reaffirm (Kaplan, Greenfeld & Ware, 1989; Emanuel & Dubler, 1995).

We believe that the doctor-patient relationship, offers a practical and effective vehicle for introducing and evaluating new ways to provide community-based health care and social supports to community-dwelling pre-frail and frail elders. To this end, the California Pacific Medical Center developed the Senior Care Connection (SCC).

In the SCC the older patient's primary care physician (PCP) collaborated with a registered nurse (RN) and clinical social worker (SW) to provide primary care, augmented by a set of new services specifically geared to persons with chronic illness and functional deficits. These services, not routinely provided in primary care, included assessing the patient's health status, functioning, and quality of life in the home and community settings; coaching the patient in strategies for successful living with chronic disease using self-management principles; monitoring the patient for specified clinical parameters between office visits; and linking the patient to available and appropriate community-based health and social supports.

In this chapter we describe the implementation of SCC and the premises underlying this intervention. We focus heavily upon the establishment of relationships among the members of the collaborative team and the implications of that collaboration.

# Project Design and Implementation

Conceived as an 18-month intervention in three counties in the San Francisco Bay Area, SCC had two objectives: (1) to demonstrate the feasibility of private practice PCPs working with RNs and SWs in providing "enriched" primary care, and (2) to reduce elders' use of acute/chronic medical services, and community and homecare services, while improving their ability to live in their communities at higher levels of physical and psychosocial functioning. Both these objectives were achieved and the specific findings are described elsewhere (Sommers, Marton, Barbaccia & Randolph, 1997).

Participating physicians were affiliated with three respective hospitals that were part of a multi-institutional health care system founded in 1986. Although each hospital had formally organized senior services programs (e.g., adult day care centers, senior education programs, nutrition and transportation programs, referral networks), private physicians had little formal interface with these efforts. In 1991, discharges of elders comprised approximately 25% of hospital discharges. At the largest hospital in County 1, approximately 25% of Medicare seniors were enrolled in managed care plans; in County 2 the percentage was below 10%; County 3's was approximately 15%. These numbers at least doubled between 1991 and 1997.

## Physician and Patient Selection

We approached 10 physicians per county, 30 total, to participate in the project. Medical leadership at each of the three hospitals had selected them as prospects because they were respected, open-minded, busy clinicians. Six physicians per county, or 18 total, agreed to participate—5 family physicians and 13 internists. Those who refused cited lack of time or insufficient numbers of older patients. Participating primary care physicians (PCPs) were randomized to an intervention and control group in each county, with practice arrangements varying from solo practice to six partner groups. On average, PCPs saw 13.5 patients per day, 4.5 of whom were 65 or older.

Prior to PCP randomization, with the assistance of the project director, each PCP used specified criteria to identify at least 32 patients out of a population of 50 to 100 English-speaking seniors seen in their office during the past two months. These patients received a pre-tested patient questionnaire, a 20-page, large-print instrument designed for the project with a cover letter from each patient's PCP. In addition to being asked about demographics, patients were asked about physical symptoms, chronic conditions, social activities, health interference in daily life, medications, physical functioning, emotional functioning, nutritional habits, health-related behaviors (e.g., exercise, smoking), use of medical and community services (e.g., home-delivered meals), self-efficacy for managing four domains of health (symptom control, depression, support from family/friends, and doctor-patient communication), proactive behavior during doctor visits (e.g., expressing concerns), self-rated health status, and life satisfaction. Several well known, validated scales were used to obtain this information.

Approximately 85% of patients at sites later assigned to the intervention category returned questionnaires. After assignment of sites to categories, and during the project's enrollment period, as these patients came to their PCPs' offices for regularly-scheduled appointments, PCPs re-assessed them, again using the original project criteria, and offered participation to those still appropriate. The intervention group was composed of 280 patients, roughly 90 per county.

Approximately 80% of patients at sites assigned control status returned completed questionnaires. Throughout the intervention period, the 263 control patients continued to receive care as usual from their PCP alone, with no additional services coming from the project.

Claims data for 1992, 1993, and 1994 were secured from payers for approximately 80% of the total patient sample. Prior to the SCC project, the patients in the control and intervention groups did not differ in use of services (e.g., hospitalization rate, mean number of office visits), but did differ across the following demographic variables: intervention patients were a year older compared to control patients, more likely to be unmarried and live alone (45% vs. 58%), and 20% more likely to use community services. The two groups did not differ on measures of self-rated health status, functioning, or self-efficacy.

# Roles and Relationships

Patients, social workers, nurses, PCPs, and their office staff were all part of SCC implementation. Each role is briefly described before focusing on relationship development among these diverse players.

## Patients

To the degree that patients were receptive to the RNs' or SWs' telephone calls or home visits, open with them about their physical, emotional, and social status, and willing to discuss their concerns, they were fulfilling their expected role. At least once a month, the patient heard from the RN or SW by phone, during which time they discussed how the patient felt compared to the last contact, the patient's current concerns (medical and non-medical), how he or she was coping on a day-to-day basis (e.g., shopping, paying bills), how the RN or SW could assist him or her to cope better, and use of medical or community-based services since the last contact, as well as level of satisfaction with those services. RN or SW advice and/or education on specific issues was given freely.

## The Nurse and the Social Worker

Our project was designed to, first, acknowledge that the traditional roles of nurse and social worker had major contributions to make to the project, and, second, to avoid confusing the patients with new names for health workers with whom they had no experience. Specifically, the term "case management" was not used since the project clinicians shared the belief that they were not managing cases but helping individual patients learn better how to manage their own health. The decision regarding who would take the lead for a particular patient, the RN or the SW, was made by the PCP/RN/SW team in the course of developing the patient's risk reduction plan. That professional would be responsible for regular contacts, initiating patient discussion at staff meetings, and calling in the other clinicians when new patient developments warranted it. On an average day, the nurse and social worker typically spent their time making telephone contacts (four to eight at approximately 10 minutes each), receiving phone calls from project patients reporting new symptoms or giving status reports (two to four a day, 5 to 10 minutes each) or receiving calls about specific patients from the PCP or office staff (one to three a day, 3 to 5 minutes each). In addition, they went on one or two home visits (each taking 40 to 80 minutes including transportation time), stopped by the PCPs' offices for meetings or ad hoc conversations with a PCP or office staff member (10 to 15 minutes), saw a patient in the office with the PCP or visited a patient in the hospital (30 to 40 minutes), contacted several family members or community-based agencies (20 to 40 minutes) and worked on special projects (e.g. reviewing office records looking for advance directive forms, 20 to 30 minutes). Finally, they would enter patient-specific data based on each contact into their computers and update care plans and logs (25 to 40 minutes), and confer with each other regarding specific patients (15 to 40 minutes).

## The Primary Care Physician

The PCPs approved the format and content of the patient questionnaire, helped develop the patient selection criteria, and with the RNs and SWs, defined their collaboration format. The latter included time and place of meeting, process for reviewing patients, and ways to communicate on an ad hoc basis regarding individual patients.

On an average day, a PCP most typically received at least one phone call, fax, or note from the RN or SW informing him or her of a new patient problem (e.g., onset of shortness of breath for a congestive heart failure patient; a panic attack in a recent widower) learned either from making routine follow-up calls or hearing from the patient directly. The PCP would usually decide one of three things: (1) to call the patient directly, (2) to ask the RN or SW to set up an appointment for the patient to come to the office the next day or even that same day if the schedule allowed, or (3) to institute therapy (e.g., new medication) or reassurance via the RN or SW, asking him or her to follow up and report back. In addition, during the average week, the PCP had an office visit with at least one project patient for whom information was on hand by fax, note, or phone call from the RN or SW, with the intention of updating him or her on patient status.

PCPs were assured that they would be involved only minimally in data collection so that project participation would not be a drain on their time. If anything, the intervention was intended to save PCP time through the nurses' and social workers' doing more patient education and reassurance. The PCP data generation role was confined to bimonthly phone interviews with the project director, 1- to 3-page questionnaires to complete two to three times a year, and an annual 1-hour interview with the project director. In the latter, the project director queried PCPs about the health status of each of their patients in the project (using a variety of scales) and asked for their feedback on project implementation and ways to improve it. Many of their comments focused on the difficulties of keeping in regular communication with the RNs or SWs and changes they had tried that succeeded or failed. One PCP, for example, discussed concerns he had about the skills of the RN in a particular physical exam area and whether he had provided helpful instruction.

## PCP Office Staff

On an average day, each PCP's office staff most typically received one or two calls from the RN or SW inquiring about the availability of the PCP for a question or update about a patient, leaving a message regarding a change in a patient's status, or checking to see if a patient came in for an appointment or was scheduled. Just as typically, the RN or SW could come into the office to review patients' charts, pull charts as part of an audit, or pick up returned questionnaires (since they were all mailed from and returned to the PCPs' offices). At these times the RN or SW would have brief, informal chats with office staff about several project patients.

## Relationship Development

Although other interventions have attempted and, in some instances, successfully reduced elders' use of health care resources through providing new combinations of services, the SCC was meant to build upon and enrich what had already been in place—a relationship with a primary care physician. This was done in three specific ways. First, the project was conceived and developed with the involvement of the PCPs in project design and pilot testing. During the 6-month start-up period, the project director spent time in five PCPs' offices observing (1) PCPs and patients in the exam room, (2) office staff with patients at the front desk, (3) office staff with the PCP, (4) work flow, (5) patient flow, and (6) patient waiting room behavior.

Project design explicitly called for few formal protocols spelling out how PCPs were to work with RNs and SWs. Each PCP/RN/SW team was encouraged to develop its own unique collaborative style. The only requirements defined by project design included (1) meeting at least monthly as a group, (2) completion of a care plan for each patient to include at least one reassessment and a final summary of project benefit, and (3) permitting the project director to sit in on one monthly meeting during the last six months of the project.

The centrality of the PCP-patient relationship was continuously reinforced. Efforts to do this included the project director's ongoing references to judging each aspect of the SCC in terms of the degree to which it could serve to enhance the PCP-patient relationship. The foundational effort was the PCP's introduction of his or her patients to the RN and SW, explaining the potential value for the patients, and encouraging them to participate. During the two-month RN and SW training program and office practice immersion, emphasis was placed on specific ways RNs and SWs could enhance the PCP-patient relationship. This included encouraging the patients to talk directly to their physicians about their health worries. The RN and SW were expected to provide the PCPs with information needed to make best use of the office visit time. During orientation, special role-plays were staged to prepare the RNs and SWs as coaches for helping patients articulate their concerns and fears to their PCPs in ways to which physicians could act in direct response.

The project was firmly planted within the physicians' offices as evidenced by the PCPs' (1) encouraging patients to see the RN and SW as "attached" to the office and not to a hospital or homecare agency (if the RN and SW saw patients outside their homes, it was in the PCPs' offices), (2) putting experienced RNs and SWs in positions to relate directly to PCPs while supporting their professional development through across-county in-services and multi-disciplinary educational sessions, and (3) at each PCP's office, placing a veteran office staff person as special liaison between the RN and SW and the rest of the office staff to facilitate the SCC work (e.g. gathering of patients' returned questionnaires, pulling medical records, facilitating appointment-making and referrals). From case analyses we learned how PCPs, RNs, and SWs responded rapidly to worrisome symptoms (e.g. chest heaviness) while tracking more vague ones over time (e.g. decreased cognition). Whereas Medicare homecare programs preclude such responses because of time-limited services, strict eligibility, and lack of close liaison with physicians' offices (Weiner & Illston, 1994), flexibility in SCC implementation allowed each PCP/RN/SW group to meet patient needs as they saw them.

## The SCC Intervention

All the older persons in our project continued to receive care from their PCPs. During project enrollment, their PCPs personally introduced the RNs and SWs to patients as their new care associates. Three intervention PCPs in one county shared one full-time RN and one half-time SW—each RN/SW duo worked with approximately 90 patients, 30 per

PCP. During the enrollment period, the PCP, RN, and SW collaborated to carry out comprehensive patient assessments and develop individualized care plans. Initially, each patient was visited at home at least once by an RN or SW to complete a set of automated assessment tools made available by specially-designed software loaded onto each RN's and SW's laptop computer. RNs visited all patients, completing those screens designed for taking a health history, a nursing review of systems (including vital signs), a functional assessment (Lorig et al., 1996), a nutritional assessment (Lee & Novielli, 1996), and the Geriatric Depression Scale (Sheikh & Yesavage, 1986). The SWs visited at least two-thirds of the patients and completed psychosocial, home support, and home safety assessments. RNs completed these screens for patients not seen by SWs.

Next, the PCP/RN/SW team met to review data from four sources: the home visits, the patient's baseline questionnaire, the nurse's review of the office record going back two years, and the physician's own perspective on the patient's health status and functioning. To help them reach consensus on a care plan for the patient, looking ahead to the next 12 to 18 months, they each ranked the patient on frailty and health risk scales. The scale that proved most useful to them was the frailty scale. It was developed to reference the burden of chronic illness experienced by the patient as he/she coped with the pain and disability of various conditions. The intention was for the PCP, RN, and SW to present how each saw the patient on this dimension; the goal was not necessarily consensus on a single frailty score, but rather discussion as a springboard for deciding upon (1) an action plan to reduce risk of hospitalization, (2) endpoints they could use to determine if risks had been reduced, and (3) a time frame for reassessment.

Care plans were completed for each intervention patient; most reassessments were scheduled for six months except for higher-risk patients, who were discussed at least monthly. The intent was for the PCPs to present the care plan to the patients as part of their overall therapeutic regimens. With the full participation of the patients, the RN and SW had the following seven options for follow-up: (1) seeing patients in the PCP's office with the PCP, (2) seeing patients before and/or after the actual PCP visit, (3) seeing patients in their homes, (4) calling patients on the phone, (5) seeing hospitalized patients in the hospital, (6) accompanying patients on non-PCP physician visits, or (7) accompanying patients on errands, or to physical therapy, and so on. Any of these occasions were called "contacts," and through contacts, the "SCC work" was done.

## Functions Performed by RNs and SWs

SCC RNs and SWs performed three interrelated functions: (1) clinical monitoring between office visits, (2) chronic disease self-management teaching, and (3) linkages to community-based agencies. We will briefly explain each function.

Clinical monitoring between office visits meant staying in touch with the patients so that proactive measures could prevent acute exacerbations of chronic conditions as well as decline in functioning. The three registered nurses were selected for clinical skills in assessing and caring for elderly persons with chronic illness (in homecare, public health center, and hospice settings). Through a pre-project, 2-month training period in the physicians' offices, they observed the practice styles of their PCPs, often going into exam rooms with them to compare findings on vital signs and other key markers of problems. Trust in clinical judgment was critical so that nurses could report findings to the PCPs via telephone from the patients' homes. The social workers' role in clinical monitoring chiefly centered on carrying out ongoing assessment of psychosocial status, soliciting patient concerns and preferences, facilitating adherence to treatment, and providing short-term therapy as necessary regarding patients' emotional problems. Experienced as therapists, they looked for signs of acute depressive episodes as well as prolonged feelings of despair and anxiety, and, in consultation with the PCP, referred emergencies, provided short-term therapy while awaiting referral, or provided therapy directly for defined periods.

The RN and SW in each county met monthly with each of their PCPs to develop care plans, monitor individual patient progress, and problem solve about patient issues. Following the individualized care plan, a regular monitoring schedule for each patient was set up based on the timing of the office visits (e.g., "Call Mrs. Baker two days after the office visit to see if she is taking her hypertension medications"), or on a routine basis not tied to office visits (e.g., "Stop by to see Mr. Stein at least once every three weeks to check on his medical adherence"). The RNs and SWs moved freely between physicians' offices, patients' homes, and the three hospitals where patients were hospitalized. Since none of the PCPs' offices had space for desks for them, arrangements were made for office space based on the RNs' and SWs' preferences. In County 1, the RN and SW preferred to work out of their homes, since they lived close to their PCPs' offices. In the other two counties, since the physician offices were located close to the hospitals, the RNs and SWs had desks in available space in the hospitals, although they, too, worked out of their homes. In

none of the three counties were the RNs and SWs organizationally affiliated with the discharge planning or homecare programs of the hospitals,
although these departments provided in-services and liaison contacts for
them. However, two of the three nurses had previously worked in these
departments.

Chronic disease self-management teaching involved using techniques
of enhancing self-efficacy, reframing, symptom reinterpretation, and
skills mastery using contracting and goal-setting, among others. The intent was to work one-on-one with the patient to jointly fashion activities
for increasing coping capacities (Lorig, Laurent & Gonzalez, 1994). For
example, in County 3 the RN and SW conducted two 6-week chronic disease self-management teaching groups (each with 12 patients) during the
SCC. In County 2 a women's support group composed of 9 patients from
three PCPs met weekly for over a year.

Establishing linkages to community-based agencies as needed to
maintain the patient in the community became a matter of course (as defined by the patient's care plan), and part of the skill set of the RNs and
SWs, all of whom prior to the project had worked in their respective
counties for at least two years. If patients were hospitalized, the RNs and
SWs worked with discharge planners and helped coordinate specialized
nursing care from homecare agencies (e.g., diabetic teaching, wound
care), ancillary services (e.g., physical therapy) and home supports (e.g.,
home-delivered meals). The RNs and SWs provided a direct link for the
homecare nurse to the PCP. The RNs and SWs augmented the traditional
linkage function with compulsive follow-up to assure appropriate service
provision, and patient coaching to become competent and assertive ne-
gotiators with community agencies.

# Evaluation and Lessons Learned

## Clinicians' Perspectives

PCPs reported impatience with the slow pace of the enrollment process
and acknowledged that PCP/RN/SW communication was time-consuming. Past the 6-month point, one PCP told the project director on more
than one occasion that she was "giving" (in time) more than she was "getting." Since it was not possible to provide her with up-to-the-moment
hospitalization and office visit rates, she did not know that she had
sharply reduced her average number of office visits, and had lowered her

patients' hospitalization rate over the course of the SCC. Another PCP was frank in his concern that the SCC was disruptive to the way he had practiced and that he had not expected to modify his practice style. On two different occasions he considered resigning because he felt he was not fulfilling project expectations. He was encouraged to continue in the interests of discovering whether he could, with the RN and SW, develop a collaborative style that fit for all of them. At the end, he commented that he was now ready for the intervention to begin since he understood what was involved in making the project work. The remaining seven PCPs believed that even if the SCC did not achieve reduced service use within 18 months, they had observed enough increased patient satisfaction to make it "worth it" for them.

Initially, the PCPs most appreciated the RNs' and SWs' role in responding to patient phone calls and helping to counter elders' social isolation. For five of the PCPs, the RNs and SWs appeared to be valued for reducing PCP isolation by providing opportunities for the three professionals to sit down together to discuss interesting patients and clinical dilemmas. Despite this overall enthusiasm, no PCP was willing to pay the nurse and/or social worker, out-of-pocket, to continue working with patients when the project had ended. PCPs in both County 1 and 2 encouraged their Independent Practice Associations (IPAs) and Preferred Provider Organizations (PPOs) to sponsor efforts to continue all or part of the project. Shortly after the SCC ended, the six PCPs in County 1 (intervention and control) began to participate in an identification and early intervention program for their high-risk elders. Although the program was considered to be based on the SCC, this was not the case since they hired only social workers and no nurses.

The three intervention physicians in County 2, the RN, SW, and project director met with their IPA's administrator and the head of the local homecare agency to lobby for program continuation through the IPA's making capitated arrangements with the homecare agency. Although this did not occur, the homecare agency committed to a pilot effort in which a specified nurse would be assigned to a group practice of five to eight PCPs; unfortunately they could not free up a social worker to participate also. The nurse assignment did go forward, and the County 2 RN, on loan from the homecare agency from the onset, continued to work with many of the patients of her three PCPs. At project end, with the exception of one RN, the other RNs and SWs continued to work with chronically ill elders either in replication efforts or in more traditional homecare or adult day health programs.

At the end of the project, *all* nine intervention PCPs wanted the SCC to continue. Many believed that 18 months was not sufficient time to test the intervention and believed that only during the last 6 months were the patient, PCP, RN, and SW functioning as a group. Data from both PCPs' mailed surveys and quarterly personal interviews regarding PCP satisfaction with the intervention during its course indicated that with the exception of two PCPs, the others coped well with the SCC's daily course.

Despite RNs and SWs overall positive feelings, they reported frequent feelings of being treated stereotypically. RNs were seen either as "handmaidens" or "Iron Ladies," whereas SWs were viewed as "bleeding hearts" or "process persons" who were prone to ask, "How do you feel about that?" Concomitantly, the project director observed that the RNs and SWs frequently stereotyped the physicians, expecting them to be godlike (and when they acted less nobly, being disappointed), or treating them as necessary evils who were needed for the medical part of elders' care but were psychosocially unaware.

## Patient Attrition and Satisfaction with the SCC

Patient attrition over the course of the 18-month intervention was similar across groups: 5% of patients switched to out-of-project PCPs; 1.5% moved out of the area; 1.7% moved to nursing homes; and 0.8% dropped out. Twice during the SCC, a 2-page patient satisfaction questionnaire was mailed to intervention patients inquiring about the intervention's usefulness along several dimensions, and asking about patients' abilities to manage their health. Eighty-one percent of the patients returned the first questionnaire and 88% returned the second. Overall, the mean usefulness score was 2 on a scale from 1 (extremely useful) to 5 (not at all useful) on both questionnaires. Of the 91% of the patients who wrote comments on the questionnaires, over 90% were positive and were categorized as follows: 35% made comments regarding general approval of the project; another 25% specifically noted how the SCC provided them with the security of knowing someone was available if they needed them; 21% mentioned the value of having someone to talk to who was interested in them; and 19% mentioned help they received with a specific problem (e.g., death of a spouse). Overall, we noted that patients did not need specific community-based, non-homecare services (e.g., home-delivered meals) as much as they needed someone who knew them (in regard to health status), to call and check in.

## Implementation Outcomes

All 280 intervention patients had at least one face-to-face contact with the RN or SW; all but one patient received an initial home assessment. Over 18 months, patients averaged 34 RN or SW contacts (range, 1 to 176).

Percentages of contacts included 69% by phone, 17% in the home, 4% in the office, 4% by mail, 3% in the hospital, and 3% in small groups. The three major reasons for contacts were clinical monitoring (65%), referral for community-based services (10%), and teaching (8%). In 26% of the contacts, the RN or SW assessed the patient as depressed; in 10% they judged that the patient's health was having a negative effect on functioning; in 6%, they believed that the patient was at significant risk for exacerbation of a chronic condition. In 12%, the RN or SW noted the need to contact the PCP within 72 hours, and in 5%, they noted the need to call a community-based agency.

On average, each PCP, RN, and SW formally met 24 times (range, 16 to 35). A common meeting time was at noon for lunch in the office or for a light supper after the last patient in the afternoon. One group met regularly at a cafe near the PCP's office. A typical meeting involved discussing patients with recent problems, reviewing the status of higher-risk patients and updating their care plans, briefly touching on patients seen by the PCP in his or her office over the last few weeks, and discussing the status of special projects or initiatives (e.g., efforts to interest patients in chronic disease self-management groups or setting up an exercise class).

The nurses and social workers met weekly with the project director for debriefing and data collection; the project director was in telephone contact with the PCPs bi-monthly in addition to a mid-intervention retreat for all participating clinicians. In the last month of the 18-month intervention, all participants attended a dinner meeting to share and review their participation in the project and discuss continuation efforts.

## County-Specific Perspectives

County 1 stands out from the other two counties for several reasons. First, from 1993 to 1994, compared to control counties, it had the largest decrease in hospitalization rates for all patients, but particularly for those with better baseline health status. Additionally, County 1 patients reported a significant increase in their social activities as well as greater self-efficacy for symptom control. Last, more County 1 patients returned the second patient questionnaire on SCC usefulness than did patients in the other two counties and showed a 13% increase in rating of usefulness.

What happened in County 1 that could account for these outcomes? Compared to other counties, the County 1 RN and SW had five times more patient contacts that took place *in the office* and three times more contacts that took place in the hospital. Additionally, the County 1 SW was the only one of the three SWs who did initial home visits on all 90 patients. County 1 patients experienced the shortest time interval between RN/SW contacts and twice as many in which the RN or SW provided advice about community services. The County 1 PCPs were part of smaller practices compared to physicians in the other two counties; one PCP was a solo practitioner. The RN and SW repeatedly praised the commitment and positive attitudes of the office staffs in the County 1 offices. Because they had smaller office staffs than their counterparts in Counties 2 and 3, there were more opportunities for consistent RN/SW interaction on a daily basis, which helped office personnel understand project objectives, particularly the importance of their pivotal role in facilitating communication among the RN, SW, and PCP. The County 1 RN and SW both felt that, although each of their PCPs had his or her own special quirks, none of them was considered challenging, difficult, or unpredictable. (In Counties 2 and 3, however, three PCPs were described with these labels at various points during the project, for doing such things as canceling monthly meetings at the last minute, not informing them about hospitalizing patients, and forgetting to update them about medication changes or the diagnosis of new conditions.)

The County 1 patients at baseline were more "sick" than patients in other counties, although baseline health status data confirming this were not available to PCPs, RNs, and SWs during the intervention. As each PCP, RN, and SW rated patients' frailty and health risks, and compared notes during across-county educational meetings, the County 1 PCPs, RNs, and SWs began to realize that they were seeing more frail and socially isolated patients than those in the other two counties. Compared to the RNs and SWs in the other two counties, the County 1 RN and SW were more likely to give patients their home phone numbers, arrange outings with patients who were more socially isolated (e.g., having lunch, going on walks), and were willing to call patients at night and over the weekend. This style of interacting could have built closer relationships, subsequently allowing the PCP, RN, and SW more latitude for influencing patient behavior.

Based on the PCP/RN/SW's frailty ratings, the County 2 patients were seen as less frail than patients in Counties 1 and 3. Their self-efficacy scores at baseline were slightly higher than other counties' patients and they reported more involvement in health-related activities (e.g., attending exercise classes). Despite the fact that County 2's baseline depression score showed less depressive symptoms than those of patients in the other counties, the County 2 SW was successful in facilitating a weekly support group.

Although all three County 2 PCPs took very naturally to collaborative work, only one of the PCPs showed a drop in hospitalization rate. What prevented more change from happening? Initially, the County 2 group began enrolling and seeing patients earlier than the other two counties. At the very beginning, the RN and SW felt very comfortable with all three PCPs. However, during the last six months, energies seemed to flag, perhaps because a number of patients with complicated health problems monopolized the team's attention. Although the majority of their patients were not as frail and/or depressed as those in the other counties, during the last few months of the intervention, a terminally ill patient and his family and an emotionally unstable patient needing inpatient psychiatric care required an inordinate amount of RN/SW time. Maintaining momentum, in retrospect, became a problem.

Even though County 3 patients were on average three years younger than County 1 patients, in the early months of the SCC, the clinicians ranked them closer to County 1 than County 2 regarding frailty. Problems in emotional functioning appeared to be more prevalent than physical functioning ones. Unlike staff in the two other counties, the County 3 RN and SW made twice as many contacts with patients with worse baseline health compared to those with better baseline status. This differential rate of contacts appears to have worked to significantly decrease County 3's intervention patients' average number of office visits, particularly for patients with worse baseline health status. This difference, however, did not affect reductions in hospitalization rate. In County 1, where there was little difference between number of RN/SW contacts for worse versus better baseline health status, hospitalization rates fell markedly but not office visits. Why this difference in effect? It may lie in the kind of relationships the RNs and SWs in the two different counties had with their PCPs. For two of the three PCPs in County 3, the RN and SW were less reliably able to reach them with patient concerns and lacked confidence that these PCPs kept them current regarding key developments for their patients. Without close coordination on patient status and ability to communicate quickly and without barriers, prevention of hospitalization cannot occur.

Office visit experiences appeared to be different, however. We observed that patients could control how often they saw the doctor based on their abilities to manage their symptoms and get the most out of the visits they did have. County 3 patients, after the intervention's end, reported higher self-efficacy not only for managing doctor-patient relationships and actually behaving more proactively during office visits, but also for controlling symptoms and asking for support from family and friends compared to County 3 controls. It appears that despite the relatively loose connection the RN and SW had with two of the three County 3 physicians, it was sufficient to allow them to make their case to the patients: "We are available to you, we understand your issues, and we have information you might need." This message appears to have come through most consistently for those patients with worse baseline status since they were the recipients of more RN or SW contacts, and were the sub-group to reduce their office visits the most.

# Implications

The findings of our project suggest directions that clinicians in practice, health professional educators, and health policy makers should consider when improving the delivery of primary care to community-dwelling elders with chronic illness and functional deficits.

## Implications for Future SCC-Based Projects

The SCC ensured access to services using a variety of service provision mechanisms but grounded the effort in the existing doctor-patient relationship in the hope of building a new one—the patient/PCP/RN/SW relationship. The original relationship—that of the doctor and the patient—became the fulcrum on which the patient/PCP/RN/SW and subsidiary ones balanced (i.e., RN/SW, RN/patient, SW/patient, PCP/RN, PCP/SW). Clinicians spoke about the timeline for relationship development. The first six months focused on enrolling patients; the next six months, in getting to know one another. Only in the last six months were some relationships strong enough to sustain meaningful collaboration in decision making. Time was needed for these relationships to develop and for each party to win the trust of the other, and each relationship affected the others. For example, an already positive doctor-patient relationship more easily allowed for the introduction of the RN and SW, or a PCP who valued social workers as therapists could persuade a patient to give the SW an opportunity to help cope with the loss of a spouse.

Structural aspects of the intervention helped the PCP, RN, and SW develop their relationships. Incorporating new data from the patient questionnaires and the RN or SW initial home visits into the PCPs' existing knowledge base for patients was a new process to the PCPs, RNs, and SWs. Together they became familiar with "rating frailty" and "risk reduction plans," the foundation for prevention-oriented caregiving that entailed identifying each patient's highest priority health care risk. Managed care risk plans usually target high-risk persons for case management based on a prior hospitalization or upon responses to mailed questionnaires reviewed by plan personnel (Padjett, 1997). In the SCC, the PCP, RN, and SW pooled information from the questionnaire, the home visit, and the PCP's prior knowledge of the patient to plan care. Patients with both good and poor baseline health status showed rate decreases or stabilizations, suggesting that it may be unwise to neglect patients with comparatively better health.

Despite one PCP proclaiming that he did not expect participation in the SCC to affect the way he practiced medicine, practice styles—and not just those of the PCPs—did change. This occurred through the gradual incorporation of the tools of the intervention (e.g., monthly meetings, care planning), but even more, through the daily exigencies of collaborative practice. Such opportunities varied markedly from responding to a depressed patient's request to cancel her office visit (because she could not get dressed) to getting an advance directive signed by the patient on the chart before surgery. In these cases, the PCP/RN/SW team was placed in situations which often called for rapid communication and coordination to achieve a focused clinical objective.

PCPs' accessibility to the RN and SW varied greatly and changed over the course of the intervention. For example, rather than be interrupted during the day, one PCP preferred faxes that she would read during the day and then page the RN or SW to discuss; another allowed the RN or SW to page him directly and began to call back more promptly as he became more familiar with the RN's and SW's levels of urgency. For RNs, particularly those with homecare experience, this meant learning to rely on phone calls as substitutes for home visits; for the social workers, it meant developing enough flexibility, for example, to do focused therapy regarding an anxiety reaction in the same visit that transportation to the doctor was arranged. But changes in practice styles came in their own unique ways, and at a rate controlled by each clinician. Certain PCPs admitted that they were only just getting "the hang of it" in the SCC's last couple of months.

In particular, "patient crises" called for fast-paced, coordinated efforts among the PCP, RN, SW, and patient to prevent an emergency room visit or a hospital admission; in such cases, all of them worked together. Sometimes, however, an admission could not be prevented. When the PCP, RN, and SW recalled these cases, they talked about how each member of the group played a unique role but acted in concert, trusting each other to identify and assess a potentially serious problem.

In retrospect we see several measures that could have enhanced the development of PCP/RN/SW relationships. The first and most important would have been to engage the social worker full-time as opposed to half-time. In addition to the message this would send—this professional is just as valuable as the nurse—it would have helped every patient to have a complete psychosocial, home-based assessment, as opposed to only those seen as needing it by the PCP or RN. Additionally, the SW could have facilitated the PCP, RN, and SW's regular meetings both by helping to organize the work to be done and encouraging more discussion of how they were doing the work. Last, a full-time SW could have facilitated formation of more patient group activities (e.g., exercise or hobby groups) which, based on those that were organized, were received very positively.

Although the RNs and SWs were involved in pre-project orientation activities, many of which involved observing in the offices, we were reluctant to involve the PCPs in formal orientation sessions other than two evening educational sessions. With hindsight, we would have involved PCPs in more educational events. Examples of issues that could have been broached during across-county sessions involving PCPs include: (1) how to work with the frailty and health risk factor scales using hypothetical cases, (2) how to objectively—without assigning blame—review a hospital admission in order to understand the factors that caused it, and (3) how to adapt principles of chronic disease self-management in helping patients better cope with a particular sequence of chronic illness (e.g., pain). Topics pertaining to the PCP/RN/SW collaboration process could have been directly addressed: (1) surmounting the natural barriers to communication in a busy office setting, (2) acknowledging professional stereotypes and how to move beyond them, and (3) inviting input on a long-time patient even though the PCP believes there is nothing more to learn. The clinicians' positive response to the mid-intervention retreat, during which much talk centered on the process aspects of the SCC, provided indication that our fears of turning off the PCPs with too much "soft stuff" might have been unfounded.

A second area where, in retrospect, we walked on eggshells was advocating for more data collection. Each time a patient was hospitalized, for example, it would have been valuable to have had the PCP's, as well as the RN's and SW's, assessment of contributing factors, and how, in retrospect, it could have gone differently. Additionally, having the RNs and SWs collect data about their contacts with patients' family members and community agencies on patients' behalf would also have been helpful. Since RNs and SWs already anguished over the time involved in entry of patient contact data, as much as they wanted the additional data to substantiate the amount of work involved, they agreed that it was not feasible. (We estimate one call to a family member or community agency for every three to five patient contacts.)

Last, the RN/SW training in the concepts and teaching of chronic disease self-management (CDSM) could have been done more explicitly. They attended three sessions during orientation as well as two more during the 18-month intervention, but they were not required to take the formal course for CDSM trainers. The County 3 RN did take the course on her own time and, with the SW, held two classes for 12 patients each. With more emphasis on teaching CDSM skills across counties, we might have seen a marked decrease in office visit rates.

## Implications for Managed Care

The Medicare HMO is again being looked at as a solution to stem Medicare's rising costs. Costs can be controlled and/or reduced by eliminating unnecessary service use, including hospital care that could be delivered out-of-hospital, hospital admissions preventable with more proactive ambulatory care, office visits to specialists for care a primary care physician could deliver, and admissions to nursing homes occasioned by the lack of coordinated home and community supports to help elders remain in their home. Costs can also be reduced by having non-physicians engage in pursuits that physicians never did or did haphazardly because such practices were not part of physician training or their concept of primary care for elderly persons. These include understanding the patient from a psychosocial perspective, eliciting health risk data and incorporating it into treatment plans, discussing treatment preferences, educating patients in self-care, and simply "accompanying" or being "present" for patients as they live with the daily anxiety of debilitating chronic illness.

In this project, the nurses and social workers explicitly concerned themselves with these tasks in the process of carrying out clinical monitoring between office visits and community-based service linkage. They did not engage in these activities independently, or according to a prescribed protocol given to them by a payer. They actively promoted these functions in collaboration with PCPs in their office settings, and without rigid role definitions and protocols. Flexibility was explicitly built in to allow patients to receive individualized care and to promote collaborative interchange among clinicians.

We believe that further analysis should be done to look at condition-specific hospitalization rate changes as a function of group assignment, particularly after the intervention ended. Would we detect, for example, increased hospital admissions for certain types of intervention patients (e.g., heart failure patients)? As a group, intervention patients' decreased hospitalization rate stayed stable during the six months following the completion of the SCC, but a more detailed analysis might reveal variable rates among sub-groups. In a managed care environment, a clear danger to quality, in the name of reducing "unnecessary" resource use, could be the actual reduction of *necessary* service use.

## Implications for Perspectives on Patient Care

At the same time that the PCP, RN, and SW engaged in efforts to individualize the SCC concept according to the needs of the single patient, each PCP's thirty SCC patients became a cohort seen by the PCP, RN, and SW as an entity in its own right. This shift in their perceptions of patients as individuals to members of a special group became more pronounced as the SCC continued.

Concepts central to a population-based perspective on health and illness were introduced. These included the idea of rating patients regarding frailty, risk of hospitalization, quality of doctor-patient relationship, and benefit from the intervention. Common problems in the care of elders—mobility, medication compliance, drug interactions—were considered on a routine basis and formulated into annual screens. With assistance from the RN and SW, the office-based PCP was able to look at her or his patients as a group with known characteristics, as opposed to a group of disparate characters. Each patient had an individualized plan to reduce health risks but, for the patient group as a whole, the PCP, RN, and SW agreed upon specific goals (e.g., a signed power of attorney for health care in the record) and clear but flexible expectations (e.g., learning self-care activities to reduce risks). As a result, one PCP reflected, "I gained an overall perspective on how this patient group aged over three years; I never noticed this before." Another observed how incorrect she was in her 1992 ratings of her patients' 2-year hospitalization risks (i.e., she expected more of them to have died by the end of the SCC). She wondered if she had been unduly pessimistic all these years about the fates of her elderly patients, unaware of their coping strengths capitalized upon during the SCC.

We asked the PCPs, RNs, and SWs to rank each patient on "benefit gained" from the intervention. We obtained valuable insights into how they defined "benefit" in the context of the SCC, and, specifically, the role of tertiary prevention (i.e., those efforts undertaken to reduce the amount of deterioration and disability in patients already suffering from disease) in the care of older persons (Lavisso-Mourey & Diserens, 1990). The PCPs, RNs, and SWs were similar across counties in their levels of congruency on benefit. For 30 to 40% of their patients, the PCPs, RNs, and SWs agreed on "high benefit"; for approximately 25% they agreed on "moderate benefit"; for 35% they could not agree at all on level of benefit, and on another 25% they agreed on "no benefit." The preponderance of patients for whom there was agreement on high benefit, however, were those who were significantly *more likely* than others to have been hospitalized in 1993 *and* in 1994. This suggests at least two interpretations: (1) although these patients were hospitalized, without good collaboration, hospital stays could have been longer, more problems would have occurred at home post-discharge, and patients could have been readmitted, or (2) the work the PCP, RN, and SW did together for sicker patients (i.e., functioning in crisis mode in and around the hospital) became defined as "high benefit," and had nothing to do with reducing service use, but quite the opposite—together, they expeditiously acted to provide care that sick patients badly needed. High benefit, therefore, in the end, became defined as ministering to acute needs.

What about patients who were not hospitalized? Why were significantly fewer of these persons considered not to have obtained high benefit? How many had hospitalizations prevented, in part, as a result of collaborative efforts? Did this not rate as high benefit? We wonder about the potential of building collaborative relationships around disability prevention as opposed to, or in addition to, saving lives (e.g., hospitalizing a patient with crushing chest pain). Physicians are trained to intervene to stop disease. Compared to stabilizing chronic disease or preventing further disability, curing disease is relatively easy to measure and makes itself apparent relatively quickly (e.g., leaving the ICU or the hospital alive). Success in tertiary prevention entails delayed gratification—attainment of small, incremental goals, such as building up a patient's confidence to exercise just a few more minutes each day. We did not attempt to directly quantify instances of tertiary prevention but rather depended on an 18-month accumulation of the many small efforts to result in a hospitalization rate or mean office visit decrease. Unfortunately, no hard data were collected—only anecdotes about a hospital admission prevented, an office visit that didn't happen, or an emergency room visit aborted. In truth, since we did not ask the clinicians to document prevention successes, we should not fault them for not recognizing them as high benefit. If we had provided them with this alternative frame of reference, we suspect the data would have been forthcoming.

## Summary

In summary, three phenomena were observed at the end of the SCC. Compared to controls, intervention patients (1) showed decreased service use, (2) stabilized or increased healthy functioning, and (3) increased self-efficacy for managing their health along several dimensions. Analyses of the relationship between number of RN or SW patient contacts and service utilization measures, as well as measures of patient self-efficacy, suggest that less service utilization and more self-efficacy were associated with more contacts. The RN's or SW's contact with the patient symbolized the reach of the PCP's practice into the patient's home, which, for the patients in this project, was construed as a positive force. The ability to extend this reach in good faith resulted from an evolved collaborative relationship between experienced nurses and social workers in partnership with willing primary care physicians. The doctor-patient relationship supplied the platform for the creation of this promising partnership.

## References

Emanuel, E.J. & Dubler, N.N. (1995). Preserving the physician-patient relationship in the era of managed care. *Journal of the American Medical Association, 273*, 323–329.

Engel, G.L. (1977). The need for a new medical model: A challenge for biomedicine. *Science, 96*, 129–136.

Kaplan, S.H., Greenfeld, S. & Ware, J.E. (1989). Assessing the effects of physician-patient interactions on the outcomes of chronic disease. *Medical Care, 17*(Suppl.), S110–S127.

Kleinman, A.M. (1978). Culture, illness and care. *Annals of Internal Medicine, 88,* 251–258.

Lavisso-Mourey, R. & Diserens, D. (1990). Preventive care for the elderly. *Occupational Medicine, 5,* 827–833.

Lee, M.Y. & Novielli, K.D. (1996). A nutritional assessment of homebound elderly in a physician-monitoring population. *Journal of Nutrition for the Elderly, 15,* 1–13.

Lorig, K.R., Laurent, D.D. & Gonzalez, V.M. (1994). *Chronic disease self-management course leader's manual.* Palo Alto, CA: Patient Education Research Center.

Lorig, K.R., Stewart, A., Ritter, P., Gonzalez, V.M., Laurent, D.D. & Lynch, D. (1996). *Outcome measures for health education and other healthcare interventions.* Thousand Oaks, CA: Sage.

McWhinney, I.R. (1972). Beyond diagnosis: An approach to the integration of behavioral science and clinical medicine. *New England Journal of Medicine, 187,* 384–387.

Padjett, Y. (1997). *Health care of seniors: Strategies for success under managed care.* Marietta, GA: National Health Information.

Pew-Fetzer Task Force. (1994). *Health professions education and relationship-centered care.* San Francisco: Pew Health Professions Commission.

Sheikh, J.I. & Yesavage, J.A. (1986). Geriatric depression scale (GDS). Recent evidence and development of a shorter version. *Clinical Gerontologist, 5,* 165–173.

Sommers, L., Marton, K., Barbaccia, J. & Randolph, J. (1997). A trial of physician, nurse, and social worker collaboration in primary care for chronically ill seniors. (Unpublished manuscript).

Weiner, J.M. & Illston, L.H. (1994). Health care reform in the 1990s: Where does long-term care fit in? *The Gerontologist, 34,* 402–408.

# CHAPTER 8

# An Effective Managed Care Strategy: Case Managers in Partnership with Primary Care Physicians

*Lynne Anker-Unnever*

The original St. Joseph Hospital in Albuquerque was founded by the Sisters of Charity in 1902, 10 years before New Mexico became a state. Today, St. Joseph is a fully integrated health care system serving the greater Albuquerque metropolitan area with three acute care hospitals and one physical rehabilitation hospital, nursing facilities, an assisted living center, a home health agency, a child care center, a physician network known as Med-Net, and a variety of community programs. Older adults comprise a major portion of patients served in St. Joseph facilities and account for over one-half of patient days in the four St. Joseph hospitals.

This chapter begins with the background of the development of the Coordinated Care Partnership, a case management program funded by The John A. Hartford Foundation. Designed to foster collaboration with primary care physicians in the process of caring for elders with chronic conditions, St. Joseph implemented this project, which lasted over three years, in partnership with selected Med-Net physicians. Background information provides a context for details of project design as well as evaluation results and lessons learned.

## Background

In 1987, with start-up funding from the Flinn Foundation of Arizona, St. Joseph developed Coordinated Care, a case management program designed to improve service delivery to elderly patients and to provide continuous coordination for those same patients in the community. The initial Coordinated Care case management was conducted by teams of nurse and social work case managers. After several years of providing hospital-based community case management services, we at St. Joseph thought that a closer link between case managers and physicians would enhance services and provide added benefit to patients. As observed by Weil and Karls (1985), case management devoid of medical participation is incomplete; establishing viable working relationships between community case managers and practicing physicians is critical.

St. Joseph realized that managing care for elderly patients presented our physicians, as well as patients and their caregivers, with complex challenges. Elderly persons frequently turn to their primary care physicians to assist them in coping not only with their health problems, but also with the confusion of the present health care system (Anker-Unnever & Netting, 1995). Physicians, in turn, are faced with a growing number of elderly patients whose needs are increasingly complex. Restrictions imposed by payers and managed care providers further complicated the lives of St. Joseph physicians.

In an effort to make Coordinated Care more responsive to the needs of physicians, St. Joseph conducted a survey of physician needs in the management of geriatric patients. The physicians identified several areas in which case management could support their practices. These areas included monitoring patients' health status at home and compliance with physician orders, reporting back to physicians, coordinating community services and benefits, and arranging for transportation to physicians' offices. The results of our survey mirrored what is often found in the literature—physicians who care for geriatric patients are confronted with non-medical as well as medical needs. As Shearer, Simmons, White & Berkman (1995) report, primary care physicians find their ability to coordinate the care of patients—especially elderly patients—limited by their traditional medical focus. While they are skilled in providing and managing medical services, they usually are not knowledgeable about the non-medical aspects of care that patients need in order to remain independent.

The design and subsequent implementation of the Coordinated Care Partnership enabled St. Joseph to further tailor case management to the needs and preferences of physicians. Building upon our existing Coordinated Care case management, our proposed project was particularly attractive to the Hartford Foundation because of physician enthusiasm and support, St. Joseph's previous experience and reputation in providing community case management, and Albuquerque's managed care environment.

## St. Joseph Healthcare in a Changing Environment

When the Coordinated Care Partnership was initially funded, Med-Net was a newly formed non-profit subsidiary of St. Joseph Healthcare and reported directly to the president and CEO of St. Joseph. As Med-Net developed, it was placed in St. Joseph's managed care division. Today, Med-Net has grown to become one of the largest group practices in Albuquerque, with more than 40 primary care providers and 13 practice sites. Med-Net includes a practice resource center and is moving to develop joint practice agreements with other providers.

Med-Net's primary care providers are a key component of St. Joseph's managed care system. The Albuquerque metropolitan area, with a population of almost 700,000, has a managed care penetration rate of over 60% and includes four active Medicare risk health maintenance organizations (HMOs). This has resulted in a highly competitive health care market. In the past five years, St. Joseph entered into several capitated, shared-risk contracts with HMOs, including one with Albuquerque's largest Medicare risk HMO. Both the development of Med-Net and the initiation of at-risk managed care contractual arrangements created a receptive environment for collaboration with physicians in managing the care of patients, particularly high-risk elderly patients.

The rapid growth of Albuquerque's older adult population also contributed to this receptive environment. Between 1980 and 1990, the proportion of the elderly population over the age of 65 in New Mexico grew by 39%, and by 12% from 1990 through 1994. This growth is due in some part to the aging of the general population, but is largely attributable to elderly retiree migration to the southwest. Almost 84,000 adults age 60 and older reside in the counties of Bernalillo, Sandoval, and Valencia, the counties which constitute the greater Albuquerque metropolitan area. These senior adults comprise 14% of the total 3-county population.

Of particular relevance is the growth in numbers of older persons over 75. Almost one-third of Bernalillo County's older adult population is 75 years of age or older, the highest in the state. Twenty-seven percent and 28% respectively of the older adult populations of Sandoval and Valencia counties are 75 years of age or older.

St. Joseph Healthcare experienced significant organizational changes throughout the more than three years of the Coordinated Care Partnership project. In 1996, the Sisters of Charity Health Care Systems, St. Joseph's national sponsor, merged with Franciscan Health System and with Catholic Health Corporation to become one of the largest health care systems in the U.S.—Catholic Health Initiatives. Catholic Health Initiatives is organized into five geographic regions nationwide; St. Joseph is in the western region, which includes New Mexico and Colorado. In the fall of 1996, the president and CEO of St. Joseph resigned and an existing senior vice president was appointed CEO. This led to a restructuring of senior management throughout the organization, including changes in the reporting relationships of both Med-Net and Community Case Management (which includes the Coordinated Care Partnership). Both were moved from the managed care division of St. Joseph to the delivery system.

Many changes also occurred in the physician practices involved in the project. Thirteen different physicians were involved in the Coordinated Care Partnership's intervention component, with a number of the physicians changing or leaving practices throughout the project's duration. The demonstration phase of the project began with six physicians in three practices. At the midpoint, it included eleven physicians in three practices and then returned to six physicians by the end of the demonstration phase.

Today, the project serves over 60 physicians in 18 different practices. The larger organizational changes at St. Joseph have also "trickled down" to the project staff level. There were 5 project managers throughout the demonstration phase. The number of case managers fluctuated from 2 to 6, with over 15 different individuals filling the case manager positions.

The environmental, structural, and project-specific changes that occurred (and continue to occur) for St. Joseph Healthcare in Albuquerque are a challenge to any project design. These multi-level changes form a context in which to understand how the Coordinated Care Partnership evolved.

# Project Design

## Development of the Model

The intent of the Coordinated Care Partnership was to demonstrate the impact of introducing a case management component into primary care physicians' practices, as well as to measure the effect of early screening and intervention on targeted geriatric patients within the practices. The

Coordinated Care Partnership's intensive case management process was designed to assist physicians in early detection, treatment, and monitoring of the health and related problems of their older adult patients.

A meeting of St. Joseph physicians actively involved in the care of geriatric patients was convened prior to the implementation of the Coordinated Care Partnership, and was attended by six of the eight invited physicians. The three separate practices of these physicians became the project's original intervention practices. The purpose of this meeting was to involve the physicians as partners, as early as possible, in jointly planning the project and in designing an effective intervention. As a result of the meeting, it was determined that screening, in-home assessment, and case management services provided to at-risk elders would complement the physician practices, as well as the hospital system. Criteria for patient selection and screening were developed at this initial meeting, and areas for case manager involvement were identified.

In the earlier Coordinated Care program, case management occurred following a referral based on identified patient need, often after the patient's condition became acute or required hospitalization, when it was too late for preventive action. With implementation of the Coordinated Care Partnership, targeted elderly patients were screened based upon criteria developed with input from the participating physicians. In-home assessment, care plan development, and case management were initiated based upon the results of the screening. It was hoped that the physician, case manager, and patient/family partnership would facilitate access to timely and appropriate care, identifying the need for intervention before that need became acute.

## Patient Selection Criteria

The criteria used to define the target population were developed as a result of the initial meeting with the project physicians. The original three criteria were (1) age 65 to 80 (at date of entry), (2) a diagnosis of one or more of the following: congestive heart failure, cerebral vascular accident, diabetes, chronic obstructive pulmonary disease, and/or hip fracture, and (3) membership in a managed care plan for which St. Joseph is financially "at risk."

Although we were aware of the fact that patients age 75 and older might have a greater need for case management than those persons under age 75, St. Joseph's intention in lowering the target age to 65 was to initiate early intervention and preventive strategies prior to exacerbation of chronic conditions. When selecting the target diagnoses, the physicians also expressed a need for assistance in managing patients with the diagnosis of dementia. However, this was not included as one of the original primary diagnoses, as patients with dementia would not have been able to participate effectively in interviews conducted for evaluative purposes.

The managed care criterion for patient selection was eliminated after the first year of the project, as physicians wanted case manager assistance for a broader population of their Medicare patients. However, the criterion was reestablished by the St. Joseph administration the following year in order to direct resources toward those patients for whom St. Joseph was most at risk financially. As the project has developed beyond the demonstration phase, the population served has expanded to include younger women and also children. Diagnostic criteria were also adjusted to include dementia, asthma, lung cancer, orthopedic replacement, and high-risk pregnancy. Each patient who meets these criteria is screened to determine his or her need for case management intervention.

## Patient Screening

The original service delivery component of the Coordinated Care Partnership included an initial telephone screening of all targeted patients, conducted by a paraprofessional case assistant. This screening process determined each patient's need for case management intervention. In addition to the telephone screening, a checklist was developed for physicians and their office staffs to readily identify and refer appropriate patients. Indicators for the screening process were developed in consultation with the project physicians. The initial telephone screening instrument was designed to gather the following information:

- ability to perform activities of daily living and assistance required
- risk of falls
- appointments with other physicians
- weight loss or gain of more than 10 pounds
- use of ambulance and/or emergency room or urgent care centers
- number of medications being taken now versus last year
- completion of advance directives (e.g., living will, durable power of attorney)
- frequency and quality of contact with family members
- presence of sleep disorders
- indicators of depression

The majority of these screening items coincide with established indicators of "high risk," although the advance directive indicator does not. However, several of the physicians felt strongly that this was an area in which early intervention by the case managers could be of benefit to them in the care of their patients. The physicians commented that they were often confronted with the need to make medical decisions for patients who were unable to do so and who had no directives in place. Rather than waiting until these "crisis situations" occurred, physicians wanted the case managers to work with patients to execute directives in advance.

During the first two years of the project, whether or not to initiate an in-home assessment and care plan was based upon the results of the telephone screening conducted by the paraprofessional assistant. Later in the project, the role of the paraprofessional position was altered and eventually eliminated. Currently, intervention is directly initiated as determined by a case manager after a review of hospital and emergency services use, followed by a telephone screening interview with the patient. The screening instrument was modified for direct use by the case managers, and several additional risk factors were added, including financial concerns, need for long-term care placement, suspected abuse or neglect, and newly diagnosed catastrophic illness.

## Assessment and Care Planning

Patients screened as needing case management receive an assessment, followed by care plan development, monitoring, and referral back to a physician as indicated. Assessments included evaluation of the patient's home setting and safety factors, formal and informal support systems, functional ability to perform ADLs or IADLs within the home setting, psychosocial status, and community resource use. Information was collected from the patient as well as the patient's family and/or caregiver. The development of care plans was a cooperative effort between patients, family and caregivers, physicians, and case managers. Each patient's status and receipt of services was regularly monitored by the case managers. Those patients not in need of active case management were also monitored to assess any changes in status and to determine possible need for intervention at a later date. The results of the screening, the assessment, and the care plan were incorporated into the patient's chart in the physician's office.

Our physicians' experience indicated that many of their elderly patients with chronic conditions waited until those conditions became acute before seeking medical attention. These exacerbated conditions were then harder to manage from both the patient's and the physician's perspective. According to Applebaum, Baxter, Callahan & Day (1985), chronic illnesses involve issues related to individuals and families as well as professional competence, and issues of daily living as well as those of medical treatment. A case management component that could provide support to patients' family members and caregivers was seen as crucial. The project's case managers supported and educated caregivers, increasing their comfort and competence in responding to patient needs. Case managers also taught patients to recognize early signs of illness and implement self-care strategies or seek timely assistance from their physicians. This process enabled the individual to remain in the most appropriate and least costly environment—generally his or her own home—containing or reducing the overall cost of care while maintaining or improving quality of life.

Demographic characteristics of patients who participated in the Coordinated Care Partnership are provided in Table 8.1. All of the 176 patients were "case managed" in the sense that they were screened and

**TABLE 8.1**

## Coordinated Care Partnership Patient Demographics (N=176)

| | Cases (N) | Frequency (%) | | Cases (N) | Frequency (%) |
|---|---|---|---|---|---|
| **Gender** | | | **Total household annual income** | | |
| male | 66 | 37.5 | | | |
| female | 110 | 62.5 | $0–$ 5,000 | 7 | 4.0 |
| **Ethnicity** | | | $5,001–$10,000 | 31 | 17.6 |
| Caucasian | 127 | 72.1 | $10,001–$15,000 | 48 | 27.3 |
| African-American | 3 | 1.7 | $15,001–$20,000 | 24 | 13.6 |
| Hispanic | 45 | 25.6 | $20,001–$25,000 | 16 | 9.1 |
| other | 1 | 0.6 | $25,001–$30,000 | 7 | 4.0 |
| | | | $30,001–$35,000 | 8 | 4.5 |
| **Marital status** | | | $35,001–$40,000 | 6 | 3.9 |
| single | 3 | 1.7 | $40,001+ | 9 | 5.1 |
| widowed | 63 | 35.8 | no response (missing data) | 20 | 11.4 |
| married | 95 | 54.0 | | | |
| divorced | 15 | 8.5 | **Housing arrangement** | | |
| **Educational background** | | | single family home | 113 | 64.2 |
| | | | apartment or duplex | 26 | 14.8 |
| elementary | 38 | 21.6 | mobile home | 21 | 11.9 |
| some high school | 19 | 10.8 | nursing home | 4 | 2.3 |
| high school graduate | 41 | 23.3 | other | 12 | 6.8 |
| technical school | 23 | 13.1 | | | |
| some college | 28 | 15.9 | | | |
| college graduate | 15 | 8.5 | | | |
| graduate school | 9 | 5.1 | | | |
| no response (missing data) | 3 | 1.7 | | | |

monitored. Of these, however, 99 received formal case management (Williams, Netting & Kirkman-Liff, 1997).

# Roles and Relationships

Selected primary care physicians' offices served as patients' points of entry for the Coordinated Care Partnership. The project's original intervention group included three physician practices with large geriatric patient populations. Each was staffed with two or three physicians. The physicians involved included both internists and family practitioners. All physicians involved were supportive of the case management process and enthusiastic about the enhanced availability of this service within their practices.

During initial implementation of the Coordinated Care Partnership, particular attention was paid to recruiting staff based upon physician-identified priorities for the case management positions. Those areas included post-hospital follow-up, patient education and support, and initiation of advance directives. Previous experience in working with the elderly, interdisciplinary teamwork, and providing services in home and community-based settings was also considered important. Additionally, bilingual ability was requested to facilitate delivery of services to the area's large Spanish-speaking population.

Considerable debate exists among both health care and aging network providers regarding who should perform case management functions. This debate often centers on medical versus social case management, usually in the form of nurse versus social worker, and the extent of professional training needed (paraprofessional, bachelor's or master's degree). The fact that social workers and nurses, as well as paraprofessionals, hold case manager positions suggests a relationship between case management and a professional body of knowledge. Based on our earlier experience with case management, we projected that the case managers would bring different attitudes and perspectives to their work depending on their professional or occupational backgrounds. Considering the identified areas, the decision was made to use both nurses and social workers in teams as case managers, and to use a paraprofessional case assistant to perform the initial screening functions.

We also felt that a critical factor in determining who would fill the case manager role was the nature of the population to be served. Many elders have psychosocial, economic, and physical problems; the majority have health concerns. As our case management component was developed to meet the complex, interrelated needs of older people, needs that might place them at risk of institutionalization, we wanted to have in place case managers who could best address those needs. Nurses and social workers were viewed as having the skills to match the case management objectives of providing both health and psychosocial care.

The Coordinated Care Partnership began by using two teams, each consisting of a nurse and a social worker, assigned to perform assessments and provide ongoing case management of patients in the selected practices. These teams were available to physicians in all three of the original intervention practices. Case managers were assigned to patients based on the geographic areas in which the patients resided. The paraprofessional case assistant worked with both teams and performed telephone screening of all referred patients. The individual in this position had an associate's degree in medical office management and had worked for many years as the office manager for several primary care physicians. When these physicians retired, this individual was trained as a discharge planner in a small community hospital which merged with St. Joseph just prior to the implementation of the Coordinated Care Partnership.

Both the case management teams, as well as the case assistant, were located in a central administrative office. The case managers, however, spent much of their time in the field visiting patients' homes. The case assistant provided in-office backup for the case managers, and assisted them with referrals to community organizations, as well as with telephone monitoring of patients.

As the project developed, the nurses began to feel that their clinical skills were not being called upon; likewise, while the physicians felt that the interventions required by their patients were more in the non-clinical areas of mental health, community resources, and other traditional social work areas. A decision was made therefore, to use three social workers with one nurse to provide consultation and/or case management for patients with complex medical needs (Netting & Williams, 1996). Therefore, the nurse/social work team structure no longer existed. At about the same time, the original target group of senior HMO patients was expanded to include any senior patients of the participating physicians, as the physicians felt that many of their non-HMO patients needed, and could benefit from, the services of the Coordinated Care Partnership.

For the first two years of the project, the telephone screening was conducted by the paraprofessional case assistant. In year three, the physicians expressed a desire for the patients to be screened directly by the case managers. In response to the physicians' concerns, the position of case assistant was eliminated from the project.

Various systems of ongoing communication between physicians and case managers were established throughout the demonstration period. These included formal meetings (often over breakfast or lunch) in one practice, and informal discussion and telephone conferencing in the other two. Occasionally, case managers met with physicians in their offices individually, or with a group of physicians and office staff. On rare occasions, case managers also met with physicians when they accompanied patients to office visits. The preferences of each physician and practice dictated which of these methods was used and the frequency of use. Other systems which were modified based on practice preference included new patient screening and charting or recordkeeping. For example, in one practice the office staff used a simple form to screen for new patient referrals, while another used the computer system. One practice included copies of all case management progress notes in their patient charts, and another included summary forms for each patient.

After a year and a half of project operation, a project manager was designated within the Med-Net organization to facilitate integration of case managers into physician practices. By this time, all the physicians were indicating a preference for having one, rather than four, case managers work with all their patients. The assignment of case managers to patients based on area of residence, rather than physician, was not conducive to physicians developing collaborative relationships with case managers. Physicians also expressed concerns that they were never sure which case manager was working with which patient, as it could be any one of the four. Therefore, some reorganization of the case management component occurred to facilitate further development of close, collaborative working relationships between the case managers and the physicians. Plans were made to physically locate the case managers within the physician practices. As three physician practices were involved in the initial intervention phase, the number of case managers was reduced from four to three, and a specific case manager was assigned to each of the three practices.

When three of the case managers were moved to the practices, the one nurse case manager was reassigned within St. Joseph. At this point, therefore, all Coordinated Care Partnership case management was provided by social workers. The physicians felt that the needs of their patients could be better addressed by social workers, and that others in their practices, such as nurse practitioners and medical assistants, could provide any medical support required. A premium was placed on certain functional capacities that are traditionally associated with social work—empowering clients through fostering development of their strengths, facilitating their use of community resources, and emphasizing appropriate utilization of resources and self-help (Fahey, 1996).

Changes occurred again in year 3. As the demonstration phase was drawing to a close, St. Joseph decided to expand case management to other Med-Net practices, other physicians in affiliated managed care organizations, and all patients for whom St. Joseph was at risk in managed care contracts. With the expansion to six case managers now serving 60 physicians in 18 practices, the case managers have been recentralized in a main administrative office to provide physicians with a single point of entry for case management referral. However, most of the case managers' work continues to take place in patients' homes, with some accompaniment of patients to physician's office visits. Case managers are now assigned to more than one physician's practice, though each practice has only one assigned case manager. Nurse case managers are once again being used, in addition to social work case managers, as many of the new physicians and the current project manager felt that both disciplines were needed to effectively manage the high-risk care of the expanded target population. In addition, assigning case managers based on patient diagnosis, a kind of "disease management" approach with case managers as specialists, is now being considered.

Physicians who have been most supportive of the case management process tend to have had a critical patient-related issue in which they witnessed a case manager's skill in dealing with complex psychosocial problems. For example, one physician had a patient whose adult daughter accompanied the patient to office visits and responded for her mother. During a physician's office visit that included this patient, her daughter, and the case manager, the case manager successfully redirected questions to the patient, allowing the patient to answer for herself. The patient and the physician both had a more satisfying interaction, and the daughter felt less pressure as a caregiver.

As a result of this project, specific in-home monitoring protocols were developed with physicians for the process of in-home assessment, as well as for each target diagnosis. These protocols, or extended-care pathways, defined the roles and responsibilities of both nurse and social work case managers and included specific guidelines for referral back to physicians. The in-home assessment pathway was followed for all patients; the diagnosis-specific pathways were followed when one or more of those diagnoses was present. The pathways have enabled the project to standardize services and better assure quality of patient care. Sample pathways are provided in Table 8.2 (on page 163) and Table 8.3 (on page 164).

---

**TABLE 8.2**

## Coordinated Care Partnership Extended-Care Pathway for In-home Case Management Intervention

---

A.  Receive referral
   1. Define presenting problem(s)
   2. Discuss with physician

B.  Review medical chart
   1. Collect general patient information
   2. Become familiar with patient's medical history

C.  Conduct telephone screening and schedule initial home visit
OR
   Re-screen at a later date

D.  If home visit is scheduled, perform assessment of patient's:
   1. home safety
   2. activities of daily living (ADLs)
   3. instrumental activities of daily living (IADLs)
   4. durable medical equipment needs
   5. chronic disease management (follow supplemental paths as appropriate)
   6. home health care needs
   7. mental health status
   8. medication compliance management
   9. support systems
   10. caregiver's support systems
   11. financial status
   12. legal needs
   13. transportation needs
   14. spiritual/pastoral care needs

E.  Refer areas of immediate concern directly to primary care physician

F.  Develop care plan
   1. Gather input from patient and family/caregiver
   2. Gather input from physician and other team members

G  Initiate care plan

H.  Monitor patient and care plan

---

**TABLE 8.3**

## Coordinated Care Partnership Diagnosis Specific Case Management Interventions for Chronic Obstructive Pulmonary Disease (COPD)

A.  Mobility/ADL Management
   1.  Assess ability to perform ADLs
   2.  Assess need for transportation assistance, if using oxygen

B.  Mental Status
   1.  Assess for disorientation and confusion
   2.  Assess for depression, anxiety, panic attacks

C.  Home Safety
   1.  Assess home cleanliness
       a. excessive dust/dirt
       b. other possible environmental hazards
   2.  Evaluate oxygen equipment/use
       a. tubing
       b. levels
       c. compliance with orders

D.  Wellness/Awareness of Condition
   1.  Assess understanding of condition and awareness of when to seek medical attention
   2.  Assess need for:
       a. exercise/exercise precautions
       b. medication management assistance

E.  Resource Options
   1.  Homemaking agencies
   2.  Education
       a. American Lung Association
       b. support groups
       c. literature
       d. smoking cessation programs
   3.  Therapeutic recreation
       a. 60+ pulmonary lunch group
       b. Publication *Traveling with Oxygen*
   4.  Pulmonary rehabilitation programs

# Evaluation

The evaluation of the Coordinated Care Partnership was conducted by a research team from Arizona State University, and focused on the effect of case management on physician practices, on patients, and on utilization. Evaluation included both qualitative and quantitative analyses. Of central interest was the effect that proactive case management had on physicians' practices.

The evaluation team monitored the health status of patients in the project, as well as that of a comparison group of patients, by contracting with a nurse specialist to conduct independent assessments of patients who met the screening criteria. All project patients were followed for at least one year. Health services utilization data were compared to and supplemented by the self-reported utilization data from the independent assessments. A sample of records of patients from affiliated HMO group practice clinics was also selected to supplement utilization analysis.

The qualitative analysis of the implementation of the Coordinated Care Partnership was conducted using semi-structured interviews and observational field methods. The research team interviewed physicians, key office staff, Med-Net practice managers, and case managers. Thirty-six different persons were interviewed over four time periods. Eight observational field visits were conducted in which an evaluator accompanied case managers into the homes of older patients. Observations revealed that case managers mobilized resources, monitored medications and health care compliance, educated patients and physicians, counseled patients, and provided caregiver support. Key players were physicians, physicians' office staff, the case assistant, case managers, project managers, and the project director. These persons regularly engaged in role redefinition and relationship-building activities. Ongoing tasks for all participants throughout project development included adjusting to and defining the case management role, structuring supervision, nurturing the intervention, and communicating with one another within diverse physician practices (Netting, 1997). Embedded in these tasks were the struggles involved in building and integrating interdisciplinary teams into physicians' practices, as well as the use of strategies such as case conferencing among case managers to maintain project integrity (Netting & Williams, 1995).

The importance of clear communication and the need for great flexibility emerged as critical themes throughout the process of qualitative evaluation. The need for clear communication existed at all levels: project directors, managers and administrators, case managers, physicians, and office staff. The ability of these individuals to communicate effectively was challenged as all involved became somewhat preoccupied with larger changes in the health care arena (Netting, 1997).

Team building required flexibility grounded in trust. Surviving within a rapidly changing health care system required flexibility, and openness to change in project design became critical, though challenging for evaluation efforts. Professional rigidity had little place in a system such as this, yet rapid change was sometimes handled by retreats to familiar professional roles and relationships. The physicians and case managers struggled with their roles in this fluid environment, but nonetheless were willing to repeatedly engage in project redesign (Netting, 1997).

Results of the quantitative analysis of the Coordinated Care Partnership focused on patients' health and functional status and on use of health care services. The health and functional ability of frail elders can generally be expected to decline over time, even with the most aggressive of interventions. In this project it was anticipated that the health status of the intervention group would decline less than it would have without intervention. Initial and follow-up assessment interviews of project patients revealed a lack of significant differences, reflecting the positive maintenance of health status and functional ability.

Due to the relatively short time of the intervention, significant reductions in physicians' office and hospital visits were not expected. Our experience parallels that of other projects presented in this book, which suggest that it takes 18 to 24 months before significant results can be seen. Nevertheless, in this project, the number of physician office visits for the more frail intervention group declined during the intervention period. By the end of the demonstration period, the rate of physician office visits by the intervention group was nearly as low as that of the comparison population. Hospital, emergency room, and hospital-based ambulatory care use also revealed positive trends. However, due to many changes within Med-Net, as well as changes in the larger managed health care market, it is difficult to attribute these results solely to the intervention. It is more accurate to conclude that the case management intervention was part of an overall strategy of cost control and improved productivity on the part of St. Joseph.

# Lessons Learned

Integration of case management into physicians' practices requires fostering physicians' "ownership" of case management, including involvement in program design and decision making. The involvement of physicians must begin on day one—during the initial program planning phase. Key areas of physician involvement in the Coordinated Care Partnership included determination of the patient selection criteria, design of the screening tool, and development of monitoring protocols/care pathways.

As the physicians began to trust and rely on the case managers, the process of centralized screening conducted by the case assistant became less effective. Also, adapting systems of ongoing communication to accommodate variations in physician preferences and practice patterns was crucial to the success of the project. Communicating the information gathered by case managers in patients' home settings to the physicians in a clear and concise manner was extremely important. This information facilitated valuable linkages between office-based and home and community-based care. The in-home assessment information proved to be particularly valuable to the physicians, as they generally saw patients only in the office or hospital and were not always fully aware of the patient's ability (or inability) to function at home, and what support was available to the patient. A variety of medical, social, and functional problems not previously identified by the physicians were initially identified through in-home assessments. These problems included differences between patient self-reports and physician observations, lack of medication compliance, and difficulties with self-management of chronic conditions.

Having employed both nurses and social workers as case managers, individually and in teams, we have learned that both professions are needed to provide comprehensive case management services—particularly for high-risk patients. It is crucial that all case managers, whether nurses or social workers, have experience in the provision of home and community-based services. Allocating case managers by physician practice aids in fostering interdisciplinary collaboration and trust between physicians and case managers. This is important for health care organizations, as they function in an environment in which facilitating collaboration among professionals of different disciplines can be challenging. However, organizations managing the care of large numbers of high-risk patients or patients with special needs may find that assigning case managers based on patient characteristics works better for the patients. For a patient with a complex chronic or terminal disease, an individual with expertise in that specific disease process may be better able to help the patient, as well as the physician, effectively manage the disease.

The Coordinated Care Partnership produced a number of positive organizational outcomes for St. Joseph Healthcare. The project created an increased awareness of issues related to geriatric care throughout our system. Closer collaboration between physicians and our health care system occurred, as well as a strengthening of teamwork and collaborative decision making among physicians and case managers. Additionally, the Coordinated Care Partnership contributed to St. Joseph's development of a continuum of patient care, strengthening our managed care expertise, particularly with regard to elders.


## Summary

Initiation of the Coordinated Care Partnership resulted in the development of closer working relationships with physicians, as well as an increased awareness of the issues they face in caring for their elderly patients. This project allowed St. Joseph to collaborate with physicians to provide a continuum of patient care, while also enhancing physicians' satisfaction. The elements of this continuum—screening, early identification and intervention, proactive monitoring, and consistent routine follow-up—have enabled targeted patients to maintain their health status and functional ability.

St. Joseph sees the development of the Coordinated Care Partnership as a strategic response that has helped our organization to adapt to many of the recent changes in health care, and to prepare for those yet to come. Medicare's rapid transition from a retroactive payment system to a prospective payment system, and the increase in managed care payer arrangements, have had a major effect on the way in which St. Joseph cares for elderly patients. These changes motivated St. Joseph to redesign inpatient discharge planning and social service functions, creating a system of inpatient, utilization-focused case management. The work of the in-patient case managers is concentrated on reducing length of stay, preventing readmissions, maximizing patients' recovery periods, and minimizing complication rates.

Through implementation of the Coordinated Care Partnership, case managers working in partnership with primary care physicians have been able to extend the physicians' practices into patients' homes. During acute episodes and exacerbations of chronic illness, case managers offer immediate assistance and coordinate with physicians to modify care regimens, schedule office visits, or arrange for hospitalization while a patient is still at a lower acuity level.

Case management functions as the hub of the St. Joseph Healthcare system, providing an interface between home-based and facility-based care. Ongoing contact with physicians and their office staffs regarding patients' progress at home and receipt of services fosters a continuum of care throughout the home, office, and hospital settings. The growth of complexity in the delivery of health care services has created the need for linkages between systems, for a mechanism that focuses on the individual patient and helps him or her navigate through the array of services, a mechanism that facilitates the delivery of quality care, and encourages the wise use of health care resources. The development of the Coordinated Care Partnership addresses these needs, by strengthening the integration of St. Joseph's provider network, and enabling our organization to respond effectively to the market forces of managed care.

# References

Anker-Unnever, L. & Netting, F.E. (1995). Coordinated care partnership: Case management with physician practices. *Journal of Case Management, 4*(1), 3–8.

Applebaum, R.A., Baxter, R., Callahan, J. J. & Day, S.L. (1985). Targeting services to chronically disabled elderly: The preliminary experiences of the National Long Term Care Channeling Demonstration. *Home Health Care Quarterly, 6*(2), 57–79.

Fahey, C.J. (1996). Social work education and the field of aging. *The Gerontologist, 36*(1), 36–41.

Netting, F.E. (1997). *Implementing the coordinated care partnership: A qualitative analysis* (Unpublished report available from author at Virginia Commonwealth University School of Social Work, Richmond, VA).

Netting, F.E. & Williams, F.G. (1995). Integrating case management into primary care physician practices. *Health and Social Work, 20*(2), 152–155.

Netting, F.E. & Williams, F.G. (1996). Case manager-physician collaboration: Implications for professional identity, roles and relationships. *Health and Social Work, 21*(3), 216–224.

Shearer, S., Simmons, W.J., White, M. & Berkman, B. (1995). Physician partnership project: Social work case management in primary care. *Continuum, 15* (4), 1, 3, 6–7.

Wasson, J. & Jette, A.M. (1993). Partnership between physicians and older adults. *Generations, 17* (3), 41–44.

Weil, M. & Karls, J.M. (1985). *Case management in human service practice.* San Francisco: Jossey-Bass.

Williams, F.G., Netting, F.E. & Kirkman-Liff, B.L. (1997). *Evaluation of St. Joseph Healthcare system Coordinated Care Partnership: Final report* (Unpublished report available from Arizona State University School of Social Work, Phoenix, Arizona).

# CHAPTER 9

# Cost-Effective Care Coordination in the Rural Physician's Office

*Carlton A. Hornung, Bernice Brewer,*
*and Millicent Stein**

The South Carolina Rural Geriatric Initiative Project (SC GRIP) was conducted jointly by the Appalachia III District of the South Carolina Department of Health and Environmental Control and the University of South Carolina School of Medicine, Division of Geriatrics. Funded by a 4-year grant from The John A. Hartford Foundation of New York, the purpose of SC GRIP was to improve the quality of health and primary medical care available to elders of rural areas, and to increase their satisfaction with care received. A second objective was to increase the professional and personal satisfaction that generalist physicians derive from treating rural elderly patients. GRIP introduced a new health care worker, a paraprofessional trained as a "geriatric technician," into the private practices of three groups of rural South Carolina physicians.

## Background

Providing quality medical care to residents of rural areas has long been a challenge to the medical community and a public policy concern (Michels, Hornung, Updike & Sheridan, 1993). Caring for rural elders is particularly difficult because their health care needs are great, while their personal and community resources are often limited. Nearly half of all older people in America with poverty- or below poverty-level incomes live in rural areas or

*We would like to thank Dr. G. Paul Eleazer, Michael D. Byrd, Dr. R. Bradford Whitney, and Dr. Thomas E. Brown Jr. for helpful comments and suggestions.

small towns, and an even larger proportion of these non-metropolitan elders relies exclusively on Medicare or a combination of Medicare and Medicaid to pay for health care. Moreover, rural elderly people report greater
physical impairments and more chronic illnesses than their urban counterparts, and a high proportion of them have multiple and complex chronic
conditions that are not amenable to "cure" (Coward, 1993). Further, their
medical conditions are often exacerbated by an array of non-medical factors such as poor education or financial and transportation problems
that limit access to primary health care. In addition, informal support
systems, such as church, family, and friends, are often non-existent or
insufficient in rural areas (Preston & Mansfield, 1984).

These complex needs can be frustrating for physicians, who are not
necessarily well prepared to recognize or deal with non-medical factors that
influence the health of their rural patients. Surveys have confirmed that
family and social issues are the most challenging problems faced by physicians caring for elderly patients (Williams & Connoly, 1990). These difficult
problems, coupled with limited medical resources, may contribute to why
physicians feel unable to deliver the quality of medical care they aspire to
provide in a rural practice. In turn, frustration and "burnout," along with
the limited financial rewards of caring for the poor, contribute to the vexing
problem of attracting and retaining physicians in rural areas.

When our project was designed, the 1990 census showed South Carolina to be a rural state with 11% of its population over the age of 65. In
recent decades the over-65 group increased in South Carolina 160% more
than than the national average. While South Carolina ranked 37th in the
proportion of older people in 1990, it is projected to rank about 18th in
the year 2020 (Tester, 1994). To address these issues, a new model for rural primary care was developed.

Four communities in the northwestern part of the state were selected; two for intervention by the geriatric technicians and two others as
comparison sites. Union, South Carolina, an intervention community
with two physician groups, had a population of 9,836 with 14.8% over
the age of 65 and a ratio of elderly patients to primary care physicians of
200 to 1. It is a small community that has always been dependent on cotton mills (now disappearing), and pulp wood farming and processing.
Each physician group in Union allocated 100 patients to the project and
housed 2 geriatric technicians each. Landrum, South Carolina, the other
community chosen as an intervention site, had a population of 2,347 that
included 18% elderly people and had a ratio of elderly patients to primary care physicians of 210 to 1. Situated at the foothills of the Appala-

chian Mountains, Landrum used to be dependent on cotton mills, but is increasingly becoming a part of the upscale "horse community" of Tryon and Columbus, North Carolina. Elderly residents of these communities find their small older homes in the midst of expensive horse farms. Their taxes are raised according to the neighborhood while their income diminishes. The single practice chosen in this community included a physician trained in geriatrics. This practice allocated 200 patients to the intervention and had two geriatric technicians assigned to its office.

Physicians' practices were chosen in two comparison communities with comparable populations and demographic profiles. Pacolet, South Carolina, is a group of several scattered communities situated at the intersection of two country roads, and Cowpens, South Carolina, was the site of an important battle of the American Revolution. Picturesque murals depicting the revolutionary armies cover the town buildings as one drives down Main Street. Each of these communities allocated 200 patients to serve as the comparison group, making a total of 800 project participants.

The SC GRIP differed from the other nine Hartford Generalist Physician Initiative projects in three important respects. First, while many of the other projects were located in metropolitan areas or had large hospital-based support, the SC GRIP was set in small towns with rural populations. Second, the physicians who participated were engaged exclusively in fee-for-service practices, as opposed to the mostly managed care settings of the majority of the other projects. Third, and most significantly, while the other projects relied on professionals such as physician assistants, nurse practitioners, or master's-level social workers to collaborate with physicians to enhance the care of elders, the SC GRIP used paraprofessionals called geriatric technicians to provide care coordination for rural elderly patients.

# The Geriatric Technician

## The Role of the Geriatric Technician

The geriatric technicians functioned as care coordinators under the direct supervision of the physicians. In the beginning they were called "geriatric specialists," but we came to believe that the term "technician" better described the position. They provided an interface between the physician, office staff, patient, patient's family, and the governmental and private agencies offering health and social services. Geriatric technicians were also an information source and contact person for the nurses and social workers in home health and other agencies.

The duties of the geriatric technician included (1) coordinating patients' medical services by scheduling appointments, reminding patients of appointments, arranging needed transportation, and occasionally even providing that transportation; (2) monitoring compliance with medication, diet, and other prescribed medical care; (3) arranging for needed non-medical and social services; (4) coordinating medical care with home health services; (5) screening for depression and dementia using standardized assessment tools; and (6) reducing the administrative burden on the physicians, patients, and office staff by assisting with the paperwork flow between service providers and payers, reception of patients, and routine filing.

Geriatric technicians contacted every patient by phone as needed, on at least a monthly basis. After the initial assessment home visits were made as needed, with each technician averaging 10 to 12 visits a month. They kept records of their contacts in the patient charts on special blue "intervention notes," where they listed the reason they had called or the topic that had been discussed. On the occasions when they provided transportation, they were reimbursed for mileage. In their small rural areas, the geriatric technicians were looked upon as neighbors and good Samaritans, so liability was never considered an issue.

In particular, those patients described as the "worried well," because they were calling the physicians many times a week for non-medical or insignificant reasons, were called proactively by the technicians. In the beginning, the technicians would call such patients every morning and say, " Dr.—— is concerned about you and asked me to call to check on how you are doing." As the patients began to feel more secure, the technicians would gradually reduce the number of calls to three and then two times a week, until the patients felt sure that the doctors had someone who looked out for them and whom they could call to "get the ear" of the doctor about their concern. Finally, the technicians cut back to routine monthly calls to these patients, just as they did for all the stable patients.

Another important role the geriatric technicians, assumed was that of "surrogate daughter" to patients whose families did not live in the area. They would keep in telephone or written contact with those families, and the families knew whom they could reach if the doctor were not available to talk to them or if they had a non-medical concern about their family members.

## Selection of the Geriatric Technicians

Input from physicians was sought in defining the criteria for selecting the geriatric technicians as well as defining the job parameters. The precarious financial viability and high failure rate of rural medical practices limit the ability of physicians in rural fee-for-service practices to employ expensive professionals. To enable the physicians to more fully "buy into" the project, they screened and chose their own geriatric technicians with the approval of the GRIP project director.

The geriatric technicians were paid by the physician with grant funds throughout the life of the project, but were eventually carried by office revenues after the project was completed. To accomplish this, the geriatric technician position's salary scale was designed to be comparable to that of clerical staff.

Experience as well as conversations with physicians practicing in rural areas clearly indicated that rural practices could not afford to hire nurse practitioners, physician assistants, or even registered nurses as care managers. Consequently, the project's geriatric nurse practitioner developed a curriculum to train individuals with a minimum of a high school education, who were self-motivated and had good "people skills," to be geriatric technicians.

In choosing to use paraprofessionals to coordinate the care of elderly patients, we were assuming that, for example,

> a person need not be specially trained in the complexities of geriatric pharmacology to participate in the elderly patient's drug therapy . . . [and that] it is not necessary for the many people caring for the elderly to understand how to calculate a specific medication dose. It is, however important that they understand the basic concepts of drug therapy and the significance that drug therapy will have on the patients and clients they care for. (Simonson, 1994, p. 11)

Four individuals were hired and began the training program. One trainee had been employed as a ward clerk in a hospital, while another had similar experience in a nursing home. Another had been a dental assistant, and a fourth had taken a medical secretary course, although her only work experience was in a textile mill.

## Training of the Geriatric Technicians

The training curriculum was developed by the project geriatric nurse practitioner and approved by the faculty in the Division of Geriatrics of the Department of Medicine at the University of South Carolina School of Medicine. It was designed to provide the geriatric technicians with the foundation needed to recognize and understand the common health problems of elderly patients, as well as to provide an awareness of the methods and resources available to address these problems. The initial focus of the technicians' training was on the aging process, functional losses associated with aging, and communication skills. However, a pre-test given at the time of hire indicated that none of the trainees had an understanding of how the human body functions. Consequently, training was modified to include a review of each body system and medical conditions common to older people.

Psychosocial issues that affect health were continuously emphasized and examples were given through case studies completed after each class. The day-to-day mechanics of recording medical information, ethical issues, ensuring confidentiality, interviewing skills, and the documentation of problems and treatment regimes were addressed on an ongoing basis. Site visits to local agencies and other area resources introduced the geriatric technicians to each agency, and alerted the agency staff that the geriatric technician would serve as a "point person" in the physician's office whom they could contact directly for information regarding individual patients. Finally, because the geriatric technicians would be making home visits to administer intake assessments, considerable time was devoted to developing interviewing skills through role play. The 15-week program involved six hours per week of lectures, case reports, and classroom discussions provided by social workers, a mental health nurse, a pharmacist, a physical therapist, a dietician, and the Department of Social Services.

There was some turnover in the geriatric technician position during the 4-year project, mostly due to family or health problems. Two of the replacements were hired while the training was being conducted, and they needed only additional make-up assistance. The third new geriatric technician was hired a year after the project began and had several tutorial sessions, a field trip to many agencies, and self-study of the extensive class handouts.

Support from peers and instructors through monthly continuing education meetings reinforced and updated the training. Much of the content of these classes was determined by the geriatric technicians themselves. This allowed them to exchange experiences and ideas, and to obtain feedback from their peers. In addition, the classes provided the opportunity to request other topics they felt they needed to increase their knowledge and/or remedy perceived weaknesses. A master's-level social worker conducted or helped plan these classes and made visits to some complex cases with the technicians. An important lesson learned from these meetings, both by project staff and by the geriatric technicians, was how very different each community and each physician's practice were and how these differences required a continuing and adaptable training program.

## Supervision of the Geriatric Technicians

Although geriatric technicians were under the direct supervision of the physicians, we always provided supervision and support. In Union, a home health nurse case manager who knew the area could be reached at all times and came by the offices on a frequent basis to review cases being followed and to make suggestions. In Landrum, the geriatric nurse practitioner from the project who lived in the area fulfilled the same role. In addition, the project director and the nurse practitioner made regular visits to the practices to confer with physicians and talk with office staff, while observing the geriatric technicians' documentation practices and progress. In the beginning these visits were monthly, but they were reduced to quarterly after the first year once the project was running smoothly.

# Role Development

The geriatric technicians consistently carried a caseload of approximately 125 patients, and as physicians assigned patients on a temporary or intermittent basis, their caseload was continually changing. They were in frequent communication with the physicians through notes, hallway conferences, and informal meetings. Periodic self-recorded time studies were conducted to track how the geriatric technicians were using their time relative to patients and the routine office tasks of reception and filing. The time studies revealed that as the project progressed, the technicians spent less time on clerical duties, usually just filling in if another employee called in sick. After being accepted by the staff (see Lessons Learned in this chapter), the geriatric technicians were referred patients by the nurses, receptionists and billing clerks, who were seeing different sides of the patients than the physicians.

The time studies also revealed significant differences in some of the ways different physicians used the geriatric technicians. One physician who had previously not been billing or documenting many of his visits had the technician accompany him on nursing home rounds, transcribe the dictation, and then submit the billing to assure that all records were complete and reconciled. Other physicians made the geriatric technicians responsible for home health billing. One practice delegated the oversight of screening charts for preventive care such as mammograms or pneumonia vaccine to the geriatric technician. In one practice, the geriatric technician became a member of the team providing a "mobile geriatric consultation service" to 55 network physicians in their primary care offices.

## Patient Selection Criteria

The project design called for a random selection of patients who were over the age of 65 and met one of three classifications: (1) the "worried well," who made weekly or more frequent calls to the physician; (2) the "chronically ill," who had a diagnosis of at least one chronic illness and met several risk criteria; or (3) the "frail elderly," who had had one hospitalization and/or admission to home health in the past year, and/or one or more chronic diseases, and/or one or more serious injuries within the past two years (e.g., hip fracture, etc.).

Soon after implementation the physicians dropped completely random selection in favor of selecting some patients who they felt would most benefit from the program. Other patients, especially those in the worried well category, were selected by the nurses or office staff, while still others were chosen at random. The fact that physicians designated some patients for services resulted in a higher percentage of intervention patients having complex medical problems or other health care needs relative to the comparison group (comparative analyses were adjusted accordingly). In addition, since increasing physician satisfaction was also a project objective, patients not meeting the inclusion criteria (e.g., a 35-year-old with multiple sclerosis) were followed if assigned by the physician, but these patients did not become a part of the project population.

As anticipated at the start of the project, case loss was significant. Over the 30-month course of the intervention, slightly more than half of the patients in both the intervention and comparison groups were lost to follow-up due principally to patients leaving the area or to mortality. At baseline, patients in the intervention group were approximately four years older than comparison patients and could independently perform fewer ADLs and IADLs. Intervention patients also scored lower on the mental status exam than did the comparison patients (Hornung, Brewer, Stein, Eleazer, Brown & Byrd, 1997).

## Patient Assessment

The intake assessment administered to each patient in both the intervention and comparison groups was a 32-page document that covered the Nottingham Quality of Life Scale (Hunt, McEwan & McKenna, 1985), the Geriatric Depression Scale (Hickie & Snowdon, 1987), a home safety assessment, an activities of daily living (ADL) and instrumental activities of daily living (IADL) deficit questionnaire, the Folstein Mini-Mental Status Exam (Pfeiffer, 1975), a health service utilization history, a consumer satisfaction survey, a health care rating survey, and the Caregiver Burden Scale (Macera, Baker, Jannerone, Davis & Stoskopf, 1993). Environmental risks (e.g., fall hazards, presence of smoke alarms) were also assessed. All project participants signed informed consent and release of information forms.

The intake assessment of intervention patients was conducted in their homes by the geriatric technicians, and by trained home health aides in the homes of the comparison patients. The intake assessment was not only a means of acquiring information to evaluate the success of the project, but also provided the geriatric technicians with the in-depth knowledge of each patient's functional status, limitations, and problems essential for effective care coordination. Scores from the ADL, IADL, mental status, and depression scales were entered on their intervention notes as a reference for all staff serving the patient.

The physicians caring for the intervention patients also obtained valuable information from these assessments. At times this led them to alter their treatment strategies, such as changing medications for some patients while referring others to home health or other agencies. Further, responses to the depression scale identified many patients in need of treatment who had not been previously identified.

The geriatric technicians were initially very apprehensive about making home visits and conducting the assessment interviews. They were assured that they would not have to make visits on their own until they felt comfortable and that until then they would be accompanied by an instructor or a staff nurse. Generally after only a few in-home assessments, they felt sufficiently comfortable to proceed independently.

The geriatric technicians developed a great sensitivity to the patients' problems and needs while making these initial home visits. As one said:

> I was very surprised at what I was seeing. I've cried when I came from many home visits. It's heartbreaking to see how some patients live. I just didn't know. When they came to the office, they were clean and dressed like they were going to church, so you don't see the other side. You don't see how they live. When they come in to see the doctor, they don't tell him they can't afford a meal today. They only share their aches and pains. It's through what I've learned by making home visits that I have been able to help the doctor help patients the most.

The geriatric technicians identified many problems during the intake assessments. One common problem involved the use of prescription drugs, including polypharmacy and patients' misunderstanding of directions. A number of patients were found not to have refilled prescriptions when the supply was depleted a week or so before a scheduled visit to the physician, because they feared they would waste money if the doctor changed the medication or dose. This alerted the geriatric technicians to schedule return visits a few days before a patient's medication supply was depleted. Geriatric technicians identified a related problem. Some patients were not filling prescriptions because they could not afford to buy the medicine and at the same time pay the rent and buy groceries. A year into the project, each geriatric technician had 40 to 50 patients enrolled in the drug programs for indigents offered by various pharmaceutical companies. Tickler files told them when the patients would be out of medication, and after asking the physician if the patient would continue on that drug, they reordered it to avoid a lapse in therapy.

Geriatric technicians also monitored the physicians' plan of care designed for each patient, conferred with families living in distant cities, and conducted additional home visits to monitor dietary, medication, and treatment compliance.

# Evaluation

## Impact of the Geriatric Technician

While the geriatric technicians experienced some frustrations with the inequities of the health care and social services system and their inability to alleviate all the problems and suffering identified, they did experience significant successes with individual patients. Three such successes are worth noting, although many similar incidents occurred during the life of the project. One involved an elderly man who did not have enough money to pay for his prescriptions and also buy the firewood needed to heat his home. The geriatric technician identified the problem, found a source in the community to donate the firewood, and also found assistance to pay for the medicine. When the geriatric technician alerted the physician to the situation, the physician wrote a prescription for an equivalent but less expensive drug, which also helped reduce the financial problem.

A second case involved an elderly woman with severe diabetic neuropathy who suffered great difficulty in walking. The driveway to her home was several hundred feet long, up hill, and covered with rutted gravel. Each day, the woman nearly fell several times on her trek to pick up her mail and newspaper. The geriatric technician wrote letters to the postmaster and the newspaper publisher and had the physician sign them. As a result, the woman's mail and daily paper were delivered to her door. Perhaps this was a small matter, but it was a major factor in improved safety and quality of life for this elderly woman, which may have permitted her to remain alone in her own home for a longer period of time.

A third instance involved the "town grouch." He had some beginning dementia and continually either changed physicians or was dropped by doctors because he refused to follow directions, became angry with the office staff and the physician for "not helping" him, or refused to pay the bill or cooperate with filling out insurance forms. The geriatric technician saw to it that she became the one who contacted him on a regular basis; he also called her directly when he had a problem. As a result, his medical regime was followed and he no longer had disputes with medical staff.

Coordinating the health care for geriatric patients can potentially affect their lives in a number of ways. Several outcome measures were studied over the course of the intervention by the geriatric technicians. Those measures related to the patients' health and well-being were functional status, quality of life and mental health, the use of health services, and patients' satisfaction with the quality of health care they were receiving.

The patients' functional status was assessed in terms of their ability to independently perform the ADLs and IADLs as well as their performance on the Folstein Mini-Mental Status Exam. These measures were collected at baseline, at 9 and 18 months on both patient cohorts, and again at 30 months on the initial cohort.

Over the course of the intervention, the patients followed from intake to exit whose care was coordinated by a geriatric technician showed significantly less decline in the number of ADLs they could perform without assistance (1.30) than did the comparison patients (1.65; <0.05). With regard to IADLs, patients whose care was coordinated by a geriatric technician showed no significant decline over the 30-month course of the study in the number they could perform without assistance (p>0.05). In contrast, there was a significant decline in the number of IADLs that comparison patients could independently perform (p<0.05).

Change in performance on the Folstein Mini-Mental Status Exam was greatest among patients in the comparison group. While the number of cognitively impaired increased from 29% to 33% in the intervention group, the increase in the prevalence of impairment was twice as large among comparison patients over the project period. Together these results suggest that introducing a geriatric technician into the physician's health care team can contribute significantly to maintaining the functional status of rural elderly patients.

The impact of the geriatric technician on the patient's quality of life is also important. Over the course of the project, patients who were served by a geriatric technician reported significantly fewer feelings of social isolation than did patients in the comparison group (p<0.05). At the same time, the number of symptoms of depression reported by intervention patients declined significantly while symptom levels among the patients in the comparison group remained the same. These findings suggest that having a member of the health care team who has time to interact with patients and encourages them to ask for assistance can increase the patients' sense of social belonging and improve their quality of life.

In an era of cost containment, the contribution of the geriatric technician to the efficient utilization of health care services is critical. Chart audits for the year prior to the introduction of the geriatric technician and chart audits of the final six months of the study revealed important changes in the utilization of physicians' services. Mean visits per year to physicians declined in both groups, but the decrease was 68% greater among intervention patients. This decrease reflects significantly fewer visits to medical specialists and occurred in spite of an increase in the rate of visits to their primary care physicians, especially for check-ups. This shift in the source of care was particularly great among patients in the intervention group who also made significantly more frequent use of telephone contacts with the physician's office and the geriatric technician. The increased rate of contact with the primary care physician by intervention patients whose care was coordinated by a geriatric technician may have contributed to the 28% decline in visits to the emergency room. No decline in emergency room use was seen among patients in the comparison group. This shift in the use of hospital and specialty medical services to a greater reliance on primary care physicians and their health care teams is likely to yield significant cost savings.

Our intake assessment included a number of questions about perceptions of the quality of health care at the start of the project. By the project's end, after the introduction of the geriatric technician, the percent of patients rating their overall health care as excellent or very good was 15 to 20 points higher in the intervention group than in the comparison group. Many of the patients sent notes of appreciation to the physicians. For example, one patient wrote:

> May I say that a person of Ms. —— caliber is imperative to act as a liaison between doctor and patient. I could call her at any time with my problems and she would talk to the doctor immediately. I feel very safe in having someone always there for me. I hope that there will be a way that such a marvelous service can one day be a part of every doctor's office.

Similarly, the daughter of a patient who had drugs for the indigent ordered by the geriatric technician wrote:

> You'll never know the feeling of relief I had last night when I was organizing Mother's medicine. We are very thankful that there are people like N —— who work hard for the elderly so families can keep them at home. —— is the most important person in the office outside of the doctors.

Many lengthy notes of appreciation and thanks have been received throughout the project, and many positive comments were reported by participating physicians. Both let us know that for many patients and families, the services of the geriatric technicians were highly valued.

## Physician Satisfaction

The eight physicians in the intervention practices all came to appreciate the role of the geriatric technician. For example, one physician stated, "When I see one of those patient's records who are receiving intervention, I look to the geriatric technician's notes and read every word. I find a lot of valuable information there." Another reported that the geriatric technician had solved a frustrating problem involving communication with a particular government office by personally channeling the messages and paperwork back and forth between the physician and the correct person in the agency. Although one or two physicians initially ignored the geriatric technicians, these same physicians said they received enough positive feedback from patients to prompt them to refer other cases to the technician. Within a year, these physicians used them as much as the other physicians. Most importantly, the physicians told us that the geriatric technicians made them aware of how critical it is to know the patient's economic and social situation in order to achieve the best possible medical care. Of the eight physicians, the geriatrician in the research project made the most productive use of the geriatric technician.

In an attempt to judge the cost-effectiveness of the geriatric technician, time studies were conducted comparing the geriatrician in the intervention group and a non-project physician seeing younger patients who did not use the geriatric technician. The time studies showed that by having a geriatric technician in the room while the physician explained the treatment plan to the patient or family and leaving the geriatrician technician with the patient and family to make sure they understood the treatment plan while the physician saw other patients before returning to answer any remaining questions resulted in increased physician productivity when measured in terms of income generated.

# Lessons Learned

We learned many lessons from developing and implementing GRIP, most related to staffing. First, the individuals selected as geriatric technicians need to be self-directed and to have good "people skills." Their training should include exposure to real situations as well as much role playing and case studies. Their introduction to the work site needs to be well thought out and prepared, and should occur after their formal didactic preparation is complete. Otherwise, they are looked upon as coming into the office without expertise or credentials. Key to the geriatric technician's successful functioning is the direction of a social worker or nurse with geriatric experience or training. Ongoing education, close supervision, and support are vital components of the technician's education, as are home visits which enhance professional judgment, as well as patient care and satisfaction.

The staff turnover in the geriatric technician position made us realize that training must be replicable for later use in one-on-one instruction. This means that video instruction or eventually a CD-ROM interactive computer program would be useful to accompany individual instruction.

One of the most important lessons we learned was that it is imperative that physicians know how to use the geriatric technicians. As paraprofessionals the geriatric technicians took their direction directly from the physicians, and yet the physicians needed to hear and understand their patients' psychosocial problems from the geriatric technicians to be able to refer them for care coordination. Most primary care physicians are not used to working on a team with social workers, nurses, and therapists. They either do not pick up on the psychosocial problems of their patients, or do not routinely address them because they are not aware of the resources available to help patients. The role and responsibilities of the geriatric technician as well as her working relationship with the physician evolved over the 3-year course of the project. Physicians gained appreciation for what the geriatric technician could contribute to the health care of their patients. Equally importantly, the geriatric technicians developed skill at identifying patients' problems and needs and learned what information was useful and important to convey to the physician and how to assist the patient in complying with the treatment plan.

Probably the most disappointing venture we undertook in GRIP was a failed attempt to recruit and train a community volunteer group that would assist the technicians by providing transportation and friendly visiting, for example. In an effort to get community groups involved, larger churches were contacted in one town selected, and a noticeable ad accompanied by a lengthy article was placed in the local paper. There was no response! We decided that the problem was in part that nearly all younger people today work, so there is no one left at home with time for volunteer work, and in part because in a rural area most of the people who could volunteer are elders themselves who may fear spending time with frail elderly persons.

# Summary

There are at least four reasons for using geriatric technicians in a primary physician's office. First, we found that physicians view the geriatric technicians as making a significant contribution to the quality of medicine. Second, our data suggest that the geriatric technicians can effectively complete many of the tasks that previously consumed physicians' time. Therefore, the increase in physicians' own productivity and efficiency more than offsets the labor costs of the geriatric technician. Third, an aging population and changes in health care financing (particularly changes that affect the care of elderly persons living in areas that are rural or under-served by physicians) enable the geriatric technician to become an income-producer within the practice. Fourth, a geriatric technician can raise the degree of patient satisfaction and comfort, and hence retention. As a result of their positive impact, the geriatric technicians continued to be employed in essentially the same role with their salary paid out of practice revenues after the grant funding ended.

# References

Coward, R.T. (1993). *Health services for rural elderly.* New York: Springer Publishing Company.

Hickie, C. & Snowdon, J. (1987). Depression scales for the elderly: GDS, Gillard, Zung. *Clinical Gerontology, 6,* 51–53.

Hornung, C.A., Brewer, B.M., Stein, M.D., Eleazer, G.P., Brown, T.E. & Byrd, M.D. (1997). The South Carolina Geriatric Rural Initiative Project. *Journal of the South Carolina Medical Association 93* (7) (July), 248–254.

Hunt, S.M., McEwan, J. & McKenna, S.P. (1985). Measuring health status: A new tool for clinicians and epidemiologists. *JR CollGen Practice, 35,* 185–188.

Macera, C.A., Baker, E.D., Jannerone, R.J., Davis, D.R. & Stoskopf, C.H. (1993). A measure of perceived burden among caregivers. *Evaluation and the Health Professions, 16,* 204–211.

Michels, P.J., Hornung, C.A., Updike, J. & Sheridan, D.P. (1993). Factors which discriminate rural and urban family physicians practicing in South Carolina. *Journal of the South Carolina Medical Association, 2,* 80–82.

Pfeiffer, E. (1975). A short portable mental status questionnaire for the assessment of organic brain deficits in elderly patients. *Journal of the American Geriatrics Society, 23,* 433–441.

Preston, D.B. & Mansfield, P.K. (1984). An exploration of stressful life events, illnesses and coping among the rural elderly. *The Gerontologist, 24,* 490–492.

Simonson, W. (1994). Geriatric drug therapy. Who are the stakeholders? *Generations, 18,* 7–12.

Tester, D.M. (1993). *Office of Research and Statistics report: South Carolina's population projections: 1993–2020.* (Available from the State Budget and Control Board, Columbia, SC.)

Williams, M.E. & Connoly, N.K. (1990). What practicing physicians in North Carolina rate their most challenging geriatric medicine concern. *Journal of the American Geriatrics Society, 38,* 123–134.

# CHAPTER 10

# How Understanding the "Patient's World" Can Improve Geriatric Care in Physicians' Busy Practice Settings

*John H. Wasson and Anne M. Jette*

More than two decades ago, Starfield (1973) reminded clinicians that medical practices achieve the best outcomes when they are responsive to patients' needs and environments. The provocative question posed by Starfield was, "How can busy clinicians be sure that they truly understand their patients' world?"

In 1983, investigators from Dartmouth Primary Care Cooperative Network, referred to as COOP, documented how clinicians inadequately understood issues that really mattered to their patients (Nelson et al., 1983). When more than 1,000 primary care patients reported their levels of emotional functioning, physicians' ratings for the severely impaired patients agreed only 20% of the time. This substantial discrepancy stimulated our primary care network to develop simple, reliable measures of patient function (Nelson, Landgraf, Hays, Wasson & Kirk, 1990). These measures, available in more than twenty languages, are now used worldwide as patient screening tools in busy office practices (Nelson, Wasson, Johnson & Hays, 1996).

In this chapter, we describe a project funded by The John A. Hartford Foundation entitled Community Centers of Excellence for the Aging (CCEAs). We designed and implemented CCEAs to bring the busy physician clinician into closer contact with the "patient's world."

## Background

Work by our group and others has led to the standardization of measures that are most important to patients and are used to improve patient outcomes (Nelson, Mohr, Batalden & Plume, 1996; Nelson & Wasson, 1994).

When simple measures are used to assess health status, such as those developed by the Dartmouth COOP Charts, the information can be readily used to "feed forward" (physician can immediately respond to patient need) and "feed back" (physician provides education to patient and caregiver). The benefits of the feed-forward and feed-back systematic approach are that the educational materials help the patient and caregiver to better understand the problem, problems can be better managed by the physician, interactions create a patient/physician partnership, and patient outcomes are improved more quickly.

The elements of medical practice necessary to improve patient outcomes have been widely studied (VonKorff, Gruman, Schaefer, Curry & Wagner, 1997; Wagner, 1996). Perhaps most essential for elderly persons and patients with chronic conditions are continuity among and meaningful two-way communication with their health care providers. In our controlled study of patients 55 years of age or older, continuity reduced costs of care by almost 30% and emergent hospitalizations by 50% (Wasson et al., 1984). From our study of provider-initiated follow-up phone calls to elder persons in their homes, we learned that we could reduce mortality and improve function for the sickest patients while having about 20% fewer clinic visits, 14% fewer medications, and 28% fewer hospital days (Wasson, Gaudette, Whaley & Sauvigne, 1992).

Increasing enrollment of older persons in managed care and Medicare risk plans is stimulating the examination of outpatient strategies to improve care (Campion, 1995; Moore & Siu, 1996; Reuben et al., 1996; Wagner, 1996; Wasson & Jette, 1993). Attributes of successful programs include standardized patient assessment tools, effective patient-provider communication, and methods to improve patient and caregiver understanding of specific problems and self-management techniques (Kaplan, Greenfield & Ware, 1989; Rubenstein et al., 1995; Wagner, 1996; Wagner, Austin & VonKorff, 1996; Wasson & Jette, 1993). Although the specific processes of care that account for the positive results of comprehensive geriatric assessment are not well characterized (Reuben, Fishman, McNabney & Wolde-Tsadik, 1996) direct control of patient care and follow-up are known to be critical factors (Stuck, Siu, Wieland, Adams & Rubenstein, 1993).

## Rationale

The Dartmouth COOP Research Team's rationale for this project was stimulated by the growing literature on how to better understand the "patient's world" and respond to their needs. Unlike the other projects described in this book, the CCEA did not use either a professional or a paraprofessional colleague as a collaborative intervention agent. Instead, our model sought to enhance physician practice by linking the physician and patient directly via patient-supplied personal and medical information and physician-supplied educational material.

We believed that a community office practice directly controls patient care and follow-up, and is in an ideal position to foster patient communication and deliver education more broadly and at a lower cost than a comprehensive geriatric assessment team. However, a busy clinician seldom has the resources to perform standardized assessments and consistently tailor care and education to individual patient needs. We nonetheless asked, "What might be the impact on geriatric care if the busy clinician were able to do this?" and we designed an approach to address this question.

## Practice Selection and Project Design

We began by mailing an invitation to participate in the CCEA project to 134 general internal medicine and family practitioner physicians who worked within a 35-mile radius of one rural, one suburban, and one urban community in New Hampshire. Forty-five physicians (including 27 family practitioners and 18 internists) in 22 practices agreed to participate. Each practice provided us with a list of their patients age 70 or older seen by a participating physician during the previous year, excluding patients residing in nursing home facilities.

The 45 participating physicians (39 males and 6 females) averaged 43 years of age. To minimize possible biases related to geographic location, practices were randomized after stratifying by size and specialty within each of the three areas (rural, urban, suburban), and were assigned within each stratum to the CCEA intervention or to usual care.

Examination and understanding of each practice's unique system for organizing care, as well as a good knowledge of interrelationships of employees' roles, is critical to effectively plan an individualized improved care approach that will be efficient and beneficial to both the practice and patients (Wasson et al., 1992). For example, in one practice the receptionist may hold the administrative key to organizing care. In another, the responsible individual might be a nurse. In yet another, there may be no such persons. The size (e.g., number of employees and services provided) and type (e.g., solo, partnership, group, fee-for-service, or managed care) of practice are also factors that will affect the responsibilities and functions of the overall system of care.

Learning who does what, when, and how, reduces misunderstandings and assumptions about roles and responsibilities, and facilitates the incorporation of new approaches. Our project team consulted with the office employees and care providers of each intervention practice, and developed a practice profile using the information they gave us to learn about their methods of providing care to elderly patients.

## Intervention Design

A patient panel typically has acute, preventive, and chronic needs (Batalden et al., 1997). Physicians' management of patients' chronic illness (e.g., asthma), and preventive needs (e.g., mammograms) is the easiest to describe, because for certain conditions a physician will generally follow a protocol. Though physicians' practice styles vary, there likely is little variation in managing a straightforward chronic condition or preventive need. Exceptions will arise depending on the acuity, complexity, or multiplicity of problems or conditions.

We used the following panel management process to design a better strategy to measure and improve geriatric care. It is important to emphasize, however, that the following steps involved small-scale pilot testing based on trial and error. Furthermore, we implemented an approach to determine the feasibility for a multi-site test of effectiveness and potential replication after the project period ended (Wasson, Jette, Johnson, Mohr & Nelson, 1997).

Using a workshop format, physicians and staff identified specific areas for improvement in geriatric care and wrote measurable objectives. Each person, whose roles within the practice varied, listed each decision he or she made and action he or she took to manage a "typical" elderly patient's chronic and preventive problems during a follow-up visit. Participants then developed flow charts to illustrate the process so that all the individuals involved in the total process of care were represented. The flow charts for each practice showed areas of duplication and inefficiency. Ideas were generated to improve patient care and to avoid failures in care.

Other flow charts were developed for each office practice system routine protocols, such as identifying all the patients' medications, assessing physical fitness of patients over 70, identifying patients without advance directives, and educating elderly women to improve compliance with gynecological cancer prevention guidelines. Beginning at the point at which the patient called to set up an appointment or to ask a question, came to the office to see the physician, or made a routine visit (e.g., blood pressure checks, immunizations, blood tests, etc.) that did not require seeing the physician, flow charts mapped out the process by which a typical response from the office practice occurred.

After completing this exercise, an overarching issue was obvious: the need to link patient-based information with an immediate clinical response (feed forward). If done well, patients and clinicians would receive direct and immediate benefits (feedback). The process would promote the patient-provider partnership and lead to improved outcomes of care most desired by the patient. In this partnership process, the clinician would become more aware of his or her patients' world. At the same time, data would be collected for the benefit of future patients and applied clinical research.

## Intervention Activities

Project staff mailed a 30-item assessment questionnaire about geriatric health and health care to intervention patients in their homes. The questionnaire was repeated 15 months later in order to measure changes in patients' responses and to direct physician's attention to new patient problems or concerns. This questionnaire was a first step in learning about the patient's world from the patient's perspective.

Intervention patients who returned a completed geriatric assessment questionnaire were mailed an 80-page educational booklet designed to provide patients with a better understanding of common geriatric problems and their self-management. The booklet was written in large print and in non-technical language and contained an index. A cover letter (generated by computer and signed by the patient's physician) provided a personalized summary of clinically significant responses, such as being very bothered with emotional problems, along with recommended sections in the booklet that would address specific individual needs. The sections in the booklet were

- Advance Directives (Living Wills)
- Assistive Devices (e.g., hearing aids, canes, walkers, wheelchairs)
- Confusion and Memory
- Constipation
- Daily Activities, Caregiving, and Support
- Eating Well
- Emotional Care
- Exercise
- Eye Care

- Preventing Falls and Accidents
- Foot Care
- Making a Medical Decision
- Hearing Care
- Medications and Overall Health
- Pain
- Immunizations
- Sleep Problems
- Oral Care
- Urinary Trouble

Recipients of the booklet—both patients and their family members—were instructed to bring it with them to scheduled office visits with their physician.

During the project period, all patients received periodic updates to the booklet, as well as additional education about advance directives, making a health decision, physical exercise, and medications. Patients were also given information about their health and well-being compared to others participating in the project. When they talked with their physicians, they could ask questions about anything they did not understand.

Patient responses to the questionnaires were summarized, printed, and mailed to each intervention physician. The summaries highlighted substantial functional problems and patients' perceptions of previous attention to these problems. Physicians incorporated these summaries into the patient's medical records and discussed results with the patients during the office visits. The patient's self-report of health care, needs, and perceptions of care received, and the education and information have obvious benefits when reviewed by attentive physicians who want to understand the patient's world. A doctor-patient partnership is established, resulting in better and more frequent communication. As a result, greater awareness and management of problems and issues can occur.

Updates on patients' health and health care, as reported in follow-up questionnaires that were mailed to patients to learn whether additional education and information made a difference, were also mailed to physicians' practices by the Dartmouth COOP Research Team. As with office staff, frequent communication between the Dartmouth COOP Research Team, the physicians, and office staff was maintained by letter, telephone, and meetings at the office practice.

The Dartmouth COOP Approach for Improving Patient Care is summarized in Figure 10.1. Based on an open systems perspective, pa-

**FIGURE 10.1**

The Dartmouth COOP Approach for Improving Patient Care

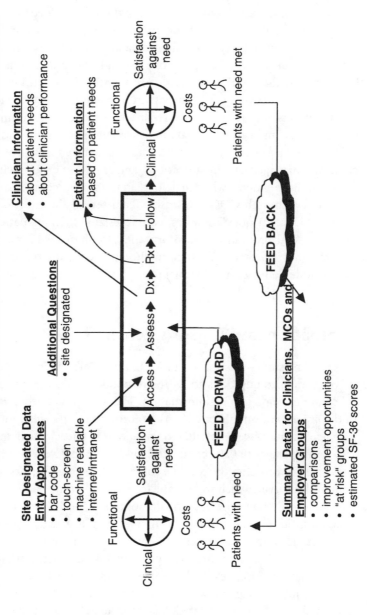

tients in need enter the system as illustrated on the left of the figure. The information they provide (clinical, functional, financial) is fed-forward to physicians, as patients complete self-assessment questionnaires. Standard assessments (along with site-specific questions added) are computerized, thus site-designated data entry approaches are shown in the upper left corner of our figure. Assessment data are reviewed by clinicians and discussed with patients as they move through the system. On the right hand side of the figure new needs are identified, beginning the cycle again. In the process of clinician-patient interaction trends are identified across patients, physicians receive feedback in the form of summary data that provide comparisons, reveal improvement opportunities, identify at-risk groups, and estimate scores. This aggregated feedback provides busy clinicians, managed care organizations, and employer groups with the big picture of how patients who participate in the system compare.

The Dartmouth COOP Research Team served the function of providing assessment questionnaires, computerizing them as patients filled them out, and providing that information to physicians. This information system was provided for busy medical practices and framed what clinicians were doing with individual patients in a broader geriatric context.

## Evaluation and Lessons Learned

The baseline survey was mailed to 5,232 potentially eligible patients. This survey contained questions about the respondents' health, previous medical care, and demographic information. The survey included a description of the project and an informed consent form indicating willingness to participate. Incentives were not offered to patients to participate in the project. Fifty-eight percent (3,050) completed the survey and were enrolled in the project. Two years after the baseline survey, patients were mailed a final patient health survey, which was completed by 1,651 participants.

Table 10.1 shows the baseline demographic, health, and care process characteristics for the 1,651 (819 intervention, 832 usual care) patients who completed the final survey. As a group, patients averaged 78 years of age; 65% were female; more than one-third lived alone. Randomization of physician practices resulted in some dissimilarities between the intervention and usual care patients. Usual care patients were older, more often female, and better educated. Self-reported clinical problems, overall health, hospital use, and measures of patient satisfaction with medical care were similar for the two groups.

**TABLE 10.1**

Baseline Characteristics of CCEA Patients
Who Completed the Final Survey, by Group (N=1,651)

| Characteristics | Usual Care Group (n=832) | Intervention Group (n=819) | p |
|---|---|---|---|
| **Demographics** | | | |
| average age in years | 79 | 77 | <.001 |
| women | 68% | 62% | .02 |
| live alone | 39% | 36% | .20 |
| high school or greater education | 72% | 67% | .02 |
| have money for more than the essentials | 65% | 65% | .90 |
| **Health** | | | |
| in fair or poor health | 19% | 19% | .90 |
| average score on CPA scale* | 2.0 | 1.9 | .40 |
| with any limits in IADL† | 24% | 20% | .09 |
| **Care process** | | | |
| hospitalized in previous 6 months | 10% | 9% | .40 |
| state medical care could be better | 27% | 32% | .09 |

*Common Problems of Aging Scale (CPA) rates how much the respondent is bothered, with ranges from 1 (never) to 5 (always).

†Instrumental Activities of Daily Living (IADL) consist of transporting self, preparing meals, performing housework, and handling finances.

Our results clearly indicate that patients exposed to the intervention were more likely than usual care patients to report improved medical care. Clinical problems and difficulties with all functional problems, including physical and daily activity limits, emotional problems, and social needs improved. Intervention patients also reported both better understanding of prevention of threats to their health, such as falls, and assistance with thinking and memory problems. The strategy appeared to have similar impacts for persons age 80 and over or in fair or poor health at the time of randomization.

In all cases, the intervention group, where patients and providers received feedback about their health care needs, showed a trend toward improvement over those receiving standard care. However, these results were significantly improved among the patients who recalled the discussion and interaction with their physician on these issues. Results indicate that a standard, easy-to-implement clinical improvement for elderly patients of primary care physicians can improve health outcomes. Detailed results of the project findings are being published elsewhere (Wasson, Nelson & Jette, in press).

The strategy was most effective for those patients who recalled that the professional staff had discussed the reports and information with them. Ninety-three percent of the intervention patients recalled receiving written materials tailored to their needs, and 74% of those patients stated that they had read 3 or more of the 20 sections of the booklet about common geriatric issues. At the end of the 2-year intervention period, 187 (23%) intervention patients remembered that their doctor or someone else in the office had specifically discussed the written materials with them. We found that improved communication had a large and positive impact on the outcomes of care; enhanced understanding, function, and prevention were particularly evident for those patients who recalled having discussed the written materials with a health professional.

The literature indicates that ongoing communication, understanding the patient's world, and making practice responsive to the patient are critical determinants of positive patient outcomes. While our approach supported these points, our results also had limitations in that both intervention and control group physicians provided high levels of continuity of care for their patients, possibly causing us to underestimate the impact of the intervention. Also, had we known how difficult it was for patients to remember specific instructions from physicians and clinical staff, we would have looked more closely at the importance of a patient's ability to recall the feedback received from physicians and staff. The intervention was based heavily upon communication between physicians, office staff, and patients, and we observed that this interactive feedback can not be used to influence the patient's world if the patient does not recall the messages given to him or her.

On-site generation of patient assessments and reports would facilitate doctor-patient communication at a much lower cost than this project's reliance on the mail. We are now using different technologies to make feed-forward and feed-back even more timely and less costly to collect (Wasson, Jette, Johnson, Mohr & Nelson, 1997). With the generous support of The John A. Hartford Foundation, the entire approach is being further tested and refined for disadvantaged and Spanish-speaking populations. We have also adapted this approach for teenagers, adult populations, and dialysis patients.

## Summary

The CCEA project, a simple system of geriatric care, was designed to incorporate high-quality planned geriatric care into everyday practice. We documented that this easily replicable strategy for elderly patients of primary care physicians could improve a broad range of outcomes. This approach serves medical practice by facilitating patient care and "front-line" improvement at a reasonable cost.

## References

Batalden, P.B., Mohr, J.J., Nelson, E.C., Plume, S.K., Baker, G.R., Wasson, J.H., Stolz, P.K., Splaine, M.E. & Wisniewski, J.J. (1997). Continually improving the health and value of health care for a population of patients: The panel management process. *Quality Management in Health Care, 5*(3), 41–51.

Campion, E.W. (1995). New hope for home care. *New England Journal of Medicine, 333*(18), 1213–1214.

Kaplan, S.H., Greenfield, S. & Ware, J.E. (1989). Assessing the effects of physician-patient interactions on the outcomes of chronic disease. *Medical Care, 3* (Suppl.), 5110–5127.

Moore, A.A. & Siu, A.L. (1996). Screening for common problems in ambulatory elderly: Clinical confirmation of a screening instrument. *American Journal of Medicine, 110,* 438–443.

Nelson, E., Conger, B., Douglass, R., Gephart, D., Kirk, J., Page, R., Clark, A., Stone, K., Wasson, J. & Zubkoff, M. (1983). Functional health status levels of primary care patients. *Journal of the American Medical Association, 249*(24), 3331–3337.

Nelson, E.C., Landgraf, J.M., Hays, R.D., Wasson, J.H. & Kirk, J.W. (1990). The functional status of patients: How can it be measured in physicians' offices? *Medical Care, 28*(12), 1111–1126.

Nelson, E.C. & Wasson, J.H. (1994, July-August). Using patient-based information to rapidly redesign care. *Healthcare Forum Journal, 37*(4), 25–29.

Nelson, E.C., Mohr, J.J., Batalden, P.B. & Plume, S.K. (1996). Improving health care, part I: The clinical value compass. *Joint Commission on Accreditation of Healthcare Organizations, 22*(4), 243–258.

Nelson, E.C., Wasson, J.H., Johnson, D.J. & Hays, R.D. (1996). In B. Spilker (Ed.), *Quality of life and pharmacoeconomics in clinical trials* (pp. 161–168). Philadelphia: Lippincott-Raven.

Reuben, D.B., Fishman, L.K., McNabney, M. & Wolde-Tsadik, G. (1996). Looking inside the black box of comprehensive geriatric assessment: A classification system for problems, recommendations, and implementation strategies. *Journal of the American Geriatrics Society, 44*, 835–838.

Reuben, D.B., Hirsch, S.H., Frank, J.C., Maly, R.C., Schlesinger, M.S., Weintraub, N. & Yancey, S. (1996). The prevention for elderly persons (PEP) program: A model of municipal and academic partnership to meet the needs of older persons for preventive services. *Journal of the American Geriatric Society, 44*, 1394–1398.

Rubenstein, L.V., McCoy, J.M., Cope, D.W., Barrett, P.A., Hirsch, S.H., Messer, K.S. & Young, R.T. (1995). Improving patient quality of life with feedback to physicians about functional status. *Journal of General Internal Medicine, 10*, 607–614.

Starfield, B. (1973). Health services research: A working model. *New England Journal of Medicine, 289*, 132–136.

Stuck, A.E., Siu, A.L., Wieland, G.D., Adams, J. & Rubenstein, L.Z. (1993). Comprehensive geriatric assessment: A meta-analysis of controlled trials. *The Lancet, 342*, 1032–1036.

VonKorff, M., Gruman, J., Schaefer, J., Curry, S.J. & Wagner, E.H. (1997). Collaborative management of chronic illness. *Annals of Internal Medicine, 127*, 1097–1102.

Wagner, E.H. (1996). The promise and performance of HMOs in improving outcomes in older adults. *Journal of the American Geriatric Society, 44*, 1251–1257.

Wagner, E.H., Austin, B.T. & VonKorff, M. (1996). Improving outcomes in chronic illness. *Managed Care Quarterly, 4*(2), 12–25.

Wasson, J.H., Sauvigne, A.E., Mogielnicki, R.P., Frey, W., Sox, C.H., Gauderre, C. & Rockwell, A. (1984). Continuity of outpatient care in elderly men. *Journal of the American Medical Association, 252*, 2413–2417.

Wasson, J.H., Gaudette, C., Whaley, F. & Sauvigne, A. (1992). Telephone care as a substitute for routine clinic follow-up. *Journal of the American Medical Association, 267*(13), 1788–1793.

Wasson, J.H., Keller, A., Rubenstein, L.V., Hays, R.D., Nelson, E. & Johnson, D. (1992). Benefits and obstacles of health status assessment in ambulatory settings: The clinician's point of view. *Medical Care, 30* (5, suppl.), MS24–MS49.

Wasson, J.H. & Jette, A.M. (1993). Partnerships between physicians and older adults. *Generations, 7*(3), 41–44.

Wasson, J.H., Jette, A.M., Johnson, D.J., Mohr, J.J. & Nelson, E.C. (1997). A replicable and customizable approach to improve ambulatory care and research. *Journal of Ambulatory Care Management, 20*(1), 17–27.

Wasson, J.H., Nelson, G. & Jette, A. (in press). A controlled trial to improve geriatric care in primary care practices. *Journal of the American Medical Association.*

# CHAPTER 11

# The Physician and Care Coordinator: A Chronic Care Partnership

*Sue Shearer, W. June Simmons, Barbara Berkman,*
*Gladys Gundrum, and Monika White*

Over a decade ago we became convinced that future health care delivery for elderly people would demand closer collaboration among health professionals and greatly improve service integration. As health care organizations began searching for innovative ways to manage the care needs of an ever older population, we began to conceive of a partnership between physicians and social work care coordinators.

We approached The John A. Hartford Foundation with our ideas and gained their support. From February 1992 to August 1994, the foundation funded Huntington Memorial Hospital Senior Care Network to explore ways to bring non-medical, supportive services to the offices of primary care physicians for their patients age 65 and older.

Although we did not design the Physician Partnership project as a research study, we hoped to show that partnerships between physicians and professionals who coordinate community-based care were both feasible and practical. The resulting model became the basis for the Hartford Foundation's Generalist Physician Initiative. Replicated by a number of health care organizations throughout the country, our model has won praise from providers and patients alike.

## Background

Huntington Memorial Hospital is a 589-bed non-profit community hospital in Pasadena, California, that provides a full range of medical and surgical services. The hospital's service area includes a group of suburban communities with a population of nearly 700,000, 12.7% of whom are over age 65. The community most represented in the project is Pasadena. Based on 1990 census statistics, Pasadena has 17,338 residents age 65 and over (or 13.2% of Pasadena residents). Of the senior population in Pasadena age 60 and over in 1990, Anglos represented 76% (but only 47% of the total population), African-Americans 14% (18% of the total population), Hispanics 4% (27% of the total population), and Asians 6% (8% of the total population). Of this older population, 9.2% were living below the poverty level and 15.8% were counted as disabled due to mobility and self-care limitations.

As part of a strategic commitment to meet the needs of the elderly residing in its service area, Huntington Memorial Hospital established Senior Care Network (SCN) in 1984 to provide leadership in a community-wide planning and program development effort. A department of the hospital, SCN is located in a hospital-owned building one block from the main hospital structure.

Within a few years, SCN became a nationally recognized model for optimizing community, inpatient, and post-hospitalization support and care for a population with growing health care service needs. The overriding goal of SCN is to ensure that community residents have the opportunity to "age well" through health promotion, life planning, coordinated health and personal care services, and in-home supports for independent living.

Historically, Senior Care Network has cultivated supportive relationships with hospital administration and key physicians. This, along with the assistance of an insightful chief of medical staff, proved invaluable when we were ready to introduce project concepts and build consensus. Our efforts also coincided with early exploration by physicians of how to better manage older patients in the face of growing challenges in health care delivery. The concept of partnering became even more acceptable among physicians as various formal health care partnerships became a popular way to integrate health care systems.

Most of the older persons in the community receive their medical care from independent, fee-for-service medical practices, which at the time of the Hartford-funded project were typically small offices of two primary care practitioners. By the end of the project, the participating physicians had become part of a larger medical practice that included consolidation of some offices and office staffs. The hospital had also joined with several other local hospitals to form the Southern California

Healthcare Systems, a non-profit integrated health care delivery system serving a 29-city area northeast of Los Angeles.

We have seen the impact of managed care steadily increase. At the start of the project in 1992, about 33% of Huntington Hospital's total admissions were enrolled in HMOs compared to more than 40% today. HMO penetration among the senior population in the Southern California Healthcare Systems service area is approximately 38%, somewhat higher than in California as a whole.

## Project Design

As the emphasis in health care began to shift from acute to chronic needs, we recognized that integrated service systems and an enhanced continuum of care were essential to preserve the functioning and independence of elderly persons. Although primary care physicians are critical access points to care systems, they are not necessarily knowledgeable about non-medical supportive services many older persons need to retain their independence. Providing easy access to this information would help reduce fragmentation of care and ensure that older adults received supportive services before a crisis developed. SCN's experience in coordinating care for older adults has consistently underscored how the timely use of supportive services can help avoid crises and prevent unnecessary hospitalization and nursing home placement.

We developed a model partnership between physicians and SCN to improve integration of medical and supportive services, and to help ensure a comprehensive continuum of care. We wanted to enhance early identification of the needs of older patients, facilitate their access to required resources, and improve care delivery. To meet these goals we developed a screening tool to identify patients at risk, easy access to care coordination services and community resources, and an emphasis on integration and collaboration.

The Physician Partnership model provides participating physician offices with rapid response for assessments, brief interventions, and linkage to home and community services through a master's-level social worker who serves as care coordinator and physician liaison. To distinguish from other existing SCN care coordinators, this project's social worker is called the "liaison," although project physicians simply refer to this person by name or as "the social worker." The liaison talks to patients in the physicians' offices, in homes, or by telephone. The liaison assesses and provides immediate information and referral, maintains short-term contact with patients and their families, or refers patients with complex situations or long-term care management needs to a community care management program. A crucial activity is making regular office rounds to maintain visibility and discuss cases.

The project involved 13 primary care physicians from six similar office practices at several locations in Pasadena and one full-time social work liaison. Two of the three social workers who consecutively staffed the liaison position during the funding period held master of social work (MSW) degrees; the third was a bachelor of social work (BSW) in process of obtaining an MSW. The project also funded a full-time licensed clinical social work project coordinator. The liaison and the project coordinator were housed at SCN, which offers a central location, adequate office space, secretarial assistance, and access to SCN resources.

Currently, the liaison is a half-time position that continues to serve the original 13 physicians, now part of a larger medical group with offices at four locations. The new group has relocated some of the physicians to other offices; however, the only impact on the project is the need to educate new office staff. The project's managerial functions have been incorporated into an existing SCN staff position.

The basic design remained unchanged throughout the project. The most significant alteration was the screening tool as a valuable risk-identifier, used not by the physician, as originally intended, but by the liaison. Physicians preferred to retain their traditional methods of identification, including observations of behavior and multiple telephone calls from concerned family members. They saw the tool as a non-medical assessment that was too time-consuming. Thus, the screening tool did not serve as the main physician referral mechanism, as envisioned. Instead, liaison visibility in the office enhanced referrals and became an essential part of the model.

As physicians began to utilize the liaison, they asked for assistance with hospitalized patients. To meet this need, the liaison role expanded during the grant period to include daily review of hospital admissions to locate patients of participating physicians who might need follow-up home care after discharge. The liaison shared information with the hospital social work department and collaborated on a post-hospital care plan.

# Physician Selection

Many older people look to their primary care physicians as the most credible sources of advice in a variety of areas. They and their families frequently ask these physicians and their staff to act as advisors on a range of personal care and custodial issues. Managed care has reinforced the primary care physician's role as advisor and gatekeeper to services.

The project targeted private primary care physicians on Huntington Hospital's medical staff whose practices consisted of at least 40% elderly patients. However, because the project was not designed as a research study, we considered any physician who expressed interest. We obtained initial support from the hospital chief of staff, who was well respected within the local medical community. We met with this "physician leader" to share understandings of the project, of the roles involved, and of a strategy for introducing the project to the local medical community.

Administrative notices, medical staff newsletters, and announcements at department meetings informed physicians of the project. A follow-up letter to the full hospital medical staff offered opportunities to be part of a one-time focus group, be on the project advisory committee, and/or be a participating office in the program.

From the response and follow-up contacts, we invited 13 primary care physicians to participate. After this selection, but before the liaison entered the offices, 12 of the physicians attended two focus groups led by an outside facilitator. We gained valuable input and support as they discussed the needs of their older patients, their methods of identifying these needs, and the benefits and inconveniences of a liaison.

The physicians expressed feelings of inadequacy and inexperience in assessing functional and community needs. They said what they needed most to help their older patients was easy access to prompt, concise, practical information on psychosocial assessment outcomes, available community, social, and health care services, and follow-up on the liaison's recommendations. Their suggestions helped refine the model design to emphasize quick response time and easy access to the liaison.

Several physicians with reputable geriatric practices joined the advisory committee to plan strategies for project support and dissemination of information. This committee offered helpful ideas on identifying and addressing potential physician resistance and on introducing aspects of the model to physicians and office staff.

Ideal physicians for this project were those who understood social work, psychosocial issues, and the impact of unmet community care needs on a patient's well-being. We preferred physicians with at least a 40% geriatric practice to ensure enough referrals and volume to demonstrate the project's value. Close proximity to the liaison's centralized office at SCN, preferably within walking distance or five to ten minutes by car, aided the goals of rapid response and liaison visibility. Physician interest in participating in research and innovations, and a willingness to be collaborative and accessible, also facilitated relationship building. An initial in-person interview conducted by the project manager with each prospective physician provided an opportunity to reinforce elements of the project, and discuss expectations of the project and the liaison.

## Roles and Relationships

We designed the liaison role in the partnership to complement the physician's medical expertise. The selection of a social worker experienced in community-based care coordination provided the psychosocial skills and understanding of community resources needed to assist patients with chronic care needs. By virtue of their training and background, social work professionals have the skills to quickly gain rapport, understand and evaluate the complexity of psychosocial needs, and do immediate problem solving. They are able to differentiate between short- and long-term needs, access appropriate community-based resources, and work across systems.

We believed the liaison role required master's-level social work expertise, experience with health and aging issues, program development skills, the ability to work independently, and sensitivity to organizational cultures found within physician offices. We felt these qualifications were necessary to facilitate acceptance of the project by the physicians and especially the physicians' office staffs. With professional social work skills and health care experience, the liaison needed no additional training except in the use of the screening tool.

It took a significant investment of time to build rapport with physicians' office staffs and to demonstrate the liaison role. Staff needed reassurance that the liaison was there to assist them, not to replace them or interfere with their duties. The project manager and liaison held an initial meeting with each physician's office staff to introduce and explain the liaison role. Thereafter, the liaison used one or two weekly informal visits as an opportunity to reinforce the partnership role, remind staff of recent patients who should be referred, and educate them about risk factors that might lead to a patient's functional decline. The liaison also discussed patient needs directly with the physician whenever possible. These educational efforts served as ongoing training for both office staff and physicians, and were a workable alternative to demanding formal training time from them.

The office staff proved even more essential than anticipated to the project's success in terms of client identification, care plan implementation, and access to the physician. As the project progressed, staff came to see the liaison less as an outsider and more as a team member who could help them solve many of their problems. Learning about office needs, understanding individual office cultures and dynamics, and adapting to the fast pace of most offices helped the liaison gain acceptance and overcome barriers to a constructive relationship. For example, the liaison respected the initial wishes of some offices, which expected the liaison to remain outside of the treatment areas (eventually the liaison was accepted in). Other ways that the liaison respected yet also worked closely with busy office staff were to ask only for crucial information on new referrals and obtain the rest of the histories from families, or to consult with staff about how to best handle patients needing a prompt intervention.

Along with the leadership of SCN, the social work project coordinator was instrumental in gaining project acceptance from hospital administration and physicians in the initial planning phase. The coordinator was visible in the hospital, communicated regularly with the chief of staff, presented project concepts and progress at department meetings, and followed up on any physician concerns with individual meetings and telephone calls. As overseer of daily operations and supervisor of the liaison, the coordinator remained a key connection to physicians throughout the project and contacted them periodically for informal feedback about their satisfaction with the project.

Physicians used the liaison as a specialist to deal with non-medical issues that arose with their patients. These issues ranged from home care needs to money management and housing concerns. With little knowledge of how to address these situations themselves, physicians viewed the liaison much like a consultant who would evaluate the patient's problem in depth, make recommendations, implement them, or direct the physician as needed. For example, the liaison might request that the physician review a patient's multiple medications, or order skilled home nursing care or medical equipment. For physicians, contacting the liaison was like writing a prescription. It was a quick action with only brief information required from the physician.

However, an important component of the model was that the liaison actively sought out indications of patients who might be at risk by talking with anyone in the office who had contact with patients. While the office nurse was a primary information source, the receptionist might be especially aware of a pattern of missed appointments or remember a patient's persistent telephone calls for assistance. The billing clerk might suspect that a patient with frequent overdue bills had difficulty managing money. Asking about patients who had any "problems" and providing feedback to staff and physicians on how the liaison had helped patients were successful techniques that led to referral of patients whose needs might otherwise have gone unrecognized.

Families, when available, were contacted and included in the assessment and care plan. Sometimes the family member was the impetus for the referral, as with an overburdened spouse or a worried adult child. When there was no nearby family, the liaison might follow up with an out-of-town relative.

# Relationship Development

Communication between the physicians and the liaison included informal office visits, telephone calls, written assessments, and summary reports. The liaison was available by beeper, and physicians and office staff were encouraged to use it to facilitate rapid response. When paged by beeper, the liaison promptly returned the call and determined whether to go immediately to the physician's office to see a waiting patient.

There were no formal meetings or rounds. The liaison tailored feedback to each physician's preference. Some physicians wanted more details about recommendations than others; others wanted to speak with the liaison before their patients received any recommendations. Telephoning the physician was limited primarily to urgent messages or requests. A concise one-page form consisting of checklists for assessment results and provided services for each patient, with space for no more than five lines of narrative, was sent to the physician for review. Physicians also received a monthly report listing referred patients, interventions provided, anticipated outcomes and contact hours spent by the liaison.

Because the physician practices were similar, cultivating relationships depended mostly on dealing with individual personalities. When a resistant office staff member denied a problem with a patient or insisted, "I can handle it," the liaison offered suggestions and asked about the patient at the next office visit. The liaison routinely shared patient progress and outcomes with staff to educate them about what the liaison actually did and to reduce concerns about "taking over" a patient. Whenever appropriate, the liaison asked staff for their advice. For example, on a home visit the liaison found a patient very anxious and breathing heavily. The liaison reported the symptoms to the physician's office. Staff indicated that the patient had a history of anxiety episodes and the liaison followed their instructions on how to handle the situation.

With physicians, the liaison took advantage of any encounter in the office or in the hospital to mention specific patients and their outcomes. On several occasions the project coordinator scheduled a lunch meeting with the physicians to discuss how the project was going and brought the lunch. These meetings were opportunities to inform the physicians of chronic difficulties in getting information from office staff or in accessing the physicians and often resulted in noticeable improvement.

The extensive efforts made to gain initial physician input and acceptance proved worthwhile. Physicians continued to remain comfortable with the project design and no significant changes were necessary. We accommodated individual physician preferences, such as the amount of feedback they wished to receive.

At the conclusion of grant funding, we decided that the project should continue because of its demonstrated value. The physician partnership concept is consistent not only with hospital administration's wish to maintain positive relationships with physicians, but supports SCN's outreach mission to locate people in the community who need help. Since 1994 SCN has underwritten the project to provide ongoing service to the original 13 physicians. Because the physicians are now familiar with the project and less education is necessary, the current half-time liaison position is sufficient to meet their needs. Limited funding has precluded adding new physicians.

# Patient Selection and Enrollment

As noted, a research design was not part of the Physician Partnership project. Beyond targeting patients age 65 and older, there were no participation criteria. Referrals were ongoing and all were accepted. Each patient was offered whatever interventions the liaison deemed necessary. Many times it was the caregiver who needed assistance. Very few patients refused to see the liaison even if some chose not to follow up with the recommendations. In those cases, the liaison persisted only if there were safety issues or if there were recurring referrals from the physician. From 1992 to 1994, the liaison served 1,300 patients. The project currently averages 25 referrals a month.

The liaison worked closely with the physician and office staff to identify older patients at risk of a decline in daily functioning. One purpose of regular office visits was to educate staff about risk factors such as medication noncompliance, isolation, and poor mobility, and to probe for indications of patients who were considered problematic or who required staff interventions. To facilitate risk indicator recognition and to help physicians and staff identify appropriate referrals, a gerontologist expert in social health care needs developed a self-administered patient questionnaire with physician, nurse, and social worker input. Designed in a simple "yes/no" format, the questionnaire covers a wide range of information including activities of daily living, recent hospitalizations, number of medications taken, financial problems, recent losses, feelings of sadness, and current service utilization. Initially patients received the questionnaire at the time of their appointment with the physician and completed it while in the reception area. This was not always effective, however, because staff were inconsistent in distributing the forms.

The most successful distribution method was mailing the form to all patients 65 and older in participating physician offices along with a letter from the physician and a return postage-paid envelope. Contrary to some physicians' concerns, patients did not complain about filling out the questionnaire and, in fact, several expressed appreciation that their physician had shown an interest in their home care needs.

Although the questionnaire was originally intended as a tool to aid physicians in identification of patients with psychosocial needs, physicians preferred to use their traditional identification and referral methods. This meant they relied on observations and patient complaints and then had the office staff call SCN or tell the patient to call. Instead, the tool became an important screening device for the liaison, who reviewed all returned questionnaires to determine the need for a follow-up telephone call for further assessment. Analysis of the screening data showed that difficulties with food preparation, light housework, and getting about the home were the main indicators that led the liaison to contact the patient (Berkman et al., 1996). The questionnaire also helped identify more subtle threats to independence, such as depression, mild mobility problems, and isolation that might otherwise have been overlooked.

The questionnaire review identified approximately one-third of patients who received help from the liaison. Physicians referred the remaining two-thirds of the patients seen. Typical patients were 70 years and older with at least one chronic condition. Physicians usually described their concerns in terms of the patient's medical condition, such as questioning how a patient with arthritis was managing at home. The liaison's assessment, however, revealed that most patients had concerns about their safety, their living situations, anxiety and depression, cognitive problems, and patient/family conflicts regarding medical care needs.

The questionnaire mailing effort both helped the liaison reach patients who were not seeing their physicians and generated referrals. The questionnaire was also a useful office staff education device. Because all referrals were assessed, however, it was not needed to screen referrals and today it is no longer used.

## Assessment and Care Planning

The liaison used the brief assessment checklist developed for communication with the physician to assess all referred patients. The assessment occurred in the office following the physician's visit, if appropriate, or over the telephone. Sometimes patients were seen at home to better determine the level of need. Seeing the patient during an office visit reinforced the liaison as part of the team and enhanced patient acceptance. Telephone assessments worked best for patients who were more independent and able to follow through with recommendations. Home visits occurred when requested by the physician, or when more information was needed about the patient's living condition and ability to cope at home.

Once the liaison determined needs, one or two contacts were often sufficient to provide information on resources and options, give support and counseling, help with decision making, or encourage action. The most common service referrals were for personal care, durable medical equipment, transportation, housing alternatives, emergency response system, and support/counseling. Many patients who were seen in the office were given immediate assistance. Seventy percent of patients, however, needed more than a resource referral and received at least one follow-up telephone call.

Because the project emphasized short-term interventions, the liaison referred patients with complex or long-term needs, or who required extensive monitoring, to one of SCN's care coordination programs. To initiate this process, the liaison notified SNC's Resource Center—the entry point to SCN's care coordination programs—helped resource staff determine the appropriate program, and provided information to the assigned care coordinator. The liaison kept in contact with the care coordinator and retained the role of providing feedback to the physician about the patient.

Physicians primarily wanted to know what services were recommended, if they were in place, and the results of home assessments. They expected the liaison to determine service needs, implement the recommendations, and inform the physician that these functions had been carried out. Because of their time constraints, which are increasing under managed care, most physicians preferred that calls about problems relate mainly to medical management issues. The one-page checklist of assessment results and provided services, along with the monthly summary of liaison contacts, kept the physicians informed in a timely and concise manner.

It is probably more appropriate to describe the physician and liaison as partners than team members. Teamwork is encouraged, however, and the integration and accountability features complement teaming concepts. The model would, therefore, seem adaptable and useful to settings that have multi-disciplinary teams. The linkage of functional and medical services that is the core of the model is also compatible with the holistic approach advocated by managed care. The project physicians' ongoing support, as they have become more involved in managed care, indicates that the project continues to meet their needs.

We use two examples to illustrate how the liaison provided brief assistance to a patient during an office visit and assisted a referred patient who needed follow-up services. See White, Gundrum, Shearer, and Simmons (1994) for additional patient examples.

## Example 1

Office staff contacted the liaison by beeper regarding the wife of a 73-year-old man who had become demented after a stroke. The wife had told the physician that she was stressed and needed some help. Although their daughter stayed with him during the day while the wife was at work, the wife was unable to get away any other time. Arriving at the physician's office while the wife was still there, the liaison determined that the wife was having difficulty managing the losses related to her husband's illness and had unrealistic expectations.

The liaison counseled the wife about the importance of maintaining her own physical and emotional health and discussed what functions she could turn over to others. The liaison explained attendant care and gave referrals to several agencies. She stressed the value of caregiver support groups and provided information on where to find them. The wife was relieved to learn she had options and was grateful for the assistance. She was able to obtain home health services and she began attending a support group where her emotional needs could be addressed.

## Example 2

The physician referred to the liaison a 66-year-old patient whom he observed to be poorly dressed and unusually anxious. An assessment conducted by telephone revealed that the man was about to be evicted from his apartment for failure to pay rent. Although he was worried, he seemed reluctant to take any action.

The liaison counseled the man about his impending loss of independence and the urgent need to address the problem and look for a positive solution. After discussion of several alternatives, low-cost housing options seemed the most appropriate. A follow-up call a week later indicated that he had contacted one facility but still had not moved. The liaison again counseled him about the need to act. As of the third call, the man had gotten a friend to move in to share the rent.

# Replication Efforts

As part of the original Hartford funding, two other hospitals (Baylor University Medical Center in Dallas and Beverly Hospital/Bay Area Visiting Nurse Association in Massachusetts) replicated our model with a total of 30 physicians for two replication and Huntington Memorial sites combined. From June 1992 through August 1994, a combined total of 1,738 patients were referred to the three physician liaisons. The liaisons provided more than 1,700 assessment and linkage hours. Three-fourths of the patients who needed interventions required only two to three contacts.

The two replication sites also participated in mailing the patient self-assessment screening questionnaire to their participating physicians' older patients. The mailings by the three sites to 3,018 patients age 65 and over yielded a 27% return rate. Because the questionnaire was an outreach method and patients who perceived themselves as doing well were probably less likely to fill out the questionnaire, we considered the response rate satisfactory.

After reviewing the questionnaires, the liaisons determined that 62% needed a follow-up telephone call for further assessment. Although a significant number of patients reported limitations in daily functioning, especially related to mobility, few were receiving assistance. Berkman and colleagues (1996; in press) provide a detailed analysis of the screening tool for risk factors that predicted the need for care management.

The Huntington Hospital model worked well in the two replication settings with very minimal modifications. Outcomes and findings were similar. Physicians were receptive and liaison visibility in the office was key to generating referrals. The sites have continued with the model and have integrated it into their existing organizational structures.

As part of a one-year extension of the project through August 1995, we developed a replication manual and invited interested sites to submit a request for technical assistance in replicating the project. Ten sites, nine hospitals and a managed care senior program, were selected nationwide based on their ability to meet project objectives. Assistance consisted primarily of telephone consultation with the project coordinators and written materials. Sites that pursued implementation were able to adapt the model to diverse settings. Experiences of three of the sites are described in Shearer, Simmons, White, and Berkman (1995). More than 75 additional sites purchased the project's replication manual (Huntington Memorial Hospital Senior Care Network, 1994).

## Lessons Learned

As the originator of the Physician Partnership model that led to the full Hartford initiative, SCN initially had to determine whether a physician and social work care coordinator partnership was possible. When it proved feasible, our challenge was to develop a prototype that would work in varied health care settings and cultures. Successful replications and ongoing partnership programs attest to the soundness and adaptability of the original model.

A number of significant insights emerged from the project. A key finding was that short-term intervention provided early can successfully solve problems that might otherwise threaten an older person's independence. This conclusion was supported by informal feedback from physicians and office staff, who noted a decrease in telephone calls for assistance from involved patients and family members and increased patient compliance. There were specific instances of patients who had fewer emergency room visits because of intervention by the liaison, such as a diabetic patient who was forgetting to take insulin.

Assistance that involved only one or two personal contacts, especially when provided before serious problems had developed, seemed to be sufficient to solve most of the identified problems. It is important to identify risk factors such as isolation, multiple medications, and restricted mobility that may lead to functional decline and intervene early to avoid unnecessary crises. Only a small number of patients had situations that required full service care coordination, so the model of limited intervention met the needs of the great majority of patients.

We found patients to be reliable self-reporters. They were generally accurate in identifying their problems on the questionnaires they returned, as confirmed by follow-up telephone calls made by the liaison. They seemed to have a good sense of their difficulties.

Another finding of the project was that building trusting relationships is essential to a successful partnership. Physicians said they wanted to be able to use the liaison as they would a professional consultant. With trust established, physicians were able to turn to the liaison for assessments and recommendations much as they would to other specialists such as a physical therapist.

Along with efforts to gain physicians' understanding and acceptance before the project began, the visibility of the liaison in the physicians' offices was crucial to the project's success. The liaison initially visited the offices two or three times a month. A shift to one or two times weekly not only stimulated referrals, but helped establish a team sense, improved accountability, and provided opportunities to educate physicians and their staff to better identify at-risk patients.

Working within the existing office culture proved more effective than attempting to change the culture. For example, the liaison discovered that office staff often had important information on a patient's functional status, such as a vision problem, that the physician did not know. Sometimes staff did not realize its importance, or else assumed the physician knew this information. Rather than usurp their role and approach the physician with the information, the liaison educated the staff about the value of what they knew and the need to share it with the physician. At lunch meetings with the physicians, the project coordinator reinforced the role of staff as valuable sources of information.

Staff were also able to assist in accessing the physicians. When there was a prompt need for a physician's order, for example, staff knew the quickest way to obtain the order. Keeping the staff informed of outcomes enhanced involvement in the process and enabled staff to reinforce the social work intervention with the patient. All in all, good relationships with staff were vital and worth the significant amount of time and energy they took to establish.

Both physicians and patients reported benefits from the project, according to satisfaction surveys. Patients in telephone interviews said they appreciated the assistance the liaison provided. Physicians responding to a written survey agreed the liaison benefited their patients and saved them time. They received fewer telephone calls from anxious family members and could spend less time addressing psychosocial issues. They said the liaison was accessible, reliable, and helpful in identifying patients in need of community services, counseling them, and facilitating linkages to services.

Physicians have commented that they like the program because it gives them "something tangible to offer patients" that need community services. "The program allows patients to be plugged into services a little better," said one physician. "Often, those people who need help the most seem to have the most trouble accessing services." Another noted, "When older patients ask questions about social issues, they can turn to someone who knows the answers. This is a great benefit."

There were very few problems with model implementation at Huntington and the original replication sites. By design the model sought to accommodate physicians and collaborate with them in meeting the needs of their patients. Most of the changes related to the distribution and use of the screening tool by the liaison rather than the physician and increasing the visibility of the liaison in the office. In addition, as the project progressed we recognized the key role of office staff in generating referrals.

The model has no built-in funding mechanisms, so sites must address financial support. During the project, we considered ways to obtain reimbursement for liaison services. A pilot study demonstrated successful billing of Medicare Part B for outpatient social work services using social work provider numbers. This does not, however, fully cover costs. After conclusion of the grant, SCN and hospital administration decided the model was valuable and should continue, even in a limited way, by incorporating costs into the existing SCN budget.

It would have been helpful to devise methods beforehand that would translate into dollars, the saving of staff time, and the improved quality of life for older patients. Because the project was designed to explore the feasibility of a partnership concept, it did not include statistical or other methods used in research studies that could empirically demonstrate the project's cost benefits. Formal evaluation of the project's success was measured by physician and patient satisfaction surveys.

The model offers a flexible, adaptable approach well suited to developing health care delivery networks. It has wide applicability as demonstrated by successful replication efforts. In addition, SCN has used features of the model in a variety of other outreach programs. SCN care coordinators have assumed a liaison role in acute care units, community centers, senior residential facilities, health maintenance organizations, and the probate court. In these locations they identify at-risk individuals and provide brief interventions and short-term assistance. These partnerships help to locate under-served populations, and have been well received in the community.

## Summary

A successful model partnership between primary care physicians and a community-based care coordinator was developed to enhance the continuum of care and improve integration of service systems. The Physician Partnership model incorporates rapid response for assessments, brief and early interventions, and linkage to home and community services provided through a social work liaison who is on call to physicians' offices. The project developed a system to provide easy access to community resources, an at-risk screening tool to identify patients in need of psychosocial help from the liaison, and a communication system to promote integration and collaboration. The demonstrated replicability of the Physician Partnership model suggests it is a viable approach for a variety of health care settings.

## References

Berkman, B., Shearer, S., Simmons, W.J., White, M., Rohan, E., Robinson, M., Sampson, S., Holmes, W., Allison, D. & Thomson, J. (in press). ADL's and IADL's: Relationship to depression in elderly primary care patients. *Journal of Clinical Geropsychology*.

Berkman, B., Shearer, S., Simmons, W.J., White, M., Robinson, M., Sampson, S., Holmes, W., Allison, D. & Thomson, J.A. (1996). Ambulatory elderly patients of primary care physicians: Functional, psychosocial and environmental predictors of need for social work care management. *Social Work in Health Care*, 22(3), 1–20.

Huntington Memorial Hospital Senior Care Network. (1994). *Physician partnership replication manual* (Available from Huntington Memorial Hospital, Pasadena, CA).

Shearer, S., Simmons, W.J., White, M. & Berkman, B. (1995). Physician partnership project: Social work case managers in primary care. *Continuum: An Interdisciplinary Journal on Continuity of Care, 15*(4), 1+.

White, M., Gundrum, G., Shearer, S. & Simmons, W.J. (1994). A role for case managers in the physician office. *Journal of Case Management, 3*(2), 62–68.

# CHAPTER 12

# Lessons Learned Across Sites

*Frank G. Williams, Bradford L. Kirkman-Liff, and F. Ellen Netting*

The chapters in this book provide an overview of 10 projects, part of The John A. Hartford Foundation Generalist Physician Initiative. Each chapter reveals a model designed to enhance primary physician care of frail elders. "Enhancing primary care" in this initiative means expanding the scope and content of the physician's practice (1) to identify and respond to the broader set of psychosocial, economic, environmental, support, and other factors affecting patient health and welfare; (2) to monitor patient health status and implement methods for early detection of health problems; (3) to emphasize health education and prevention; (4) to support patient self-management of chronic disabilities; and (5) to increase lines of communication and access points for patients, practice physicians, and staff.

Each chapter focuses on a specific site nested within a distinct local and regional environment. Projects vary in many ways, one of which is the penetration of managed care in their respective geographical environments. For example, Wasson and Jette (Chapter 10) describe sites in New Hampshire barely touched by managed care even as the grant period ends. This is in radical contrast to Anker-Unnever's vivid portrayal (Chapter 8) of the rapidly changing managed care environment into which her project is introduced in New Mexico. All sites, however, witnessed changes in their environments as traditional fee-for-service and managed care approaches intertwined within physician practices.

Given the changing Medicare managed care environment and the diversity among the 10 projects presented, it is a challenge to identify the lessons learned from the Generalist Physician Initiative. We approached this challenge by making numerous site visits, conducting over 200 interviews, and by engaging in hundreds of informal dialogues with the key players at each site. What is remarkable is that there are definite lessons that emerged across sites, even amid the diverse situational factors that influenced the design of each model. Nonetheless, there is no one prescription for success.

## Consider the Context

Embedded within an emerging and changing Medicare managed care environment, these 10 projects were initiated by approaching medical systems with strong track records in caring for older persons and asking each to independently design a model to meet the initiative's objectives. All but one model added persons to the primary care team to broaden the scope of practice. The exception to this approach was New Hampshire, where an expanded survey process was used to better inform physicians about wider patient needs and issues (see Chapter 10). However, even though the approaches to enhancing primary care by adding personnel were similar in a conceptual sense, there was no single prescription for success. A diversity of models resulted due to differences in local conditions, including the cultures of the health care systems, their traditions, prior experiences, and even influential personalities. For example, as we traveled to the various sites, we discovered that some models were built around the concept of making home visits, with care coordinators being the "eyes and ears" of physicians in the homes of older persons. However, for reasons of safety and because their practice cultures did not assume that home visits needed to be made, two projects in inner-city neighborhoods were originally designed to do virtually no home visits. Another example was the selection of the type of care coordinator—nurse, nurse practitioner, physician assistant, social worker, or trained lay person—that was very much determined by past relationships and availability of personnel. The design of projects funded by previous grants was also an influential factor. The lesson we learned early in our site visits was that local situational factors are critical to understanding model design.

Three categories of projects emerged as the result of local factors. The first category included projects that were more medically based, in which assessments were more often completed in the physicians' offices, and in which home visits were limited in number or scope. In this type, nurses, nurse practitioners, and physician assistants played major roles, and social workers were used primarily in consulting roles. These models were developed in Cleveland, Detroit, Miami Beach, and Binghamton. The Carle Clinic in central Illinois was also a medically based program, but it included more home visits. These projects were featured in Chapters 2 through 6.

Projects in the second category were located in Albuquerque, San Francisco, and Huntington. These projects were more externally oriented, with assessments and patient contacts most often occurring outside the physicians' offices. Addressing psychosocial needs through the use of social and mental health services received greater emphasis. MSW-level social workers, often teamed with nurses, played more prominent roles in these projects. Chapters 7, 8, and 11 provided overviews of these projects.

The third category provided alternative models to the highly "professionalized" types in categories 1 and 2. Although quite different in their approaches, the projects in South Carolina (Chapter 9) and New Hampshire (Chapter 10) did not hire additional professional staff to work with physicians. Hornung, Brewer, and Stein describe their rural South Carolina project as focused on the use of indigenous paraprofessional staff who addressed concrete service needs and often visited patients' homes. Wasson and Jette, on the other hand, used patient self-assessment in an attempt to link physicians more directly with patients, in the hope that greater communication would occur as a result when patients came to their physicians' offices.

Projects in these three categories developed models that fit with their local environments and that were feasible within their health care systems. For example, in rural South Carolina it was not feasible to design a highly professionalized project that would stand little chance of continuation when grant funds ended. In Detroit, however, it was logical to design a model that used the skills of nurse practitioners in busy inner-city clinics, particularly since these professionals were already being introduced into the Henry Ford Health System. In Albuquerque it was reasonable to build on a previous foundation-funded grant and to expand the case management model with which key stakeholders within the system were already familiar.

Project implementation and continuation is influenced by a complex interplay of systems and sub-systems. Not only is the national context changing, but there are regional variations among provider networks. States vary in terms of professional credentialing and licensure, and local communities are the arenas in which changing provider relationships and competition develop. Employing organizations vary across projects, with across projects, with some physician practices solo or group, others part of managed care groups, and others hospital-based. It is within this array of changing systems that one must consider the uniqueness of physician practices.

The importance of understanding the local environment and the culture of the physician practice can not be stressed enough in designing models that will work. Equally as important to project continuation is demonstrating that the intervention is cost-effective.

# Coordinated Care Can Be Cost-Effective

## Decreased Utilization of Acute Care Services

Coordinated care models cannot be expected to reverse the declining health and functioning of frail elderly persons. The models demonstrated in this project do not represent "fountains of youth." Furthermore, when these projects began, much had to be learned by the participants about operational details and how to work together as teams. The achievement of desired outcomes was determined by the slope of the learning curve at each site and the time required for projects to become integrated into routine practice operations. More structured systems, such as the Carle Clinic, whose physicians all work for the organization, had an advantage over projects with independent private practices.

Once projects became operational it generally took another 12 to 18 months for intervention effects to be measurable. Since the evaluation period for these projects was no longer than two years, the only reasonable expectation for the projects is to reduce the rate of decline in the health of the intervention patients, compared to a control group. Measuring a decrease in the rate of decline was difficult, as the sample sizes were small and patients in the intervention groups were generally in poorer health than those in the comparison groups. Nevertheless, there is evidence from some sites that patients in the demonstrations reduced depression and reduced declines in their functional abilities.

In the Albuquerque, Binghamton, Carle, Cleveland, and San Francisco sites significant lower emergency room and hospital utilization was observed toward the end of the evaluation period. The Albuquerque and Binghamton sites have been able to document that the lower utilization resulted in lower overall costs, even when the costs of the intervention are considered.

## Financial Incentives for Physicians and Provider Organizations

Projects with traditional fee-for-service Medicare patients benefited from the improved physician and patient satisfaction, quality, and productivity that resulted when care coordinators were able to meet many of the complex, time-consuming needs of certain patients. In the long run, however, it is important that the physicians and provider organizations who implement enhanced primary care also benefit financially, if for no other reason than to recover the costs associated with implementing enhanced primary care. Payment to support program costs must come from physicians and providers who benefit from reduced utilization. Some success has been achieved in obtaining insurance coverage for program services, most notably by the Senior Care Network at Huntington Memorial in Pasadena featured in Chapter 11. For most organizations, however, incentives to save utilization costs are derived from capitated reimbursement under managed care. The incentives from capitation, moreover, assume organizations have high-risk frail elderly patients. Although some managed care companies have profited from discouraging enrollment of high-risk patients, a more common situation is that chronically ill and frail patients have established physician relationships, and are thus reluctant to join managed care plans. This situation is expected to change as Medicare encourages more elderly persons to join managed care plans, and as Medicare expands the services it expects to be included for fee-for-service reimbursement. Therefore, the organizational incentives for expanding the scope of primary care practice for elders can be expected to increase.

# Flexibility Is Needed
## Patient Targeting

All projects set age criteria, with a few having an upper age limit. Beyond age, sites varied in the criteria they established. There was no consensus about the type of elder likely to benefit from these models. Whereas the project in Detroit (see Chapter 2) included elders at the end of life, the project in Albuquerque (see Chapter 8) embraced a proactive model that focused on persons who needed less intensive services. Depending on the site, "at risk" was defined differently.

No matter how careful project designers had been in selecting enrollment criteria, physicians inevitably referred patients outside the established criteria to care coordinators. This led us to realize how difficult it is to establish criteria for patient enrollment prior to project implementation. Day-to-day medical practice and patient problems can defy attempts at predictability. At most sites, care coordinators readily admitted that they had chosen to respond to physicians' referrals, even if they did not meet established criteria, rather than to adhere rigidly to pre-established guidelines. Obviously, this flexibility made it difficult for the persons attempting to evaluate these projects.

Most revealing is that as grant monies were no longer available, project after project diversified its population to be more inclusive and therefore less targeted. Including younger persons with disabilities was most typical, and often projects began to accept patients across the age span. This was logical since physicians care for panels of patients across the age span and they saw opportunities to have care coordinators involved with issues that transcend chronological age.

Efforts to expand the types of patients treated to meet provider preferences may have limited project outcomes. Better results were achieved, for example, during the first phase of the Albuquerque-based project when telephone screening was used, compared to the second phase when patients were referred directly by physicians. During the first phase, case managers were able to identify patients with potential risks that could be alleviated, whereas in the second phase, referrals were generally not made until problems were obvious. In general, an effective approach is to have both a proactive process for patient identification, assessment, monitoring, and case management, and a "quick response" process for direct referral. The proactive process will likely yield better outcomes with respect to utilization, health, and functional status; the latter will maximize physician, staff, and patient satisfaction while minimizing subsequent costs and difficulties.

## Practice Operations

Geriatric care is different from the care typically provided to older persons by most primary physicians. In addition, collaborative practice requires time and effort if is going to work. All practices that participated in the initiative were required to make significant changes in practice operations and treatment protocols. At first the grant projects were seen as special activities outside of the normal routine. However, it soon became evident that project success depended on integration of the projects into the practices.

It was also important that project efforts to coordinate care for frail elders be integrated into their host health systems. Integration is limited when there are separate care coordinators for hospitals, payers, and, in this grant, physician practices. These models were built on the premise that the physician's practice was the point on the continuum at which care should be managed. Accordingly, success in integration was achieved when services such as care coordination and home care were decentralized to the physicians' practices. Integration improved when physicians and care coordinators worked with a small number of home care nurses for a defined group of patients. This led to the development of working relationships, familiarity, and trust.

# Geriatric Training and Knowledge Is Limited

It will not surprise those with backgrounds in gerontology to read that we found that most participating physicians and office staff across sites were initially not knowledgeable about or appreciative of the care needs of elders. Many felt they understood geriatrics, when it was clear they did not. Others did not believe there was anything special or different about caring for frail elderly persons. Still others were perplexed to have so many elders among their patients. The major challenge was not implementing the initiative itself, but educating participants about why the projects were necessary. A major goal of the initiative was to enlighten primary care providers about geriatrics. Indeed, the models served as a means to this end.

Our experience with these projects strongly reinforced the need for more geriatric training for physicians. Today's medical school and residency curricula do not generally appear to reflect the growing numbers of chronic and frail elderly patients that will be treated by physicians in the future. Geriatric practice deserves more respect in the professional and academic communities, but this is not easy to achieve in a youth-oriented culture. As with previous grant projects in long-term care, we again encountered in this initiative many administrators, physicians, nurses, office staff, and others who did not choose their careers in order to work with "old people."

Office staff and physicians had to recognize that much of primary health care is shifting from acute to chronic care. Expanding the scope of practice, emphasizing patients' psychosocial needs, developing a focus on care by helping patients adapt to their declining physical capabilities, and using a team approach were difficult tasks to incorporate into the daily routines of busy practices. Yet these changes became critical to successful project implementation.

## Successful Collaboration Requires Tact, Preparation, and Time

Essentially, the physician's practice is embedded in multiple systems, each with its own different cultural norms, values, assumptions, and behaviors. In order for a project to succeed, it is important that the practice in which an intervention is introduced has a culture that will accept the intervention. It is within the office practice that older patients meet their physicians and other professionals, and where the project must be integrated.

Regardless of project design, each site's office staff had to get beyond initial impressions and learn to work with project members. A project care coordinator talked about the importance of observing for two weeks in order to get "a general feel for how the practice operates." One advanced practice nurse from the project worked as a medical assistant while the staff person who normally assumed that role was out sick. This provided an opportunity to gain the trust of office staff and to demonstrate a willingness to "pitch in" regardless of training. Across sites, it was important for the project care coordinators to be seasoned by experience in health care, flexible as they entered office practices, attentive to the norms and values within each practice, able to develop good working relationships with office staff (and sometimes to win them over), and extremely skilled interpersonally.

Just as developing relationships with office staff is important, relationships must develop between project staff and physicians. Throughout the previous chapters are descriptions of the roles and relationships played by those persons involved in interventions. At first, physicians were typically somewhat bewildered and uncertain about what these persons would do in their practices. Most of this was due to project staff's initial hesitance to interfere too much or to disturb busy physicians. Observing these patterns, we realized the importance of orientation to and reinforcement of project roles and goals for physicians and their staff. We also realized how very difficult it is to find a time when physicians can meet with project staff. Having participated in multiple meetings, one physician laughed when he told us that he wondered if the project's evaluation was designed to study physicians as much as older patients.

Communication, familiarity, and trust became the ingredients for developing relationships. Physicians commented that they began to appreciate the feedback from their project care coordinators much more than that from home health agency nurses. As they got to know the care coordinators, physicians began to understand how they viewed home situations, how to interpret their feedback, and to trust their judgment. At the same time they were also developing an appreciation for non-medical information they were receiving.

# Each Team Is Different: Lessons Learned

Team building was a constant challenge throughout the initiative, as the following sections show. As a result The John A. Hartford Foundation later funded the Geriatric Interdisciplinary Team Training (GITT) program at academic medical centers across the country to address team issues. In GITT projects, students in medicine, nursing, social work, and other professions are taught to work as teams and to appreciate and learn how to care for geriatric patients.

## Learning to Work in Teams

As participants became more educated about long-term care, they began to understand the importance of interdisciplinary teams. However, few knew how to work as part of a team. Physicians, in particular, were educated to work and make decisions independently. While establishing what works well with a particular physician is key to defining a relationship with care coordinators, all members of the team must feel integral. Many physicians, however, saw themselves as the captains of the teams. In these situations the degree to which other professionals had input varied, and nonmedical input, such as that from social workers, tended to be underappreciated. Decisions were not usually made collectively.

Physicians were not the only professionals who valued autonomy, however. Some staff viewed the projects as ways to substitute less educated, lower-cost personnel for physicians and nurse practitioners. The professionals felt pressured to expand and protect their scopes of practice. To prove their value, many nurses, for example, felt the need to become more directly involved in the delivery of primary medical care, while also assuming the duties of social workers. There was a tendency in these situations to use the team as a means to organize and define professional "turf." Effective team interaction and collective decision making were clearly limited in these situations.

## Proximity

The socioemotional factors in building teams were important, and these factors were enhanced by the physical environments in which projects were housed. Some projects located care coordinators in physicians' offices, whereas others were located in nearby office buildings. The chance for informal exchange of information was hampered if the care coordinator was not on site. The opportunity to build team collaborations was enhanced by physical proximity, even if the care coordinator had only a small work space. For example, the care coordinators in Binghamton had offices located in renovated supply closets. Social workers in Albuquerque were able to claim space in physicians' offices when physician turnover occurred. Nurse practitioners in Detroit shared office space with physicians and one another. It was not the size of the office, but the physical location that contributed to integration and team development.

## Effective Information and Communication Systems

In order to assimilate project staff into physicians' practices, information gathered by care coordinators must be communicated in a usable form. Practice staff and physicians must then figure out how to use this information to respond better to patient needs. Often the success of grant projects can be determined by whether an information system is developed. In order to do so, participants must agree on terminology, protocols, measurements, and outcomes. It is not sufficient to have a "system" in which one simply enters individual progress notes into a word processor, since this type of data cannot be easily analyzed. It is also not reasonable to collect so much information on each patient that physicians are overwhelmed.

Asked how much information they would like about their patients, physicians varied greatly. Some simply did not want to know more, as illustrated by the physician who told us, "The problem with this project is that it tells me more about my patients than I want to know," or another who said that the care coordinators at that site were "opening up cans of worms. We'd just like one worm at a time!" Most physicians were glad to know more, however, because new information explained why patients behaved in certain ways. One physician explained that he couldn't ignore the issues faced by older patients—even if they were overwhelming—because "they come back every day, they come back with the same problem. You'll get stuck if you don't deal with the problem."

Because these projects had rigorous evaluation components, a great deal of data was collected, often more than staff were able to handle or incorporate into records. Most of the practices in this initiative were still in the early stages of computerizing medical records. All still relied on the paper record in normal practice. Adding psychosocial and other assessment data was often awkward and difficult. As projects matured, we were often told that staff planned to reduce the number of forms used and the amount of information collected when projects were no longer grant-dependent. Because of this "culture clash," most care coordinators kept separate "shadow records" containing their notes and assessment data.

The lack of computerized systems meant that the patient records kept by the care coordinators were not routinely accessed by physicians and other providers, so communication of these data depended on informal interactions, such as color-coded notes attached to charts and conversations in hallways. The more successful sites found that scheduled team meetings in which case reviews were conducted was a highly effective way to communicate to physicians the care coordinator's assessments.

## Project Leadership Is Critical

The importance of leadership to project success cannot be overemphasized. Both administrative and clinical skills were essential for project directors. The clinical and hospital administrators of the participating systems had neither the time, nor often the motivation, to manage these special projects. Project directors had to provide stability and direction during times of constant change in parent organizations' objectives and management. Flexibility was essential to adapt to environmental changes and to redesign the projects as lessons were learned during implementation.

It was important for projects to distinguish between administrative and clinical supervision. Project directors typically focused on administrative oversight, although most were very available to project staff. Most projects also designated a clinical supervisor or a project manager who directly supervised the activities of care coordinators. This role became very important in buffering the project director from having to deal with day-to-day problems, and provided a source of guidance and nurturing for persons working directly with patients and their families. When this role was not evident or when staff turned over in this role, it was clear that care coordinators felt somewhat uncertain in their roles.

On a day-to-day basis, clinical leadership also came directly from care coordinators who were hand picked for their knowledge, experience, and leadership. Their primary role during the early phases of the projects was to educate physicians and office staff on the projects and collaborative primary care. In this regard, their role was critical to project success, and therefore it turned out to be quite important that the care coordinators be located within the physician practices.

Leadership strategies were demonstrated in a variety of ways. In San Francisco (see Chapter 7), the project director held meetings with nurse/social worker teams, and in Albuquerque (see Chapter 8) the clinical supervisor led regularly scheduled case conferences at which case managers pooled their expertise in group problem-solving. These meetings were held in locations other than physicians' offices. In Detroit (see Chapter 2), nurse practitioners and physicians (one of whom was the clinical director) met on a regular basis within the clinic setting to case conference and to develop their team. In central Illinois (see Chapter 3), a supervisor made visits to monitor the activities of care coordinators, and in New Hampshire (see Chapter 10) project staff stopped by physicians' offices on an ongoing basis. In South Carolina (see Chapter 9), the project provided ongoing training by nurses and social workers for paraprofessional staff. In Cleveland (see Chapter 6), the project director made himself available "on call" to physician assistants so that they could consult with him as needed.

Throughout our site visits we asked how quality assurance was provided, and we found that none of the projects had put a quality assurance system in place for grant-related activities. Administrators and project directors even in highly structured health care systems often viewed a foundation grant as something "set apart" from normal operating procedure. Care coordinators expressed a sense of freedom from the constraints of rigid rules and oversight, which they had rarely experienced in a health care setting. Typically, physicians had not even considered the possibility that care coordinators were seeing patients for whom physicians were ultimately responsible if a problem arose. Physicians told us that their patients would tell them if anything was wrong, and that this was how they held the care coordinators accountable. It was very typical to have a physician say that he or she had no idea who was supervising project staff and then to ask us, "Am I supposed to be doing that?" The lesson we learned from these interactions is that it is very easy to suspend normal procedure when new projects are funded and that supervisory lines and relationships need to be clarified.

## Applied Research Is Difficult in Health Care

This initiative once again demonstrated the difficulty of conducting research in today's dynamic health care environment. During the five to six years from project conception to completion hardly anything remained constant. Since care was determined by physicians, it was the number of physicians, not patients, that determined statistical power. Practically speaking, this number was usually small. It was also difficult to randomize or match patients in the intervention and comparison groups. Research efforts were a casualty of project success. Practices often did not stick to protocols or enrollment criteria when positive outcomes were achieved.

Many lessons were learned (and reinforced) about the difficulties in evaluating projects that are "moving targets." First, research designs can become constraints to project staff who are not involved in the design process. We often heard comments such as, "Oh, we've got to collect that for the study." If "that" was not something that clinical staff perceived as relevant, then the collection of those data was a tribulation to busy practitioners. It is critical that the designers of research protocols work with project staff so that the persons collecting data know exactly why it is being collected and how it will be used.

Second, determining what outcomes are important to measure is a value-based process. The outcomes that are important to health care administrators (such as reduced utilization) are often organizational, not clinical, outcomes. Clinicians, on the other hand, view outcomes as quality-of-life changes for patients and focus on whether the intervention worked for the person served, even if that intervention placed the person in the hospital for an expensive stay. In other words, it is important to distinguish between organizational and client-centered outcomes since they are not always the same.

Third, all projects reinforced the importance of both formative and summative evaluation. Formative or process evaluation is very labor intensive in that someone has to be responsible for tracking what happens as projects develop and change. Qualitative approaches to process evaluation were incorporated as part of the research design for several sites and were very helpful in developing an understanding of what actually happened on a daily basis. Summative evaluation focuses on what was achieved, and all sites were very intentional about collecting the appropriate quantitative data to determine whether interventions actually "worked."

# Managed Care Can Foster Improved Primary Care

In our view, the results of the 10 projects presented in this book have utility in the changing world of Medicare and managed care. They point out a number of directions that physician groups can take to better provide primary care services to the Medicare population. As demonstrated in several sites, these interventions will achieve reductions in hospital and emergency room use, potentially result in lower rates of decline in health and functional status, and improve physician and patient satisfaction. All of these outcomes are intended consequences of the expansion of managed care into Medicare. These projects indicate approaches by which physicians and other professionals can work together to improve primary care and reduce the occurrence of high-cost episodes. A collaborative approach focused on prevention and meeting the broad health needs of the elderly person is, in our view, more likely to produce long-run cost savings under capitation arrangements than the current micro-management approaches.

Managed care has both advantages and disadvantages in implementing these models. We believe that the advantages outweigh the problems, which should decline as the managed care market matures. The concept of the primary care physician serving as a gatekeeper is being reassessed. In recent years most plans have changed their procedures for behavioral health services, and patients can obtain counseling and other related services without first seeking approval from their primary care physicians. Many plans have taken this concept further by developing "open access" models, in which patients can self-refer to a number of medical specialties. In our view, a number of the models presented in earlier chapters can be used by managed care to further refine the appropriate role for the primary care physician. In managed care systems, patients could be allowed direct access to case managers, without requiring a referral from their primary care physicians (of course, physicians could always refer patients as well). Many managed care organizations and physician group practices already have team structures in place which would allow the integration of the approaches described in this book. One of the most important advantages of managed care is that the incentives are already in place to encourage the adoption of methods that produce utilization reductions. Capitation under managed care provides the right incentive for organizations employing teams of providers to develop more comprehensive approaches to primary care for the elderly.

The major disadvantage of these incentives is that investments in improved primary care for frail elders do not produce positive outcomes for 18 to 24 months. Medicare, however, allows beneficiaries to change plans monthly. Current market-driven pressures on health plans for short-term profitability also make long-term efforts at improving care and outcomes of limited financial value. In the Generalist Physician Initiative, a consistent finding was that positive outcomes are not immediately apparent. It takes time to realize the full potential of enhanced primary care. We hope that managed care in a less tumultuous environment will have the stability to make long-term investments in enhanced primary care.

## Summary and Conclusions

We believe that the projects of the Generalist Physician Initiative have provided valuable lessons about the complex multiple variables which must be considered when the scope and content of primary care is expanded in elderly populations. A fundamental difference among sites was a lack of consensus on the type of patient to be served. A better understanding of who can most benefit from a collaborative primary practice approach is critical before enrollment criteria can be somewhat standardized. This is an important area for future research.

We have learned that projects must be considered in their local environments, for managed care penetration varies greatly as do local conditions such as cultures of health care systems, their traditions, prior experiences, and even the personalities involved. We have learned that coordinated care of high-risk elders is cost-effective, and that developing the appropriate incentives is critical. To work well in a Medicare managed care environment, significant operational changes are required to achieve effective primary care of frail elders. These changes are based in a service

delivery system in which physicians and other professionals need to negotiate and define their roles and relationships, as they learn to work as
teams. Teamwork does not always come naturally to professionals who
have been schooled to identify with their own, rather than other, professions. For teams to work, effective ways to communicate must develop,
including efficient management information systems that "make sense"
to clinicians who must use them. Critical to pulling all this together are
the skills of leaders who may often wear multiple hats, but who recognize
the differences in administrative and clinical supervision. For teams to
work well, they must feel that they have leadership that supports what
they are trying to do. Last, in evaluating work with older persons in primary care, it is important to recognize both process and outcome objectives so that a full understanding of why and how models develop is
documented. Then others can learn from the successes, as well as the failures, that occur in working within complex systems.

In many ways the most important lesson learned from this initiative
is that it is possible to expand the scope of primary care for the elderly in
ways that improve outcomes. Every site achieved the objective of improving the quality and comprehensiveness of services. Every site that measured patient or physician satisfaction found increased satisfaction with
the primary care system. Further evidence of physician satisfaction is that
a number of sites (Huntington, Binghamton, Carle Clinic, South Carolina, Henry Ford, Dartmouth) have institutionalized their models. These
overall results are very positive considering the variety of approaches and
complex situational factors involved.

Underwriting all the lessons learned, however, is the importance of
practitioners' advocacy for the older persons who are the recipients of
primary care, so that they do not get lost in its complexity.

# Contributors

**Philip A. Anderson,** M.D., is Associate Professor of Medicine at Case Western Reserve University School of Medicine. He is board certified in internal medicine, and has a certificate of added qualifications in geriatrics. For six years, he practiced at the community health centers described in Chapter 6; during part of that time he also served as Chief of Adult Medicine and then as Assistant Medical Director. Since 1988 Dr. Anderson has been on the full-time faculty at Case Western Reserve University School of Medicine, where he practices general internal medicine and teaches primary care medicine. The author of numerous journal articles, he served as the principal investigator for the Senior Health Connections project described in Chapter 6.

**Lynne Anker-Unnever,** M.P.A., has over 25 years' experience in the health and human services field. Currently, she is the Administrative Director of Community-Based Services for St. Joseph Healthcare (SJH) in Albuquerque, New Mexico, working with the State of New Mexico and a consortium of public and private organizations to develop Program of All-Inclusive Care for the Elderly (PACE) sites. Prior to this position, Ms. Anker-Unnever was the Director of Managed Care Development for SJH. With SJH for over 13 years, Ms. Anker-Unnever has developed, implemented, and administered services for older adults and the community, including case management, a senior membership program, and corporate eldercare benefits. She served as the project director for the St. Joseph Coordinated Care Partnership described in Chapter 8.

**Linda J. Battaglini,** M.S. in Accounting, is Senior Vice President for Strategic Planning and System Development at Melrose-Wakefield Healthcare Corporation in Melrose, Massachusetts. She has worked in health care since 1977 and in strategic planning since 1979; she served as the corporate planner for the United Health Services system in New York from 1986 to 1994. She was project director for two projects that have established innovative systems of Care Program Management (1982–1985) and System Case Management (1992–1995) for United Health Services, the latter of which is described in Chapter 4.

**Barbara Berkman,** D.S.W., is the Helen Rehr/Ruth Fizdale Professor of Health and Mental Health at Columbia University in New York City. Dr. Berkman has directed many federal and private research projects. Her professional contribution to the knowledge base of social work in health care is evidenced in her publications, which include books, chapters, and over 90 articles. She is a fellow of the Gerontological Society of America, a Distinguished Practitioner of the National Academy of Practice in Social Work and has received numerous national awards. She played a research role for the Physician Partnership project described in Chapter 11.

**Bernice Brewer** is Director of Special Projects at the South Carolina Department of Health and Environmental Control in Spartanburg, South Carolina. She has directed several highly successful research projects, both federal and private. She currently directs programs providing educational and therapy services to frail elderly persons, elder day care services, and case management services. She has written and published several journal articles pertaining to case management and spoken at numerous national and international meetings. She was a site director for the South Carolina Rural Geriatric Initiative Project described in Chapter 9.

**Teri Britt,** B.S.N., M.S., is a research analyst for the Health Systems Research Center at the Carle Clinic Association in Illinois. She has extensive clinical and research experience with geriatric patients and nursing case management. She has published in a variety of health-related journals and books. Currently a doctoral student in health policy and administration at Penn State University, Ms. Britt was first a nurse partner and then a part of the research analysis team in the Geriatric Collaborative Care project described in Chapter 3.

Phyllis Collier, M.S.N., M.S.A., is a Certified Nurse Practitioner currently practicing at the Henry Ford Health System's ambulatory clinic in Livonia, Michigan. She has achieved professional certification as an Adult Nurse Practitioner, a Geriatric Nurse Practitioner, and a Clinical Specialist in Gerontological Nursing from the American Nurses Credentialing Center. She participates in precepting graduate students from Wayne State University. She has co-authored a how-to manual titled "Sharing the Care" to assist in replicating the Complementary Geriatric Generalist Practice model of care described in Chapter 2, for which she was a nurse practitioner.

A. Judith Czerenda, M.S.N., is a health care services consultant in Miami, Florida. Certified as a Family Nurse Practitioner, she taught in both the undergraduate and graduate nursing programs at Binghamton University from 1979 until 1985, when she joined United Health Services (UHS) in New York as the Director of Patient Services for their Long-Term Home Health Care Program. During her tenure at UHS, she was Assistant Vice President for Long-Term Care and Administrator of the UHS Extended Care Facility. In 1990, she became the Vice President of Ideal Senior Living Center, a multi-level geriatric campus operated by UHS. Ms. Czerenda was a member of the development team for System Case Management, described in Chapter 4, and served as its program manager until 1996.

Alice Early, M.S.N., is a Nurse Practitioner at Henry Ford Medical Center for Seniors in Detroit. She is certified as an Adult Nurse Practitioner through the American Nurses Credentialing Center, and has worked as a nurse practitioner in geriatrics since 1982. She is a clinical educator for nurse practitioner students from Wayne State University, Oakland University, and the University of Michigan. For the Complementary Geriatric Practice initiative, described in Chapter 2, she served as the lead nurse practitioner.

Richard H. Fortinsky, Ph.D., is Associate Professor of Health Care Policy in Medicine at Case Western Reserve University School of Medicine. He has directed or co-directed numerous applied research projects aimed at improving the organization and delivery of health and social services to adults with chronic illnesses. Currently, he is studying the impact of hospital and post-hospital care interventions on older patient outcomes, the impact of interdisciplinary geriatric team care on ambulatory patient outcomes, relationships between home care resource use and patient outcomes over defined episodes of care, and how to increase physician referrals to community services and help family caregivers provide better inhome care to persons with dementia. He served as a major co-investigator for the Senior Health Connections project described in Chapter 6.

**Gladys Gundrum**, M.A., is a special projects coordinator for Senior Care Network at Huntington Memorial Hospital in Pasadena. A communications professional for over 13 years, she developed a comprehensive communications program for Senior Care Network and has written extensively about its innovative models. She is also a licensed speech-language pathologist. For the Physician Partnership model, described in Chapter 11, she played a dissemination and publication role.

**Carlton A. Hornung**, M.P.H., Ph.D., is Professor of Medicine and Professor at the Center for Health Policy and Research at the University of Louisville School of Medicine. He is also Director of the Epidemiology Core at the Louisville Veterans' Administration Medical Center. Previously he was Professor of Medicine and Director of Research for the Department of Medicine at the University of South Carolina. From 1991 to 1995 he was co-director of a USAID-funded Partnership in Health Care with the Nicolac Stancioiu Health Institute and the University of Medicine and Pharmacy in Cluj-Napoca, Romania, where he also served as visiting professor. His current research includes health policy issues and cardiovascular disease epidemiology. Dr. Hornung was co-principal investigator of the South Carolina Geriatric Rural Initiative Project described in Chapter 9.

**Anne M. Jette** has more than 20 years of broad experience in the health field. Currently, she is research associate at the Center for the Aging at Dartmouth Medical School in New Hampshire. Her areas of expertise include office-based research and continuous quality improvement. She has also been instrumental in implementing continuing education programs for physicians and nurses in northern New England, and in overseeing research projects with the Dartmouth Primary Care Cooperative (COOP) Project. Ms. Jette was research associate in the Community Centers of Excellence for the Aging project described in Chapter 10.

**Bradford L. Kirkman-Liff**, Dr. P.H., is Professor in the School of Health Administration and Policy, College of Business, Arizona State University. He teaches graduate courses at home and abroad in the organization and management of health insurance and managed care plans, the use of quality improvement and management information systems in health care organizations, and the reform of health care systems in industrialized nations. He has published more than fifty papers on access to care, physician payment, managed care, and health reform. He has been a World Health Organization Fellow and has served as a consultant to governments, foundations, hospitals, physician group practices, health care trade associations, bio-technology businesses, and health insurers in the U.S., Canada, England, Belgium, and The Netherlands. He is a member of the resource center team for The John A. Hartford Generalist Physician Initiative.

C. Seth Landefeld, M.D., is Professor of Medicine at the University of California, San Francisco (UCSF), the Chief of the Geriatrics Division, and the Director of the UCSF–Mt. Zion Center on Aging. His postdoctoral training included medical residency at UCSF, where he was chief medical resident, and a Henry J. Kaiser Family Foundation Fellowship in general internal medicine at Brigham and Women's Hospital and Harvard Medical School. Dr. Landefeld was previously Professor of Medicine at Case Western Reserve University, Senior Research Associate in the Department of Veteran's Affairs, and the head of the Division of General Internal Medicine and Health Care Research at the University Hospitals of Cleveland and the Cleveland Veterans Administration Medical Center. At UCSF, Dr. Landefeld leads efforts to develop clinical education and research programs to improve the care of older persons and to integrate geriatrics into the mainstream of medical training. He was co-principal investigator in the Senior Health Connections project described in Chapter 6.

Ida Nagele, B.S.N., is a Nurse Partner with the Carle Clinic Association in the Monticello, Illinois, branch. Ms. Nagele has experience in home health care and medical oncology nursing, as well as nursing case management. She is certified in gerontological nursing. Ms. Nagele continues to be a nurse partner for the Geriatric Collaborative Care project described in Chapter 3.

F. Ellen Netting, M.S.S.W., Ph.D., is Professor of Social Work at Virginia Commonwealth University (VCU), where she received the University's Distinguished Scholar Award for 1997. She taught both social work and gerontology courses at Arizona State University for ten years before coming to VCU in 1993. She has written several books, numerous book chapters, and over 90 journal articles in the areas of case management, continuing care retirement communities, the long-term care ombudsman program, and other areas specific to aging and service delivery issues. She is a Fellow of the Gerontological Society of America and a Distinguished Scholar in the National Academy of Practice in Social Work. A member of the resource center team for The John A. Hartford Foundation Generalist Physician Initiative on which this book is based, she co-conducted interviews with key stakeholders at all sites with Dr. Frank G. Williams.

**Janeane Randolph,** M.S.W., is Chief Executive Officer of Elder Care Alliance, a newly formed organization to support the development and affiliation of non-profit, long-term care programs and facilities serving older adults. Working collaboratively with Catholic Healthcare West, Elder Care Alliance will focus its development efforts in California, Arizona, and Nevada. Ms. Randolph was involved with the development and management of two of San Francisco's adult day health care programs and the development of a citywide case management program for San Francisco's frail elders. She was also a founding member of the San Francisco Elder Abuse Prevention Consortium. She was the project adminstrator in the Senior Care Connection project described in Chapter 7.

**Mark A. Sager,** M.D., is Associate Professor of Medicine in the Geriatrics Section at the University of Wisconsin, Madison, Medical School. He is also the Interim Director of the Wisconsin Alzheimer's Institute, the Director of the Memory Assessment Clinic at the University of Wisconsin Hospitals and Clinics, and the Director of the Geriatric Evaluation and Management Program at the William S. Middleton Memorial Veterans Hospital in Madison, Wisconsin. Dr. Sager is a health services researcher with interests in the areas of long-term care, primary care for older adults, inpatient geriatric units, and dementing disorders. He is a member of the resource team for The John A. Hartford Generalist Physician Initiative.

**Cheryl Schraeder,** Ph.D., is Head of the Health Systems Research Center for the Carle Clinic Association in Illinois. She has extensive experience in case management, medical research, and directing innovative delivery systems for elderly at-risk patients. She is also an adjunct faculty member with the University of Illinois College of Medicine. She has been or is currently project director for several research studies. The themes of Dr. Schraeder's publications include nursing case management, geriatric nursing, community health education, applied research in the clinical setting, and nursing roles and functions in managed care. She was the project director for the Geriatric Collaborative Care project described in Chapter 3.

**Sue Shearer,** M.S.W., is a licensed clinical social worker with 15 years' experience in health care as a clinician and administrator. In 1992, she returned to Pasadena's Huntington Memorial Hospital Senior Care Network as project manager for the Physician Partnership project, designed to create partnerships between primary care physicians and community-based social workers, as described in Chapter 11. In 1995, Ms. Shearer was appointed the Assistant Director of Senior Care Network. In this role, she is responsible for the clinical and administrative oversight of six core coordination programs, totaling nearly 1,600 clients served a year. She has also developed, in conjunction with Jewish Family Service of Los Angeles, The California Network, Inc., a statewide network of care advisory services designed to serve clients with long-term care insurance.

**Paul Shelton,** Ed. D., is Research Analyst for the Health Systems Research Center at the Carle Clinic Association in Illinois. He has over 20 years of experience in health care education and training, conducting health services research, evaluation, and data management. Dr. Shelton has been involved with several funded programs that provided health-related services to Medicare beneficiaries and has published on a number of health care delivery and research topics. He is a research analyst for the Geriatric Collaborative Care project described in Chapter 3.

**W. June Simmons,** M.S.W., has enjoyed a long career in human services, most of it in leadership posts in healthcare settings. She spent many years as an administrator at Huntington Memorial Hospital in Pasadena, including the period of the founding of the Senior Care Network and the Physician Partnership project, described in Chapter 11, for which she was the principal investigator. Since 1993, she has worked for the Visiting Nurse Association of Los Angeles, and was appointed President/CEO in 1996. She has focused her energies in three main areas: (1) the creation of a workplace that supports and encourages excellence, (2) program development for evolving and newly identified patient needs, and (3) network development to integrate inpatient and community-based services for a full continuum of care with choices of setting and care options.

**Lucia Sommers**, M.S.S., Dr. P.H., is currently Associate Program Director of the Internal Medicine Training Program in Medicine at St. Mary's Center in San Francisco and principal investigator on research efforts in primary care and chronic disease in elderly persons. Coming from a background in epidemiology, quality of care research, and postgraduate and continuing medical education, Dr. Sommers has published and directed numerous multi-site, longitudinal studies on physician retraining and team building for clinical decision making, physician and non-physician collaboration in patient care giving, and interventions for patients with chronic illnesses. She was the project director in the Senior Care Connection project described in Chapter 7.

**Millicent Stein**, R.N., G.N.P., has worked in nursing for over 45 years. After retiring from nursing, she has been employed at the South Carolina Department of Health and Environmental Control. In addition, she serves as a consultant for nursing homes and hospitals for nursing home placement. As a member of the South Carolina Geriatric Rural Initiative Project team, she was responsible for the education and supervision of geriatric technicians (see Chapter 9).

**Mary Beth Tupper**, M.D., is the Division Head of Geriatrics and Medical Director for Senior Services at Henry Ford Health System (HFHS) in Detroit. She is also the Medical Director for the Center for Senior Independence, and the Program Director in Detroit for the Great Lakes Geriatric Interdisciplinary Team Training program. Dr. Tupper has been instrumental in the development and implementation of interdisciplinary care for geriatric patients in ambulatory, acute care, and nursing home settings within HFHS. She was clinical director for the Complementary Geriatric Practice model described in Chapter 2.

**Robert Turngren**, M.D., is a family physician with the Carle Clinic Association in Illinois, a member of the clinic's Board of Governors, and a Vice President with Health Alliance Medical Plans, Inc., Carle's managed care entity. Dr. Turngren served as a participating intervention physician for the Geriatric Collaborative Care model described in Chapter 3.

**John H. Wasson**, M.D., is the Herman O. West Professor of Geriatrics and Professor in the Department of Community and Family Medicine and Medicine at Dartmouth Medical School in New Hampshire. In addition to his directorship of Dartmouth's Center on Aging, Dr. Wasson is also the Research Director of the Dartmouth Primary Care (COOP) Research Network and the co-principal investigator for the Prostate Patient Outcomes Research Team. In 1996, the fourth edition of his book—*The Common Symptom Guide*—was selected as "outstanding for practice" by the *American Journal of Nursing*. Dr. Wasson was principal investigator for the Community Centers of Excellence for the Aging project described in Chapter 10.

**Gloria B. Weinberg,** M.D., is Associate Professor of Medicine and Chief of the Section of Geriatrics at the University of Miami School of Medicine/Mount Sinai Medical Center campus in Florida. As the Program Director of the Mount Sinai Internal Medicine Residency Program, her main interest has been training future primary care physicians and most of her publications have involved the development of more effective teaching programs. As the principal investigator in the Intervention Pathways to Integrated Care project described in Chapter 5, she promoted an interdisciplinary approach to geriatric care within Mount Sinai Medical Center and recently implemented a Geriatric Evaluation and Management Consultative Service at the Medical Center.

**Monika White,** Ph.D., trained in social work and has extensive experience as an educator, researcher, consultant, and administrator. Since the mid-1970s, Dr. White has concentrated her work on case management program development and community-based service delivery systems for older adults and their families. A nationally recognized author and lecturer in the aging field, Dr. White is the President and Chief Executive Officer of the Center for Healthy Aging (formerly Senior Health and Peer Counseling) in Santa Monica, California. She served as the administrator for the Senior Care Network's Physician Partnership project described in Chapter 11.

**Nancy A. Whitelaw,** Ph.D., is Associate Director of the Center for Health System Studies and Director of Health Services Research, Health Alliance Plan, at the Henry Ford Health System (HFHS) in Detroit. Her research and programmatic interests are in the areas of integration of health care services for the elderly, especially Medicare managed care, measurement of health status in older populations, and delivery of health care to underserved urban populations. She is the principal investigator on two projects: an evaluation of the outcomes of care in the Geriatric Complementary Practice model described in Chapter 2, and a program to improve geriatric interdisciplinary team training for both current and future practitioners.

**Frank G. Williams,** Ph.D. is Professor in the School of Health Administration and Policy, College of Business, Arizona State University, and a Clinical Professor in the Arizona Graduate Program in Public Health, University of Arizona Health Sciences Center. Dr. Williams' professional interests are primarily in long-term care. He teaches graduate courses in chronic care management, human resources management, and health care finance. Dr. Williams is active in the Arizona Chapter Board of the American College of Health Care Administrators and the Arizona Regent's Advisory Committee of the American College of Healthcare Executives, and he is a board member of the Healthcare Administrators Forum of Arizona. In 1992, Dr. Williams was inducted into Beta Gamma Sigma, the Honor Society for Collegiate Schools of Business. Dr. Williams is principal investigator for the resource center for The John A. Hartford Foundation's Generalist Physician Initiative.

# INDEX

('i' indicates an illustration; 't' indicates a table)